PRINCE MARKO

PRINCE MARKO

The Hero of South Slavic Epics

TATYANA POPOVIĆ

SYRACUSE UNIVERSITY PRESS

The paper used in this publication meets the minimum requirements of American National Standard for Information Sciences—Permanence of Paper for Printed Library Materials, ANSI Z39.48-1984. ∞™

Library of Congress Cataloging-in-Publication Data

Popović, Tanya
    Prince Marko: the hero of South Slavic epics.

    Bibliography: p.
    Includes index.
    1. Epic poetry, Southern Slavic—History and criticism.   2. Marko, Prince of Serbia, 1335?–1394, in fiction, drama, poetry, etc.   I. Title.
PG573.4.M37P6   1988   891.8′1   88-4885
ISBN 0-8156-2444-1 (alk. paper)

To my husband
NENAD
and to my children

Tatyana Popović is a librarian at LeMoyne College in Syracuse, New York. She received her M.A. in Slavic linguistics and literatures at the University of Belgrade. She obtained her M.S.L.S. and later her Ph.D. in Slavic Studies from Syracuse University. Dr. Popović is an United States citizen. Her native country is Yugoslavia, where she was one of the editors of the *Yugoslav Survey*. She is included in *International Who's Who in Community Service*. Dr. Popović resides with her family in Syracuse.

Contents

ILLUSTRATIONS

Note on Pronunciation and Translation

Cyrillic transliterations into English have been done according to the usage by Library of Congress for Russian, Ukrainian, Bulgarian, and Macedonian. The following Serbo-Croatian consonants are, however, printed with diacritical marks and their closest English equivalents are:

ć, č	= ch as in church
dj, dž	= j as in James
š	= sh as in shape
ž	= zh as in treasure

Epic songs quoted in this book are given in the English translations of David H. Low and of George R. Noyes. Unless otherwise stated, the remainder of the songs and quotations are my translation.

Preface

E ver since my childhood I have been fascinated with the epic figure of
Prince Marko. The same is probably true for many South Slavs growing
up in the Balkan Peninsula where, as early as grade school if not before, children acquire a firsthand awareness of this hero. They learn songs about his
adventures and read tales of his exploits and Herculean strength. The lore
of a great hero who protected the South Slavic peoples from injustice and
oppression during their long history of hardship is deeply entrenched in the
hearts of both the young and the old.

In the 1950s, when I was a student at the University of Belgrade, a
strong tradition of heroic poetry existed in scholarly circles. It was a time
when the image of Prince Marko was being reevaluated by many scholars.
Dr. Dragolyub Pavlović, a well-known medievalist, spoke to me of writing
about Prince Marko and stressed that the greatest number of published
studies either were dated around the turn of the century or had appeared
mainly in the 1930s. Quite a bit of new research had taken place, with the
results scattered throughout numerous scholarly journals. During this time
I undertook a preliminary examination of the available sources and collections of epic poems, published mostly in South Slavic but also in other languages, including Russian, German, and French.

I became disconcerted by the complexity of Prince Marko's heroic profile and by his seemingly paradoxical behavior, which ranged from the fantastic to the naturalistic, from the heroic to the opportunistic. In addition,
my studies were thwarted by family matters, including a change in lifestyle
as I joined my husband in his diplomatic activities and travels. All this contributed to a long delay in paying tribute to my favorite folk hero, Prince
Marko, and it was not until the late 1960s that I resumed serious, sustained
study.

This book is the result of many years of research on Prince Marko, a
figure standing at the center of the South Slavic folk tradition. Slavic folk
literature represents a masterful mixture of pagan, Christian, and historical

elements. In addition, traditional Slavic poetry is a living specimen of a still-extant oral tradition providing us with a rare opportunity to closely analyze the specific processes of oral composition which are analogous to other epics of the past, especially the Homeric.

Tatyana Popović

Syracuse, N.Y.
Spring 1988

Acknowledgments

A special note of appreciation is due to Cambridge University Press for permission to reprint excerpts of the songs from *The Ballads of Marko Kraljević* translated by David Halyburton Low. As Serbo-Croatian is my native tongue, I was impressed with Low's in-depth knowledge of the language and the quality of his translation, which greatly enhanced my own research.

Grateful appreciation is also given to the Yugoslav Press and Cultural Center in New York, and especially to Mr. Damir Grubiša, its director. Mr. Grubiša was very cooperative and supportive in providing advice, information, and assistance regarding the documentation and permission for the use of the illustrations. It was invaluable to find that the Yugoslav Center sustained my intent to acquaint the American reader with heroic Prince Marko and the Yugoslav cultural heritage.

My thanks go particularly to my family, who supported me in many ways. As it happens, there was a symmetry in terms of aid proferred: I conducted early research at Harvard's Widener Library in the 1970s while staying with my older daughter, Gina, who also provided valuable assistance in editing initial versions of the text; I carried out the final stages of research while staying with my younger daughter, Sanya, who was studying at Harvard University in 1987. I am also indebted to Professor Albert B. Lord for pointing out to me the collection of Yugoslav poems at Harvard that were recorded by Millman Perry, which I was able to consult while I conducted my research.

Introduction

This book contributes to the rediscovery of the entire folkloristic and ethnic past of the South Slavs. The last quarter of this century is witnessing a renaissance of interest in medieval times. The goal is to illuminate the heroic past, researching human relationships which are expressed in Slavic myths and legends.

This study introduces Prince Marko, who has been nearly unknown to American readers until now. It bridges centuries of tempestuous South Slavic existence. The saga of Prince Marko is a South Slavic odyssey of medieval times in the Balkans.

This book attempts to meet the interests and needs of both general and specialist readers. The Slavic epic tradition is relevant for those readers seeking knowledge of distant cultures. The subject of Prince Marko is also attractive to anthropologists, ethnologists, psychologists, sociologists, and students of Slavic studies and comparative literatures.

The book is arranged in three chapters. Chapter 1 opens with a brief historical summary of South Slavs, followed by a description of general characteristics of South Slavic folk literature. This serves as the central framework for the monumental heroic figure of Prince Marko. The book presents Marko in terms of ancient Slavic patriarchal civilization up to modern times; in many ways he is the product of both. I have emphasized the creativity of anonymous Slavic bards whose oral compositions expressed the dissatisfaction of a people living under bleak conditions, but who, nevertheless, cherished dreams of a great future. The role of such bards was essential in the formation and spread of Prince Marko's epic glory.

Chapter 2 identifies factual and fictional images of the folk hero. It traces the earliest available historical records relating to Marko's royal Mrnyavčević family, Marko's acquisition of his small fourteenth-century kingdom in Macedonia, the conditions prevailing during Marko's rule, and his vassalage to the Turkish sultans Murad I (1359–1389) and Bayazet I (1389–1403). It also considers problems resulting from the Turkish conquest and interference in Balkan domestic affairs. Finally, the chapter covers historical information relating to other epic personages who appeared alongside Prince Marko in his many dramatic encounters. The second part of chapter 2 presents the process of Prince Marko's poetization from a historical nucleus to the shaping of a legendary figure, two images which differ from each other substantially.

Chapter 3 deals with Prince Marko's heroic activities, both general and particular themes and motifs. These themes encompass the major stages and facets of Prince Marko's life, including his genetic ties with his epic uncle, Duke Momčilo, and his consistent opposition to his own father, King Vukašin. Vukašin has been blamed for the national discord and loss of the medieval Serbian Empire, while much glory and patriotic feeling were instead directed toward his son, Prince Marko. In the poems, Marko sometimes behaves as an impeccable chivalric knight *sans peur et sans reproche,* but at other times he quickly shifts to a brawling rogue, or a fierce-blooded Robin Hood type of outlaw. Although Prince Marko was a historical king, he was frequently described in the poems as neither a knight nor a gentleman but rather as an exact replica of his peasant compatriots. These peasants recoiled from their Turkish oppressors into somewhat barbaric shells although their hearts forever dreamed of freedom.

Prince Marko represents a faithful projection of the major traits of the South Slavs. In the folk songs, he often appears as capricious, quarrelsome, and from time to time ruthlessly cruel. He was impulsive and prone to drink. On the other hand, he was always benevolent and soft-hearted toward those who suffered, particularly toward women and children. He reacted ferociously against injustice, while consistently showing respect for noble adversaries. Above all Marko passionately hated his Turkish oppressors and loved his own people.

The central point in chapter 3 is a study of the mother-son relationship, a theme permeating South Slavic epic poetry. This book approaches the topic of the heroic mother from several viewpoints, with particular attention to her traditional role. The serene, yet firm love of Queen Yevrosima is fully reciprocated in the warm response of her dutiful son. She guides his conscience toward noble ends.

I have attempted to present the Prince Marko legend as a living force, ever changing and continuously adjusting to the needs of every generation up to the present. Popular interest in the legendary Prince Marko has persisted through the centuries, and contemporary enthusiasm about him remains high. The people's faith in the Prince Marko legend is still very strong. In 1912 Serbian soldiers stormed Marko's fortress in Prilep during the Balkan War of Liberation against the Turks. According to a war report, the Serbian forces were stationed below the fortress at Prilep, then held by the Turkish garrison.[1] Voyislav Petrović, a war correspondent, provided a vivid account of the situation. Knowing the strength of the legends in the minds of the Serbians, the commander-in-chief issued a special caution against any impetuous heroics.

During the early morning the infantry kept quiet, but at the first cannon shots we noticed an effervescence among our troops, and soon afterward we heard them shouting frantically and saw them running like wolves straight to the castle of the royal Prince Marko. I could hear the voice of our captain, Agatonović, commanding them to stop and await the general's order. When the immediate commanders saw that discipline proved futile, they essayed in vain to appeal to the soldiers' reason, assuring them of certain death if they would not await at least the effect of our artillery. Our warriors, deafened by the roaring of the Turkish siege cannon and mitrailleuses, ran straight into the fire and appeared to fall in dozens! The sight was horrible. I was unable to stop my soldiers. My blood froze, I closed my eyes. Disastrous defeat! Demoralization of other troops! My own degradation was certain!

In a little while our artillery ceased firing, lest they should kill their own comrades, who were now crossing bayonets with the Turkish infantry. A few minutes later we saw the Serbian national colours fluttering on the donjon of Kralyević Marko's castle. The Turks were fleeing in greatest disorder. The Serbian victory was as complete as it was rapid!

When we arrived on the scene a little later, a parade was ordered. After calling together the troops, we found our loss to be comparatively insignificant. I praised my heroes for their brave conduct, but reproached them bitterly for their disobedience. At my last admonishing words, I heard from thousands of soldiers in majestic unison: *"Kralyević Marko commanded us all the time: FORWARD! Did you not see him on his [horse] Šarac?"* It was clear to me that the tradition of Kralyević Marko was so deeply engraved on the hearts of those honest and heroic men that, in their vivid enthusiasm, they had seen the incarnation of their hero.

In his commentary, Cecil Stewart states, "Serbian history is complicated by the influence of the legends upon the actions of the people. Gods intermingle with humans in classical fashion."[2]

In World War II, from this small town in Macedonia, the first attack was launched against the Nazi forces of occupation on October 11, 1941. The Macedonian uprising against the enemies had begun. Every year, even to the present day, an international painters' conference takes place in the monastery where fresco portraits of King Vukašin and his son Marko are still visible.[3]

The book does not attempt to deal with the myth of Prince Marko as it appears in the neighboring folk literatures of Albania, Greece, and Romania, which go beyond the specific boundaries of the South Slavic language region. I occasionally compare other epic poetries, particularly those of Russia, the Ukraine, Byzantium, and Western Europe. A companion volume devoted exclusively to the relationship between the Prince Marko saga and other comparable national poetries would be highly useful. References might include the Anglo-Saxon *Beowulf*, the Babylonian *Gilgamesh*, the Armenian *David of Sasoun* and *Mher of Sasoun*, the Old Norse epic of the *Elder Edda* and the hero *Sigurth*, the Old German *Hildebrandslied*, and the Russian Ilia *Muromets*, as well as the Middle High German *Wolfdietrich*, the Karakirghiz poems of *Manas*, the Byzantine *Digenis Akritas*, the French *Chanson de Roland*, the Spanish *El Cid*, and the heroes of Homer. Such a comparative study would yield interesting and even fascinating results with regard to mutual influences and similarity of motifs in the international family of great heroes. However, this ambitious task remains to be faced sometime in the future.

I have avoided narrow regional approaches, except in those cases requiring minute analysis. Instead, Prince Marko's figure, delineated in broad strokes, portrays him as a typical representative of all the South Slavic nations. Despite Prince Marko's historical insignificance and the relatively limited geographic region in which he lived, the South Slavs treasure him as their hero. He reflects the many views and attitudes of the people who created him.

The South Slavic epic narrative form with regard to language and stylistic devices can be compared to the Homeric tradition. However, this topic deserves more intensive treatment than is possible in this book. The literature of the poetics of oral expression has already been discussed extensively by experts on folk literature.[4] Oral formulaic theory applied to Prince Marko's epic poems would be a worthwhile venture, especially since those poems are a part of a still-viable oral tradition in the Balkans.[5]

I hope this book will serve as an updated approach to the South Slavic epic tradition which occupies a special niche within the repertoire of great European folk literatures. As Professor Svetozar Kolyević says in *The Epic in the Making*, "the richest oral epic material in any single European language, comprising a continuous tradition ... of epic singing, can be fully appreciated in its comparative aspects only after it has been properly understood in its own context and studied in its own right."[6]

1

South Slavic Folk Literature

*The Sclavonians disdained to obey a despot, a prince, or
even a magistrate; but their experience was too narrow, their
passions too headstrong, to compose a system of equal law
or general defence. Some voluntary respect was yielded to age
and valor; but each tribe or village existed as a separate
republic, and all must be persuaded where none could be
compelled.*[1]

SOUTH SLAVIC CIVILIZATION IN THE BALKANS

The present South Slavs came from central and eastern Europe, from
north of the Black Sea and from around the Dniester and Bug Rivers,
in what is now the Western Ukraine. They arrived on the Balkan Peninsula
in the fifth and sixth centuries to fill the territory of the Eastern Roman or
Byzantine Empire, particularly the Roman provinces of Pannonia, Illyri-
cum, and Moesia.[2]

With the exception of a few peripheral coastal strongholds which still
contained remnants of an indigenous Romanized and Hellenized population, all of the Balkans had been solidly settled by Slavic tribes by the end of
the seventh century. The Slavic people settled in the Balkans not through
sudden conquest but by a process of persistent penetration. They achieved
this by peacefully following in the wake of other more warlike conquerors,
such as the Avars. Their motivation in acquiescing to such a secondary role
probably stemmed from a distaste for the organizational forms which en-
dangered the tightly preserved autonomy of their clans and tribes. These
territorial defensive units were called *župa* which were further subdivided

1

into extended communities based on family relations, or *zadruga*.[3] The *zadruga* functioned through the authority of its chief, who was generally the oldest and most experienced member of each family unit. The *zadruga* represented the primary social and economic unit and has managed to survive almost to our time.[4]

By the end of the tenth century the Slavs had become largely Christianized. Their language became recognized as an official church language and they obtained their own Glagolitic and later, Cyrillic scripts. This was primarily due to the efforts of such missionaries as St. Cyril and St. Methodius. This language, known as Old Church Slavonic, also became the literary language of the Slavs through which they joined other civilizations and created their own states.[5]

Arab pirates, West European Crusaders, and Asian Turkish conquerors preyed upon the Byzantine Empire from the eighth to the fifteenth centuries.[6] The Slavic states, though somewhat spared because of Byzantine debilitation, were in no better position. In 1102 the Croats became incorporated into the Hungarian kingdom under the rule of King Koloman. The Slovenes maintained silence beneath the suppression of the German feudal lords, the Venetians continued their control of coastal areas, and Bulgaria, after great initial growth, stood exhausted and docile. The creation of a national state in Serbia was much delayed until the end of the 12th century by the resistance of the autonomous clans and *župe*. Due to a number of able rulers such as Stevan Nemanya and church leader St. Sava, Serbian development quickened after the 12th century. It climaxed at the time of Emperor Dušan the Mighty (1331–1355), whose power stretched over all of Serbia, Bulgaria, and a vast section of Albania and Greece. After Dušan's premature death in 1355, the Serbian state disintegrated into dozens of small independent and semi-dependent states and principalities.

In addition to territorial division, the Balkans were also split by differing religious persuasions. The Bulgarians, Serbs, Macedonians, and Greeks were Eastern Orthodox, while the Croatians and Slovenes were Roman Catholics. The Bogomils, mostly in Bulgaria and Bosnia, represented not only a separate religion but a separate social ideology as well.[7]

The Turkish invasion profited from the disunity of the South Slavs. The Turkish conquerors were strong and well-organized, but their success was also due to the feebleness of the Balkan feudal system and to the fact that Turkish rule, though alien, appeared less harsh to people.

Within a mere century and a half (1350–1500) the entire Balkan Peninsula was, with minor exceptions, conquered by the Turks. This included nearly the whole South Slavic population in those areas. Bulgarians, Serbs, Macedonians, and Bosnians lost their estates, kings and national institutions. The Church was the one exception. The Turks interfered little with the Churches in Serbia and Bulgaria and they came to be not only religious institutions but the carriers of what remained of culture, the arts, and education.

Turkish rule was accepted as a fact which people could not change. The Turks symbolized the state and the Sultan ruled by the same principles and indeed from the same location as had the Byzantine emperors of the previous thousand years. In time Turkish administration deteriorated to the point that it became oppressive.

It was not by chance that Marko* Mrnyavčevič (1335?–1394), in folk tradition usually called Prince Marko (*Marko Kralyevič*), stands out in popular lore as a dichotomous personality. The Sultan's faithful vassal, he symbolized the incarnation of the uncompromising fighter against Turkish injustice. He represented the primitive patriarchal society which was restored after the collapse of the feudal order.

The levelling of the people to the status of peasants and sheep-raising nomads in the mountains contributed to the formation of the epic mood and epic poetry. These mountains stretched from Albania across Montenegro into Western Serbia and Hercegovina toward the Bosnian-Dalmatian borderland, and this entire area became known as the Dinaric Mountains.

There in the poor, craggy mountains grew the image of Prince Marko, an image which was inextricably entwined with the customs of blood revenge (*vendetta*), the bartering and abducting of brides, raiding, duelling, and fighting. People created artificial family ties, such as "god-brothers" or "god-fathers."

Family and clan affinity and hospitality were important, as was the emergence of an acute sense of honor and dignity. Memories of the Nemany-čes dynasty and nobility were assimilated into a relatively new democratic equality. All were peasants, and epic kings dined on onions and bread, and queens did their washing with the common women at the nearby creek. This equality among people who possessed little and lived in scarcity, who were conscious of a glorious past, who remembered each injury and never forgot an insult, slowly made them aware that they could and should be free. These were the elements of a heroic climate. With no other cultural or aesthetic outlets, folk songs, tales, and oral tradition in general lent the initial motivation for the creation and perfection of epic poetry.

---

*Whenever the historical person of Marko Mrnyavčevič is referred to he is called "King Marko," while the epic person is called "Prince Marko."

SOUTH SLAVIC FOLK LITERATURE AND PRINCE MARKO

*In them breathes a clear and inborn poetry such as can
scarcely be found among any other modern people.*[8]

The folk literature of the South Slavs is living documentation of their historical, social, religious, ethical, and ethnic conceptions of life. Various parallelisms within the folklore of South Slavic peoples are a direct result of mutual ties, common origin and language, similar tribal organization, and patriarchal family relations. Similarities also exist in the forms of common folk customs, rituals, and ancient or pagan myths which the South Slavs brought along with them when they came to the Balkan Peninsula. These were all Christianized over time. In addition, South Slavs were exposed to strong cultural influences, first from the Byzantium and later from the West.

Serbs, Bulgarians, Macedonians, Croats, and Slovenes all participated in the formation of South Slavic folk literature. The epic poetry which we know followed the flourishing of South Slavic medieval states in the fourteenth century. The oldest South Slavic heroic poems have not been preserved, their origin dating back to remote antiquity. The poems dealt with various events and persons particularly connected with warfare. One of the oldest available pieces of heroic poetry is found in the report of the fifth-century Greek historian Priscus Rhetor, who had been visiting Attila the Hun (A.D. 433–53) on a diplomatic mission. Gibbon mentions the event in his *History of the Decline and Fall of the Roman Empire*.[9] Priscus was present at one of Attila's feasts when "two Scythians [possibly Slavs][10] stood before Attila's couch and recited the verses they had composed to celebrate his valor and his victories. A profound silence prevailed in the hall; the guests' attention was captivated by the vocal harmony, which revived and perpetuated the memory of their own exploits; a martial ardor flashed from the eyes of the warriors, who were impatient for battle; and the tears of the old men expressed their generous despair, that they could no longer partake the danger and glory of the field."[11]

Here is a clear case of heroic poetry. It is, however, a matter of conjecture whether the poetic narrative may have included both heroic and lyric ingredients in earlier times. A classical example of the conjoint situation is represented in the genre of laments. According to the Serbian folklorist Voyislav Djurić, laments had lyric-epic-dramatic character.[12] Lament songs expressed strong emotions with regard to the loss of loved ones as well as praise of their past heroic feats, all permeated with the dramatization of the funeral reenactment of their deaths. Among the laments which were collected and published by Vuk Karadžić is a very remarkable one titled, "It is Terrible to Behold You."[13] Here a sister expresses both her bereavement for the fallen brother and her pride with his heroic deeds:

> Why are you laid down,
>> My hero!
> You are dressed handsomely,
>> My joy!
> In knightly garments,
>> My falcon!
> Armed as a warrior,
>> My hero!
> Ready as for a wedding,
>> My splendid wedding guest!
>> . . . .
>
> Why did you leave your home,
>> Woe, my home!
> You have left your weak children,
>> Woe, me!
> Yet, the glory will arise again,
>> Oh, Lord have mercy!
> Children are growing,
>> Praying to Lord!
>> (Vuk Karadžić, *Ethnographic Papers*)

Gradually a separation took place in which the distinct lyric and epic genres developed. Although each genre maintained its essential features, emotions could appear in epic poetry and heroic events could be found in predominantly lyric poetry. Bulgarian songs often employ both genres, and among them is one song which is rich in both emotions and action. It deals with Prince Marko recognizing in a Sultan's outlaw his sister who was taken into captivity when she was young. The song titled, "Šaina the Slave Girl and Marko," describes how

> Marko weeps and Šaina sobs, brother and sister,
> They cannot part one from the other,
> . . . .
>
> They did not turn to the city of Sultan,
> They took the road to the town of Prilep.

When they returned home, they found their mother still grieving for her abducted daughter. She greets them with a dramatic lament:

> Today are thirty years, spoke the Mother,
> Since my Šaina was captured,
> Captured her the Turks Janissaries,
> I cry and drink my own heavy tears.
>
> (Brothers Miladinov, No. 146)

The oldest preserved South Slavic lyric poem, according to Milivoye Knežević, was dedicated to the harvest cult. Knežević quoted the Arabic traveller and geographer Idrisi (died A.D. 1154), who allegedly recorded the poem as follows: "O, Lord! Thou art the One who gave us our daily bread. Give it to us until our end."[14] Knežević believed that the lines of the song in prose which reached us in Idrisi's translation were originally chanted in verse.[15]

After the twelfth century, reports and historical records about oral poetry became more reliable, although they did not distinguish whether songs were epic or lyric in nature. The hagiographers of Rastko (the youngest son of the Serbian Grand Lord Nemanya) were two monks—Domentiyan (1210–64) and Theodosius (1246–1328). They wrote about feasts at the court of Nemanya and about the heroic songs that were performed.[16] Theodosius described Rastko, who later became the head of the Serbian Eastern Orthodox Church and was canonized as St. Sava. He mentioned that Rastko, even before his ordainment, avoided listening "to indecent and harmful songs of youthful desires which weaken the soul."[17] This report corroborated the existence of folk songs in the thirteenth century, probably lyric in nature, which were sung by young people at their gatherings.

Another well-known record of the existence of folk songs in the fourteenth century comes from the Byzantine historian Nicephorus Gregoras. The writer was a member of a Byzantine delegation sent by the Emperor Andronicus II to the Serbian King Stephen Uroš III (1322–1331). While travelling in the area of present-day Strumica in Macedonia, Nicephorus mentioned in his *Correspondance* that he heard people singing. His account is as follows:

> The servants who were following us ... were talking in high voices and some of them intonated tragic songs celebrating their illustrious heroes, of which "We know glory, but we have never seen it." Ravines along our path and caverns which hid surrounding hillocks, were absorbing sounds of

piercing elegies as if they were living beings. They kept them as they were, unchanged, with the same intonations, and repeated them, sending them back successively as echoes. Like in a chorus, the strains followed each other and responded to the previously given melody.[18]

The first definitive evidence of South Slavic epic poetry was established by the Slovenian traveller Benedikt Kuripešič in the sixteenth century. In his book, *Putopis Kroz Bosnu, Srbiyu, Bugarsku i Rumeliyu 1530* [Itinerary . . .] Kuripešič described his travels across Bosnia and Serbia and noted hearing folk songs along the way. In 1531 he recorded people in the Kossovo region singing about epic heroes—especially Miloš Obilič, who was the most popular Serbian folk hero after Prince Marko.[19]

Some of the records referring to South Slavic folk songs also mention the musical instruments used by the folk singers to accompany their recitations. One of the earliest such observations (noted by the Greek historian Plutarch), was the Scythian custom of listening to the sounds "of the twanging bow-strings during their festivities."[20]

The historian Theophylaktos Simokattes stated in A.D. 592 that Slavic singers used the instruments called *kitharai* to accompany their songs. *Kitharai* appear to have been the South Slavic *gusle* (cithara). He also noted that the Slavic envoys travelled unarmed, carrying these instruments with them instead.[21] In *Sermon Against the Heretics*,[22] the earliest Slavic source referring to Bogomils in A.D. 972, the Bulgarian priest Cosmas accused the Bogomils of being "lovers of *gusle,* dancing, and singing licentious songs."[23]

Gusle became very popular music instruments, inseparable from decasyllabic songs in so-called "*guslars'* singing." According to the Serbian folklorist Svetozar Matič, the South Slavic epic singing with *gusle* comes from the very ancient "pre-Slavic" period adapted in the feudal times.[24] The Russian folklorist Nikolai Kravtsov stated that the melody of *gusle* is monotonous and that "*gusle* give forth an impure sound of low tone, in the elegiac manner."[25]

South Slavic oral and written literatures interacted with one another.[26] Folk literature was exclusively secular in character, anonymously composed and orally transmitted, and relied heavily on the vernacular language. It modelled itself to large audiences of common people who were, as a rule, illiterate. Written literature, on the other hand, was largely sacred, addressed to the educated few, and practiced in monasteries and churches.

Educated monks supported by medieval rulers on the Balkans also developed written literature which was somewhat secular in character. The purpose of the secular literature was to amuse the South Slavic nobility and

instruct future rulers in the courts. From the repertoire of the courtly literature, which was a mixture of the fantastic, miraculous, symbolic, and al-
legoric, some motifs migrated and found their way to the oral tradition. Bib-
lical and other religious themes were manifested in the medieval romances
and tales of the written literatures but gradually became evident in popular
folk literature as well.[27] The legend of St. George slaying the dragon, which
is a part of sacred literature, was very popular in the medieval times because
St. George was the protector of Christian knights. This legend is also found
in the epic poems about Prince Marko, as in "Marko and the Moor" (Low,
No. 21).

The other example of such western influence is the medieval romance of
Beuves de Haumtone which reached the South Slavic region in the fifteenth
century and is connected with the epic song, "The Marriage of King Vukašin," (Low, No. 1). Professor Dragolyub Pavlović, member of the Serbian
Academy of Sciences and Arts, observed that in both cases the plots dealt
with kings, knights, and tournaments, intending to entertain and satisfy the
interests of medieval nobility.[28]

The *Alexandriad* of the so-called pseudo-Callisthenes relating to Alexander the Great was very popular medieval reading, especially because it
depicted the figure of an ideal ruler and conqueror. This romance was believed to be translated from Greek into Serbian at the end of the tenth or
beginning of the eleventh century, and then from Serbian into Russian.[29] According to Pavlović, later opinions maintained that the romance about Alexander entered South Slavic written literatures from Latin sources by way
of translations of the Glagolitic priests in Dalmatia.

Popular romance of Alexander the Great spread from written literature
into South Slavic epic songs and folktales. One finds it in the song, "Stephan
Dušan's Wedding" (Vuk, 2, No. 28), in which the bride's name, Roxana,
had been taken from the romance of Alexander the Great. Emperor Dušan's
historic wife was Yelena. Influence from the Alexander romance is also preserved in the South Slavic folktale, "The Land of Gloom," which contains
motifs about a magic ring which makes a man invisible, along with motifs
of the water of immortality and other fantastic features.[30]

The legend about Acyrius the Wise reached South Slavs from the Byzantine translation which originated from the story of Wise Heikar in the
Arabian Nights.[31] There is a parallel between this story and the song,
"Marko and Musa the Outlaw" (Low, No. 22). Both Acyrius and Prince
Marko share the motif of incarceration in dungeons and eventual rescue;
both were emaciated and unkempt beyond recognition and required
months of healing and recovery.[32]

Various forms of secular medieval entertainment were performed in
feudal courts, including one about historic King Marko. The professional

entertainers were commonly referred to by any of the following terms: co-medians (*skomorosi*), performers (*špilmani*), entertainers (*zabavlyači*), ac-tors (*glumci*), players (*svirci*), singers (*pevci*), dancers (*igreci*), or jesters (*začinyavci*).[33] The epic bards were very prominent among these varied groups.

In their roles of singers, recitors, and heralds, epic bards entertained both feudal nobility at courts and people who gathered during family and clan celebrations. Bards extolled the deeds of the feudal nobility, describing their courts and particularly their feats in war and knightly combat. Bards satisfied peoples' curiosity by telling them of heroic achievements and hap-penings in the world. They were well informed because they traveled from court to court, visited fairs, and took part in pilgrimages and church feasts. Bards often converged at monasteries and other public places.[34]

While oral poetry implied an anonymity of the poet, it was the individ-ual personalities of the bards which played a primary role in their creations. The individuality of great poet-bards emerged and was preserved in their work as is the case with every genuine piece of art.[35] The poet-bards seemed to shed their own individualities in traditional epic singing. In referring to the significance of the bards, the German historian Leopold von Ranke stated that "the very song which is disliked when given by an inferior singer, excites enthusiasm when sung by a more successful performer—by one possessing more of the national sentiment and spirit."[36]

The performer of an epic song was obviously known to the audience. The art was of primary importance, not the performer's immediate iden-tity.[37] Emphasis was clearly placed on tradition so that each epic song gained in value the more it conformed to recognized epic rules and followed well-trodden paths. The importance of epic songs increased with their antiquity, perhaps because heroic events appeared more believable and glorious when placed in a more remote past. Epic bards endeavored to associate with well-established folk materials, thereby dressing new epic songs in familiar, rec-ognizable, and respectable garments.

The anonymity of the bards becomes even more understandable in light of the medieval convention which emphasized modesty and humbleness. A composer-bard of the oral tradition endeavored to contribute as much as possible to the collective value of the art, all the while remaining within the confines of the heroic tradition.[38]

When the Turks invaded in the fourteenth century, the level of learning, formerly maintained by the clergy, sharply declined, with written literature suffering the most. On the other hand, conditions became much more fa-vorable for the further development of oral literature. The heroic climate was marked by struggle with the Turks and hatred of this enemy. The spirit of resistance was best channelled through the oral tradition which grew stronger as literacy and educational levels diminished under Turkish rule. In addition, the Turks did not interfere in oral literature because they did not know the languages of the South Slavs. The South Slavic people took advantage of this neglect and put their hearts into the creation of beautiful epic poems. The fact that oral poetry was anonymous gave the bards even freer rein in expressing themselves.

The Balkan Slavs also developed a balladic genre especially cultivated by the Bulgarians.[39] Prince Marko was cast in both the epic and balladic genres; in heroic poetry great emphasis was put upon his valor, physical strength, and noble actions, while in the ballads he was rewarded with a diverse abundance of emotions. The balladic Prince Marko's true character emerges in the emotional context of patriarchal family relations. Such balladic elements are visible in the motif of Marko's unfaithful wife Angelina, who turned out to be faithful in the end, as we found in a song from Kyustendil (Bulgaria), "Prince Marko Goes Visiting" (M. Arnaudov, *Ocherki*, no. 104, p. 323).

The Macedonians, situated somewhere between the Bulgarians and the Serbs, exploited both genres. Macedonian ballads introduce fantastic creatures, such as the hag-fairy *Samovila* who imposed a levy on the use of potable water on Smoke Mountain. The Mountain complains to Prince Marko in the song, "Veligdenska," from the Prilep area (Brothers Miladinov, No. 9):

> The Mountain of Smoke, thus to Marko spoke:
> Hey, Marko! Good hero!
> Don't curse me, Mountain of Smoke.
> The witch *Samovila* you ought to curse!
> ....
>
> Seventy-seven wells, she dried up,
> To sell a barrel of water,
> A barrel of water for two beautiful dark eyes.

According to Djurić, three stages can be identified in the development of epic poetry. The first stage is "characterized by broad, free improvisations of songs among popular audiences. Poetic forms were not yet stabilized, and epic songs continued to change." In the second stage songs were repeatedly performed in the same form. The third stage in the development of epic poetry is characterized, according to Djurić, by a confluence of songs into a major single epic, such as the Iliad, Nibelungenlied, etc.[40] This final third stage of the growth of epic poetry, the formation of major heroic epics, is achieved through the clustering of individual outstanding epic songs around a central theme. Great epics are a rare and exceptional accomplishment.

South Slavs never developed this level of achievement in the growth of oral poetry. If a singer talented enough to integrate a large number of songs into a single great epic ever existed, the work has not survived. South Slavic epic poetry developed as far as the border between stages two and three. The themes and motifs relating to Prince Marko were developed into more or less permanently accepted songs, while plots were consolidated and grouped around a cycle of the epic person, Prince Marko.

Prince Marko was also the subject of numerous fascinating folktales. Oral poetry and prose often share their origin in the same oral tradition and can even emerge from one another. The relationship between folk poetry and folk prose was very close, and characters and motifs migrated from one genre to the other, the motif of Prince Marko's immortality, for example. Another example is the folktale, "After Death Prince Marko Goes to the Cavern," in *The Folktales* (Matica Hrvatska, No. 158). Yet another motif of fighting a giantess can be found in the song, "Prince Marko and the Djid-Maiden" (Matica Hrvatska, 2, No. 49), as well as in the folktale, "Marica, the Tavern Keeper, Hits Prince Marko with a Spindle," *The Folktales* (Matica Hrvatska, No. 159).

Folk prose, however, tended to be more conventional than the poetry, and in the process of schematization a poetic motif could easily lose its specific features. Whenever Prince Marko and other South Slavic heroes emerge in the folktales, they seem quite generalized, having been detached from their historical context. In the folktales Prince Marko becomes almost any giant, and his heroic actions can be only vaguely recalled, for the most part being descriptions of the fantastic, the miraculous, and the legendary. For this reason, folktales about Prince Marko, and folktales in general can be of interest to us only when they illustrate or support a topic already treated as a main theme of the epic poems.

By virtue of their very form, epic songs were more stable than folktales, assimilating motifs in fixed patterns which, in turn, became entwined in the very structure of the songs themselves. In this way epic songs remained less prone to change. Aesthetic and ethical criteria were much more emphasized in the epic poetry than they were in the folktales. Bards cultivated epic poetry with great pride, and the poems were readily accepted by heroically minded audiences.

The Serbian Uprising against the Turkish Janissaries which began in 1804 provided a new power to heroic poetry. Serbian victories and new heroes among the rebels inspired the epic singers to create original and forceful poems of the time. A group of South Slavic bards that appeared at that time impressed the strong mark of their individuality on folk epic poetry, although they endeavored to keep their talent and their epic poetry within the confines of traditional form. It was also the time when the folk literature was collected, edited and published extensively by several folklorists, among whom the most prominent was Vuk Stefanović Karadžić.[41] It was fortunate that Vuk recorded the best of the heroic poetry, folktales, and proverbs. In his collection are some names of epic bards from whom Vuk obtained the songs. Among them the best were Tešan Podrugović from the village of Kazanci in Hercegovina, Filip Višnyić from the village Medjaši in Bosnia, and the Old Man Miliya and Raško, both from Kolašin in Montenegro.[42] With his straightforward, uncomplicated ranking system, Vuk rated all bards according to their degree of talent: "Just as one man may talk better and clearer than another, so he may be better at reciting and singing songs."[43]

Vuk Karadžić selected about thirty of the most beautiful epic songs about Prince Marko and included them in the second volume of his collection. Later folk song collectors gathered the epic songs about Prince Marko into a cycle (*ciklus*) which increased to about sixty to seventy major songs. These collectors were less discerning in their criteria for inclusion than Vuk Karadžić. There are approximately two hundred South Slavic epic songs including variants about Prince Marko. These songs can be found in the collections *Matica Srpska, Matica Hrvatska, Matica Slovinska,* and *Bulgarsko Narodno tvorchestvo,* as well as in Macedonian, Bosnian, Hercegovinian, and Dalmatian songs. In addition, Prince Marko is found in the Bosnian Mohammedan songs, in which he appears as an adversary.

The Prince Marko cycle of epic songs has to be understood as a group of relatively loosely integrated songs which nevertheless achieve a unity of actions and events throughout his heroic life. According to Nikola Banašević, a well-known Serbian literary critic, in the process of development "it is much more difficult to find the constituent elements in the cycle of Prince Marko, because the songs of the most diversified origin have been attracted to the cycle."[44]

South Slavic epic poetry mirrors the incessant national struggles which characterized Balkan life for the more than five centuries of Turkish occupation, from 1354 when Orkhan occupied Gallipoli to 1913 when the Balkans were liberated. The songs about Prince Marko reflect several stages of Turkish rule, ranging from an almost tolerable reign at the beginning to the unbearable oppression after the late 1600s when the Turkish system began to deteriorate into lawlessness and corruption. For this reason it is not surprising to find the image of Prince Marko undergoing drastic changes of character and mood. These images include the faithful Turkish vassal; the uncompromising fighter against all oppression, Turkish or otherwise; the protector of the weak and poor; the feudal knight, the democratic leader of his people; and the primitive Viking-type warrior who slaughters and ravages. Each projection represents specific views taken from different time periods and by different groups of South Slavic people. Yet all focus upon the same person, contributing to the complexity of Prince Marko's image. Despite all the additions, subtractions, and alterations, the epic Prince Marko sustained a certain unity in the sense that any of the numerous South Slavic groups were able to identify themselves with certain and sometimes all aspects of Prince Marko's character.

The role which Prince Marko played in South Slavic folklore was far out of proportion to his actual historical stature. Marko's intense fame, which managed to survive through the centuries, cannot be accounted for historically. In the South Slavic oral tradition Prince Marko emerged as the incarnation of national sentiment formed through many generations. Historians such as Jireček, von Ranke, and Temperley, however, depict Marko as merely one of several fairly nondescript feudal lords who, as a result of internal feuding, contributed to the disintegration of the Serbian medieval empire and let it fall prey to the Turkish conquerors.

How and why Prince Marko happened to become a major epic hero is still an unsolved puzzle. Once he was established in the role of hero, Marko's fame increased with each successive generation of admirers. The people never held his royal and feudal ties against him. Prince Marko appealed so strongly to the South Slavic peoples that despite his royal origins, he was accepted by them as the dominant force of an entire oral tradition. Consequently Prince Marko came to reflect diverse qualities, embodying both the strong and weak traits of the people who created him. Through the single character of Prince Marko, the South Slavs were able alternatively to praise and blame themselves. Today, the epic figure of Prince Marko stands as a fine aesthetic creation of the South Slavs. In the absence of more reliable sources, Prince Marko's epic life, replete with countless exploits and heroic deeds, serves as a viable means for tracing medieval events of South Slavic history. Through the interaction of epic and history, national ethical values were formulated, creating a central national ideal embodied in the heroic person of Prince Marko.

The role of South Slavic epic singers was paramount in building and spreading a powerful legend which symbolized popular aspirations. The Prince Marko legend has survived as a moving force due to the strength of the oral tradition.

2

Factual and Fictional Images of Prince Marko

> *But Marko is, above all, an historical person, though history knows very little about him.*[1]

South Slavic history has little to say about its folk hero, Prince Marko. The paucity of historical data renders it necessary to rely to a great extent upon oral tradition which has been accepted by audiences as a substitute for actual historical fact. Oral tradition relied on history and history drew on oral tradition. Under such circumstances, it is vital to distinguish between reliable historical data and the seemingly realistic substitute supplied by the oral tradition.

The Mrnyavčević Family

All historians, from Constantine the Philosopher in the fifteenth century to writers in the nineteenth and twentieth centuries, seem to concur that King Marko (1335?–1394) was the first son of King Vukašin Mrnyavčević.[2] Marko was the ruling king from 1371 to 1394, with his capital in the town of Prilep in Macedonia. During his entire reign King Marko was a vassal of the Turkish sultans. Marko's genealogy is not long, the available information being scarce and often vague. According to a citizen of Dubrovnik, Mauro Orbini, who wrote *The Kingdom of the Slavs (Il Regno degli Slavi)* in 1601, Marko's grandfather was a provincial nobleman called Mrnyava. According to Mikhail Khalanskii his name was actually Nenad with the nickname Mrnyava,[3] and he was from Bosnia by origin.[4] He moved to the Serbian royal court when invited by the then King Dušan.

Mrnyava had two sons, Vlkašin and Uglyeša, although folk tradition and poetry indicate a third son by the name of Goyko.[5] Both Mrnyavčević brothers were very successful at Dušan's court.[6] There are indications that Vukašin was an able though aggressive statesman. During the year following the premature death of Emperor Dušan the Mighty in 1355, the Serbian princes and high clergy met at a state convention in Skopye and made Vukašin a regent to the heir Uroš, who at the time was nineteen years old.[7]

We find more about Vukašin in the decree which he issued on April 5, 1370, at Poreč near Skopye. He described himself as "the Lord of the Serbian Lands, of the Greeks and of the Western Provinces," further alluding to his wife Queen Alena (Yelena) and his sons Marko, Andriya, and Dimitar.[8]

During these times Vukašin intended to marry his son Marko to the daughter of the Croatian nobleman Gregor Pavlović Šubić. Vukašin negotiated the matter with the Bosnian King Tvrtko at whose court the girl lived as a protégée. This match had been a clever design of King Vukašin to have his son Marko marry a Šubić, who was a grandniece of the Emperor Dušan (a granddaughter of Dušan's sister Yelena) and a descendant of the Nemanyić dynasty in the female line. The match was never realized because of the opposition of Pope Urban V who refused to allow a Catholic princess to marry the schismatic Prince Marko. The matter was concluded by a letter of dissent in April 1370 which Pope Urban V sent to King Tvrtko.[9]

Vukašin was concerned that the Turks, who had crossed over from Asia Minor, were pressing ever deeper into the Balkans. Vukašin sought to create a defense alliance with the Greeks and, in order to cover his western flank, went to a camp near the town of Skadar in June of 1371. According to Jireček, his son Marko was with him.[10] On September 26, 1371, the Turks totally defeated the Serbian army in a forested area called Černomen near Adrianople. During this battle both Vukašin and his brother Uglyeša were killed.[11]

Later Serbian chronicles such as the *Karlovci Annals* and *Tronoša Genealogy* from 1791 made a case against Vukašin as the murderer of Emperor Uroš, a charge which is historically unfounded since Vukašin died in September 1371. Uroš died in December of the same year. The roles of the older Mrnyavčevićes, Vukašin and Uglyeša (father and uncle of Prince Marko) have been diminished in folk tradition.

The relationships between Prince Marko and both the Emperor Uroš and his father King Vukašin were complex. It is known historically that

1. Emperor Uroš and King Vukašin, fresco in the Monastery of St. Nicholas in Psača, painted 1365–1371. Reprinted by permission of V. Djurič, from *Recherches sur l'art* (Novi Sad: Matica Srpska, 1968).

Uroš personally relied on Marko and as early as 1361 on at least one occasion sent Marko to Dubrovnik on a diplomatic and business mission.[12] At the same time the Patriarch Paysiy reported in his chronicles that Vukašin and his son Marko had mutual frictions as seen from these words: "Somehow Marko erred against his father Vukašin, who tried to kill Marko. And Marko escaped to the Turkish Emperor at Adrianople. After Vukašin was killed [in the battle] Emperor Bayazet appointed Marko a low ranking pasha in Prilep and Ohrid."[13]

It is evident that this chronicle tried to compromise the characters both of Vukašin and Marko: the former for attempting to kill his son, and the latter for having become a Turkish vassal. There are no firm historical records which confirm such a split between King Vukašin and Prince Marko.

As with the Emperor Dušan's death sixteen years earlier, the death of Vukašin and Uglyeša in 1371 created a vacuum within the Serbian state. The situation worsened to the point where princes and powerful magnates rushed to seize as much land as they could. After Vukašin's death, Balša II, the ruler of Skadar, promptly took over Vukašin's town of Prizren, while the rest of the region was occupied by the Turks. Then the Turks gave the land to Marko who became the Turkish vassal King in Prilep.

King Marko's domain was bordered by Mt. Šar on the northwest and the Vardar River on the east. It embraced the Lake Ohrid area and the town of Kastoria in the southwest. As a Turkish vassal, Marko had to serve the sultan in various military campaigns and he paid regular dues in tribute. Otherwise, it appeared that Marko enjoyed relative freedom in the domestic affairs of his little kingdom. He availed himself of the royal right to mint coins, one of which carries the inscription "In Christ the Lord, the faithful King Marko."[14]

According to Kravtsov, a Serbian state convention or *sabor*, took place at Peć on September 25–26, 1374, to settle the discord which had arisen in the Serbian state.[15] Marko declared himself King at the convention, while Lord Vuk Branković supported Prince Lazar Hreblyanović for the same title. Tvrtko of Bosnia also proclaimed himself King. Ironically, two Serbian kings accepted the overlordship of two different foreign countries—Marko of the Turkish sultan, and Tvrtko of the Hungarian king. The other Serbian rulers kept mostly to themselves, plotting against each other when they were not fighting. What had once been the great Serbian Empire now degenerated into an indefinite and ever-changing region which is vaguely described on historic maps as being ruled by "Serbian princes."

According to Mauro Orbini, Marko married Yelena, the daughter of Radoslav Hlapen, Lord of Berria and Voden. His married life was turbulent and he abandoned Yelena because of her immoral life.[16] Then, in 1380,

КРАЛЬ МАРКО (1371—1394 г.)

По фреската въ мънастиря Св. Димитри — Скопско.

(Изъ спис. „Минало". кн. 7 и 8. 1913 год., на г. Баласчевъ.)

2. Historical King Marko, fresco in his Monastery of St. Demetrius. From Veliko Iordanov, *Krali-Marko: istoriko literaturen priegled* [King Marko: a historical literary survey] (authenticity of fresco is in question) (Sofiia: Tsarska Pridvorna Pechatnitsa, 1916). Courtesy of the Bulgarian Writers Union.

while Marko was fighting in campaigns on the Sultan's behalf, Yelena ceded Kastoria to Balša II Balšić and to the Albanian magnate Andriya Musaki.[17] Marko tried several times to recapture Kastoria by force and, although he had the support of the Turkish troops, he failed.

Yelena was not the only woman in King Marko's life. He was known for his love affairs. According to a fourteenth-century South Slavic manuscript in the collection of Aleksei Ivanovich Khludov (now in the State Historical Museum in Moscow),[18] King Marko gave his father-in-law, Radoslav Hlapen, a certain Todora,[19] the wife of Grgur, in exchange for the return of his own wife Yelena. King Marko historically had no offspring, although Bulgarian folk tradition hints that he did have an illegitimate child. The atmosphere of King Marko's court was lighthearted. Thus we hear from one of King Marko's subjects, a certain Dobre, son of Rade from Poreč (who reports the above exchange of women), that King Marko was inclined to drink and indulge in a lascivious way of life. The same Dobre describes himself as having been present at King Marko's parties. According to Lyubomir Stoyanović, Dobre's observations appear as an annotated gloss in the Khludov manuscript and read as follows: "This is being written in Poreči ... during the days of the faithful King Marko who gave Todora, wife of Grgur, to Hlapen and took back his first wedded wife Yelena, daughter of Hlapen ... written by novice Dobre, son of Rade ... and if they sin somewhere ... or get drunk ... do not condemn them."[20]

Another historical fact sheds light on King Marko and on the moral climate of his court. Of the folk singers who celebrated the achievements of Marko's contemporaries, one was a man who was both historically known and the subject of folk poetry. His name was Ostoya Rayakovič, and he was related to King Marko and married to a daughter of Marko's friend Gropa, Lord (*Župan*) of Ohrid.[21] Epic bards praised Ostoya during his lifetime, giving him the nickname "Ugarčić," and they mentioned that epic singing was accompanied by the instrument called a *gusle*.[22] The fact that an epic song about a contemporary and relative of Marko was preserved until today proves, according to Kostić, that epic poetry was not only alive in Marko's time but that epic songs also existed about King Marko which were not preserved. It is logical to assume that epic bards were more likely to sing about the royal Marko than about his insignificant relative Ostoya. Marko's local popularity spread with time across the provincial boundaries and became accepted by all South Slavs, as can be seen in oral literatures from Macedonia, Montenegro, and Dalmatia, as well as from Serbia, Croatia, Slovenia, and across Bulgaria to the Black Sea.

Another important question remains to be examined—the relation between historical King Marko and the Battle of Kossovo which was fought between the Turks and the Christians in 1389. This was one of the most decisive battles in the Balkans, but one in which the historical King Marko did not participate.

A loose Christian alliance of a majority of the Balkan principalities was arraigned against the Turks. These principalities included Serbia (Vuk Brankovic̀), Bosnia (King Tvrtko), Croatia (Ivan Horvat), and Zeta, present Montenegro (Vlatko Vukovic̀). Led by the Serbian Prince Lazar Hreblyanovic̀, they were defeated, and the fate of the Balkans was decided for the next five centuries.[23] Sultan Murad I was killed by Miloš Obilic̀, and Prince Lazar was beheaded after the Battle of Kossovo by the Turks on orders of the new Sultan Bajazet I. The Croatian scholar Maretic̀ speculated that both King Marko and his neighbor Konstantin Deyanovic̀-Dragaš remained neutral during this battle because they were Turkish vassals. According to Maretic̀, Sultan Murad I did not pressure King Marko and Konstantin, because he did not trust that they could fight against their own people.[24]

The death of Prince Marko is reported by Constantine the Philosopher in his biography *Život Despota Stefana Lazarevic̀a* (1431). He described the 1394 campaign of Sultan Bayazet I against the Wallachian Duke Mirchea. Several Serbian vassals stood with the Turks: Lord Stefan Lazarevic̀, son of the beheaded Prince Lazar; Konstantin Deyanovic̀-Dragaš, who was related both to the Nemanyic̀es and to the Byzantine emperors; and finally King Marko. The battle between the Wallachians and the Turks took place at Rovine on May 17, 1394, and both King Marko and Lord Konstantin Deyanovic̀ were killed.[25] Thirty-seven years later Constantine the Philosopher reported how Marko prayed to God to give the victory to the Christians even at the price of his own life. This, in fact, is what happened.

A Composite Image of Prince Marko

> *Songs about Marko's imprisonment by Arabs . . . are about the other historical person of the sixteenth century, "Knight Marko" (Viteazul), . . . and songs about him merged with songs about Prince Marko.*[26]

Stories of other historical personages have been added to the descriptions of King Marko, who himself was the first of the four dominant images of Marko. King Marko Mrnyavčevic̀, who lived in the fourteenth century, acquired some of the characteristics of Deli Marko Viteazul, the second dominant Marko prototype, who lived at the end of the sixteenth and the beginning of the seventeenth century.[27] Both these historical Markos contributed their share to the creation of the poetic image of Prince Marko. The second Marko, Marko Viteazul, was a *condottière* in the service of the Wallachian Prince Michael the Brave, who ruled from 1593 to 1601. Marko Viteazul, or Deli Marko, held high military posts and distinguished himself by courageous and spectacular deeds in the war against the Turks. He fought on both sides of the Danube River in Romania, Serbia, and Bulgaria. Songs dealing specifically with him can be found in the Romanian epics published in 1893 by Professor Ovid Densusianu, linguist and folklorist, in *Revista critica literara*. The poems were analyzed by A. I. Jacimirski, though somewhat onesidedly, since he explained the Romanian legend of Marko Viteazul exclusively on the basis of South Slavic epic poetry.[28]

The Romanian Marko Viteazul was quite a heroic personality in his own right. Regardless of his Serbian origin and the fact that he fought primarily with his own Serbian bands, Marko Viteazul was accepted and celebrated as a Romanian national hero. Many of the Serbian refugees living in Wallachia at the end of the sixteenth century were attracted to Marko Viteazul for reasons of revenge against the Turks or by prospects of booty; perhaps by both. This Marko's origin is uncertain. Some sources trace it to Dubrovnik, others to either Szeged or Kanyža in Hungary. Romanian collectors of his songs tend to pinpoint his origin in the Wallachian mountain villages of Transylvania, while others refer to a ruined castle near Haceg in Transylvania.

Aleksa Ivić, in his book, *The History of the Serbs in Voyvodina*, has compiled a body of data on Marko Viteazul.[29] According to Ivić, the first historical record relating to Marko Viteazul can be dated to 1594 when he raided Turkish territories. In his first raid, Marko Viteazul penetrated as far into Turkey as Adrianople, moving through Bulgaria. He and 500 Serbians plundered, sacked, and burned towns along the way. Another raid was soon undertaken with 1500 men, who captured and sacked the town of Plevna in Bulgaria. On his return from this last raid Marko Viteazul was wounded, captured, and sent to prison in Constantinople.[30] The sources vary concerning the year of Marko Viteazul's capture, placing it between 1596 and 1600. In any case Marko succeeded in escaping or being released during or after 1601. Upon returning, Marko Viteazul entered the service of the Austrian King Rudolf II and later of the Hungarian Prince of Transylvania, Count Gabriel Bethlen. Marko remained with him from 1617 to 1619, during which time he was sent to Constantinople as an envoy. He was rejected by the Turks when he was suggested for the post of Prince of Moldavia. The last time Marko Viteazul was noted as being alive was in 1619.[31]

The common elements in the lives of Marko Viteazul and King Marko Mrnyavčević unavoidably led to the combination of the two figures into a single epic character. The Prince Marko prototype augmented the legend of Marko Viteazul. Both men were Serbs, both disliked the Turks and fought against them, yet both were Turkish vassals. The two Markos shared the qualities of adventure and chivalry, and they were popular knights. Another prominent common detail was that both men were fond of drinking. Marko Viteazul was renowned for his nights of revelry with another Serb, Djura Rac of Slankamen in Srem, who is known to us from such epic songs as Djura the Drunkard.[32]

A contributing factor in the ultimate fusion of the two Markos into a single epic figure might have been that Marko Viteazul of the sixteenth century lived in Wallachia in the very vicinity where King Marko Mrnyavčević had been killed about two hundred years before. The memory and lingering legend of Prince Marko's death at Rovine inspired the South Slavic and the Romanian traditions. Both complemented each other and eventually merged into a single legend. Seventeenth-century poems about Marko were readjusted and new elements were introduced, giving a novel vitality to the existing epic tradition of Prince Marko Mrnyavčević. The historical fact of Marko Viteazul's imprisonment explains the whole series of epic poems dealing with Prince Marko's sojourn in the Sultan's jail in Constantinople, an event which otherwise tended to contradict other poems describing Marko's generally good relations and sense of duty toward the Sultan.

The epic figure of Prince Marko may have gained support from yet another historical personality, that of Marko Barbadigo, a Venetian nobleman; the third Marko prototype. When Marko Barbadigo, a contemporary of King Marko, married, he received in dowry the town of Kroya, Albania, as Prince Marko had acquired Kastoria. Marko Barbadigo is also reported to have had poor luck with his wife, who, like the wife of Prince Marko, is represented in the chronicles as being unfaithful. Furthermore, during Barbadigo's absence from home, his wife left him and even managed to transfer Kroya over to her lover, Konstantin Balšić,[33] a relative of Balša II who took Kastoria from King Marko.[34]

The fourth Marko was known in Ukrainian epic poetry as Marko the Accursed (*Marko Prokliatyi*).[35] Khalanskii asserts that Marko the Accursed was a Ukrainian version of Prince Marko and that those songs dealing with him as the central figure evolved under direct influence of the Balkans.[36] According to this view, the oral epic tradition of Prince Marko travelled from the Balkans to the Ukraine. This epic migration is supported not only by the historical and social similarities existing between the Balkans and the Ukraine but also through the close cultural relations and particularly the high mobility of the respective populations. Thus the massive Serbian exodus in the 1700s from Southern Hungary to the Western Ukraine becomes of outstanding importance in the eighteenth century. For some time a seg-

ment of the Ukraine was known as Little Serbia and thus the Serbian epic
tradition may have played a role in influencing and motivating the growth
of the legend of Marko the Accursed. Khalanskii found that a majority of
Ukrainian songs about Marko the Accursed, with the exception of his journey to the Underworld, were variants of Serbian epic songs about Prince
Marko and almost exclusively dealt with the outlaw (*hayduk*) cycle, and
that these motifs readily corresponded to the Cossack period of Ukrainian
epic poetry.[37] In the process of assimilation, Serbian influences were
adapted to the needs and circumstances of the Ukrainian people who during this period were faced with a struggle against foreign oppression similar
to that of the South Slavs. From this emerged a new epic personality of
Marko the Accursed who was characterized quite differently from Prince
Marko. He was known to be unhappy, orphaned, and homeless; frequently
guilty without cause—in a word, an accursed man. In this sense he fit the
prototype of a Cossack, who corresponds to the South Slavic idea of the
hayduk.[38] Cossacks began as outlaws and escapees from their domestic and
foreign (Polish) feudal lords. Later they served in Russia as border rangers,
known by their violent and brave conduct.

The Ukrainian cycle of Marko the Accursed did not, however, develop
to an advanced stage of epic poetry nor was it infiltrated by various universal motifs. It failed to become the vehicle for numerous other epic themes, in
contrast to the case of Prince Marko. The epic songs dealing with Marko
the Accursed did not evoke a sufficiently strong response from the popular
audiences. In the Ukrainian environment, memories of South Slavic epic
past were falling into oblivion, and Marko the Accursed could not develop
the epic qualities powerful enough for peoples' identification. After all,
Prince Marko was providing people with the feeling of greatness, while
Marko the Accursed was burdened with guilt and unhappiness.

Marko's Companions

As a hero Prince Marko usually appears alone and without a retine, his
adversaries often enlarged into the whole Turkish army. At times he is seen
with a companion who fights alongside him against a common enemy.
Sometimes Prince Marko appears in a trio with other heroes. At wedding
parties he is usually in a large group of brave warriors, distinguishing himself as the one who overcomes obstacles and wins the bride for another man.

One of the warriors related to Prince Marko is Duke Momčilo, whose
bravery and strength were objects of great admiration by epic bards.[39] Over
time Duke Momčilo was transformed into Prince Marko's uncle. Within the

framework of epic structure Duke Momčilo instills in Prince Marko the qualities of intrepid gallantry, valor, and chivalry. When the presumed bond between Marko and his epic "uncle" surfaces, the archaic reminiscences and motifs of the matriarchal order become more evident expressed in the relationship between the maternal uncle and nephew which is stronger, more binding and important than even that between father and son.

The proof of Momčilo's historical existence can be found in two of his Byzantine contemporaries: Nicephorus Gregoras, who called Momčilo "Momitilas," and John VI Cantacuzene, who refers to him as "Momicilos."[40] Momčilo lived in the first half of the fourteenth century in the fortified town of Peritheorion in Aegean Thrace. From this town Momčilo used to set out on raids into surrounding areas with his band of marauders. In South Slavic epic poetry the Greek name for Peritheorion was changed to Pirlitor, which is a mountain in Montenegro. This provided a Slavic territorial frame for Momčilo and his activities.

Momčilo's historical origin is obscure. It is generally accepted that he was a Bulgarian and that his early unlawful activities took place in the inaccessible high Rhodope Mountains in the general vicinity of the triangle between the towns of Drama, Plovdiv, and Samokov. He was helped by the fact that at the time that particular area represented an undefined and highly disputed border between Serbia, Bulgaria, and the Byzantine Empire. Yet Momčilo's extralegal successes eventually proved useful and perhaps even justifiable, since he was made a Lord of the area as well as Margrave (*Sebastokrator*). Many of his earlier outlaws turned into mercenary soldiers.[41]

Momčilo's death was dramatic. His plundering raids had annoyed the Greeks so much that they found it expedient to ask the Turks, who had just crossed over from Asia Minor into Europe, for help. Thus the Greeks together with the Turks attacked Duke Momčilo in an effort to subdue him. Momčilo was killed in 1345 by the then Emperor John VI Cantacuzene (1342–1355) and his Turkish allies in Peritheorion.[42]

Djurić described the battle which took place beneath the walls of Peritheorion. The citizens, in their fear of the Turks and their uncertainty of who would win, had closed the gate of the fortress so that Momčilo could not get in. He was killed just outside. According to Djurić this betrayal of Momčilo was widely and deeply remembered in the popular tradition, and since the guilt had to be transferred and made as heinous as possible, Momčilo's wife was selected as the culprit instead of Peritheorion's citizens. Historical records, however, are clear in their description of what really took place, because John VI Cantacuzene indifferently reports in his chronicle that Momčilo's widow was allowed to leave freely and return to her native Bulgaria.

Historical sources do not mention the existence of Momčilo's sister who later appears in the epic South Slavic tradition as Yevrosima, the mother of Prince Marko, and as advisor, critic, and guardian of his faith. Such songs, for instance, are from the Brothers Miladinov collection: "Marko's Confession," No. 54; "Seven Heroes and the Arab," No. 143; and "Marko Abducts the Bride," No. 147.

There are several trios of heroes in which Prince Marko is the central figure. The most common trio is that of Prince Marko-Miloš Obilić-Relya Krilatica. Miloš Obilić is one of the most prominent Serbian epic heroes. He and Prince Marko often appear together in epic poetry as blood brothers, as in "Marko and the Fairy," in Vuk 2, No. 37.

History knows little about Miloš Obilić but is quite positive about the deed which brought him glory—the famous slaying of the Turkish Sultan Murad I in the Battle of Kossovo. Miloš' true name was Kobilić or Kobilović, derived from *kobila* which means "mare."[43] According to popular tradition, the name "Kobilić" comes from Miloš having been nursed by a mare.

Miloš Obilić did not belong to the gentry, although it is possible that he was a lower nobleman or a courtier. In order to set the stage for his dramatic conflict with the "traitor" Vuk Branković, Obilić was portrayed in epic poetry as being the son-in-law of Prince Lazar, although in fact he was not.[44] Vuk Branković was the real-life son-in-law of the Prince. Miloš Obilić won his place in South Slavic epic poetry and by the sixteenth century his memory was strong, even in Bulgaria. This was confirmed by Benedikt Kuripešić, who collected so much material about Miloš while travelling through the Kossovo region, that he was able to dedicate an entire chapter to him in the book *Putopis* [Itinerary].[45]

Relya the Winged often appeared in the company of Prince Marko as the third of the Marko-Miloš trio. Relya lived before Prince Marko, but bards have rendered him Marko's contemporary, a common anachronism with many other heroes who lived centuries before or after Marko. The two Byzantine historians, Gregoras and Cantacuzene, call Relya *Chrelis*, while Slavic sources refer to him as *Hrelya*.[46] Stoyan Novaković reports that Relya was a nobleman who lived during the late thirteenth and early fourteenth centuries, having held the Byzantine court title of First Regent (*Protosebastos*) which he probably received from Andronicus II (1282–1328). Later, Relya supposedly used the title *kesar* or *kaisar* and ruled the region around the Struma River from Strumica, its Macedonian capital.[47]

Relya seems to have occupied various important positions in the courts of three Serbian kings of the fourteenth century. He seceded from Emperor Dušan (1331–1355) to the Byzantines, and then later returned. Dušan, however, did not forgive his earlier disloyalty and sent him to the monastery Rila where Relya was ordained as Father Chariton and where he died in 1343.[48]

Relya acquired the nickname "winged," and his family's coat of arms contained the emblem of an eagle's wings. He is often described in epic poetry as having used "winged" body armor.[49] Kravtsov and Maretić both agree that these two factors are sufficient explanations for the use of such a nickname, although Kravtsov went further and entertained the possibility that in the popular tradition Relya was considered to have been the son of a dragon.[50]

In numerous poems Prince Marko appears in yet another trio, with the Hungarian heroes Sibinyanin Yanko and Banović Sekula, both of whom lived in the fifteenth century, about hundred years after Marko's death. Among heroic poems about the trio are the following songs from Matica Hrvatska: "Prince Marko at the Wedding of Sibinyanin Yanko," No. 51; "Prince Marko Rescues Sibinyanin Yanko," No. 52; "Sibinyanin Yanko and Sekula Rescue Prince Marko," No. 63.

The epic Sibinyanin Yanko is the historical figure of Yanoš Hunyady, who was born around 1387 in Transylvania. In South Slavic tradition he is called Sibinyanin for the city of Sibiu. His father was of low birth, and was knighted by King Sigismund.[51] As a result of his incessant struggle with the Turks, Yanoš Hunyady became one of the most celebrated men of his time. He was particularly popular in Hungary, Serbia, and Bulgaria where he participated in wars against the Turks. He served the Serbian ruler Djuradj Branković and later the Hungarian King Ladislaus (*Laszlo*) III. When the king was killed, Yanoš Hunyady was elected to rule as regent on behalf of the young king Ladislaus V.[52]

Both historically and in epic poetry Hunyady stands out against the Turks in the second Battle of Kossovo which took place in 1448. He was forced to flee through Serbia, where he was imprisoned by Djuradj Branković, who charged Hunyady with confiscating his estate in Hungary and plundering Serbia. While Hunyady had done both, they were only as a retaliation for the Branković refusal to participate in the war against the Turks. Hunyady was eventually released and remained very active in his struggle against the Turks. His most glorious deed was the valiant defense of Belgrade in 1456, which staved off the Turkish conquest of Central Europe for more than half a century.

In several poems epic Yanko is referred to as "Ugrin," meaning the Hungarian. South Slavic bards and epic audiences accepted Sibinyanin Yanko as their own national hero, while always aware of his non-Slavic origin. This can be understood within the overall struggle of the Christians against Islam, when national differences were considered of secondary importance at best. It is also a universal trait of the heroic epic to feature foreign heroes. The Homeric epic has several of them, as does the Russian *bylina*.

The other Hungarian champion of the fifteenth century who was absorbed in the second trio of heroes was Banović Sekula (*Szekelyi*). Sekula Banović appears fighting alongside Prince Marko in the epic poetry and is sometimes mentioned as Marko's son. According to the historical record, Szekelyi was a nephew of Yanoš Hunyady. He served as the Lord (*Ban*) of Dalmatia and Croatia in 1446. Szekelyi did not live a long life. He was killed in the second Battle of Kossovo in 1448. Throughout the popular lore he is remembered as a young man who is on occasion made out to be a child hero, Sekula the Child, barely twelve years of age.[53]

It is characteristic for both epic trios to be unstable in terms of the personalities which appear in epic songs. Other heroes enter in the trios replacing each other in various combinations. Thus Vuk the Fiery Dragon is a new hero who was frequently introduced into the second trio. He is a mixture of two figures—one mythological, the other historical. Vuk the Fiery Dragon appears side by side with Prince Marko, although he was not a contemporary of Prince Marko, having lived in the fifteenth century.

The historical Vuk was the grandson of the Serbian ruler Djuradj Branković and the illegitimate child of Grgur, who was blinded as a hostage by the Turkish Sultan Murad II. Grgur's sister Mara was the wife of Murad II but was unable to help either her family or her country which had in the meantime become almost fully occupied by the Turks.

When Vuk, who was born around 1440, came of age, he entered into the service of the Hungarian King Matthias Corvinus (1458–1490), the son of Janoš Hunyadi. During this service Vuk distinguished himself in the war still raging against the Turks. King Corvinus bestowed on Vuk the title of Lord, allotting to him estates in Croatia and Srem, and the fortress of Slankamen.[54]

Popular songs describe Vuk's birth and death as supernatural. Vuk probably stimulated the people's imagination with his bravery and spectacular escapades against the Turks.[55] Epic poets were so overwhelmed with Vuk's victories that a great number of heroic songs were composed and dedicated to this hero, placing him next in rank to Prince Marko and Miloš Obilić.

PRINCE MARKO'S FICTIONAL IMAGE IN EPIC POETRY

The giant bones of Marko Kralyevič have found their resting place somewhere in that Holy Mountain where nothing has changed since the Middle Ages.[56]

Departures from the Historical Bases

The epic poetry generally draws from and expresses the oral tradition of its people. The heroic plot develops within the framework of an existing epic tradition. Such epic tradition, in turn, may absorb historical elements to eventually become an oral historical tradition on the ground of which the folk history is built. Historical persons and events merely represent the starting point from which poetic imagination begins the process of developing the epic songs. At times bards have produced almost impossible combinations of plot and character, and epic singers have come to treat history by giving subjective interpretations, very much in the manner of the modern writer. The historical reminiscences which did find their way into epic poetry have frequently undergone such extensive modifications by bards that what remained of real history is changed beyond recognition. Indeed, it was a common practice, as in the case of Prince Marko, to adjust and combine attributes of various historical persons into one composite whole. The reason for such a procedure can be found in the attitude of epic singers toward their work. They praised Prince Marko's heroic deeds or historical events, and they also celebrated other archetypal persons and events which still lingered in the popular tradition. The epic poet begins with the real King Marko and moves toward the realm of the fantastic while retaining a semblance of reality. In the absence of historical materials, epic poetry came often to serve as a "primary" historical source, as in the case of the *Tronoša Genealogy,* dating from 1791, which represents history written on the basis of the popular tradition.[57] In the development of the genealogy genre, history emerged from the epic, which in its turn drew to a large extent upon medieval chronicles and other similar sources.

Epic singers selected and inserted certain historical facts about Prince Marko into folk poetry, which succeeds in illuminating history from the popular viewpoint. Historical elements in epic songs should not be considered as accurate accounts but rather as what was *believed* to have happened or, under certain conditions, what *might* or perhaps *should* have happened.

The epic songs about Prince Marko tended to present historical events in the light of the ethical and societal outlook of a given period. Balkan society underwent constant and profound change, so that the differences in the social conditions before, during, and after feudalism or the Turkish oc-

cupation came to be reflected in the manner in which history was interpreted in epic poetry. The epic songs were like a living organism in which
the historical elements underwent many evolutionary changes, depending
on the views of successive generations. The figure of Prince Marko became
a nucleus around which differing popular views clustered, so that Prince
Marko eventually came to denote everything from a traitor to a protagonist
of national liberation.

Songs which belong to the Prince Marko cycle display a great range of
differing and often contradictory views. Thus the passing of centuries could
have profound impact on the same song. It is of outstanding importance, as
Djurić stated, to analyze songs to see how they "show the spirit of each ep-
och itself and all epochs together; their differences and their commonali-
ties; their harmony or disharmony between heroes and their time; influence
of social and historical circumstances on the course of this or another event,
and on the actions of a specific individual."[58]

The Turkish conquest of the Balkans was gradual, taking over one
hundred and fifty years, from the mid-fourteenth to the end of the fifteenth
century. Several songs linked Prince Marko to the Sultan and the Turks as if
they were allies, for example: "Marko's Hunting with the Turks," Vuk 2,
No. 34, and "Marko and Mina of Kostur" Vuk 2, No. 28. Such songs de-
scend from as early as King Marko's lifetime or soon after. They reflect the
prevailing atmosphere of King Marko's own time when the Turkish occupation had not yet instituted a severe and tyrannical rule over the Balkan
people. Some of the songs show the old discord which prevailed among the
South Slavic noblemen, their mutual fights over land and property rights,
and their arrogance and petty quarrels, conveying the extent to which these
domestic feuds became a burden for the people. Songs like: "Uroš and the
Mrnyavčevićes," Vuk 2, No. 33, and "Prince Marko and Bogdan the Perilous," Vuk 2, No. 38, exemplified such behavior.

Later songs or later layers of epic songs, particularly from the seventeenth century, display an idealization of the South Slavic medieval states
with their often exaggerated glamor and splendor. Such descriptions took
place in light of growing dissatisfaction with Turkish rule which became
more and more unbearable as time passed. Many of the fresco paintings in
churches and monasteries depicted Slavic medieval rulers in all their gran-
deur. These could have rekindled the popular imagination and introduced
such attributes into the later songs. This view is asserted by Djurić[59] and
substantiated by Svetozar Radoyčić in his contribution to the book, *Texts
and Frescoes* entitled, "About Some Common Motifs of Our Folk Song and
Our Ancient Paintings."[60]

If the frescoes from church walls reminded people that they once had a
national state and kings such as Marko, then they needed a hero in their

3. King Marko, damaged fresco in the Monastery of St. Archangel Michael in Prilep, painted about 1380. Reprinted by permission of V. Djurić, from *Recherches sur l'art* (Novi Sad: Matica Srpska, 1968).

own image to protect them from Turkish oppression. They made Prince Marko superior to Turks in his bravery, justice, honesty, and honor. Prince Marko's superiority over the Turks was what they wished, dreamed, and needed for themselves. As Djurić noted, "Marko was to the Turks what a hawk is for terrified sparrows. Marko was a giant for whom the world was too narrow, who has a strength unquenched by combat. Marko is the embodiment of strivings of an oppressed nation which is gathering its indomitable force to break out of the boundaries of an enslaved life."[61]

Prince Marko's historic vassalage to the Sultan was handled masterfully by epic singers. They accepted it as unavoidable and were not afraid to make this clear. Despite his vassalage, Prince Marko was increasingly represented as protecting his people from Turkish injustice. Sometimes he was a dutiful vassal who used his influence through regular channels and fulfilled this role without conflict. He was also shown as an outlaw who fought the Turks along with the popular brigands from the sixteenth to eighteenth century (commonly called the *hayduci*).

With the passage of time Prince Marko was reduced from royalty and transformed into a commoner. The epic Prince Marko became accepted as one of the people and as one who worked on their behalf for justice. Once presented in this manner it was easy to remember and identify oneself with Prince Marko, since he stood precisely for those elementary ideals which were universally held sacred. While the basic heroic core of Prince Marko's poetic personality was preserved (honor, justice, filial respect), new generations would add something from their own values. Thus in the song, "Betting of Prince Marko," in Matica Hrvatska, 2, No. 15, Prince Marko's mother performs menial house duties and errands, the singer having forgotten her royal status. The other song, "Marko and Beg Kostadin," Vuk 2, No. 59, contains the theme of friendship between the two feudal lords. The bards presented Prince Marko as a commoner with traditional values who reproaches his friend for not respecting his own parents, for having contempt for the poor, and for only selecting rich friends.

Epic poetry about Prince Marko interacted with history, resulting in a forceful cycle of epic songs which are mainly grouped according to whether Marko is presented as Turkish vassal or not. The Prince Marko cycle has a shortcoming in that its songs are loosely connected, and that Marko appears in other cycles as well, such as the Nemanyić and Kossovo.

The grouping of songs by motifs is a rather difficult task because there are some songs with two distinct motifs next to each other, e.g. the unfaithful wife and the wedding in the song, "The Marriage of King Vukašin." In *Morphology of the Folktale,* Vladimir Iakovlevich Propp notes that "the fully objective separation of one theme from another ... is by no means a simple task."[62] He states that "the themes of the tale are closely linked to one another, and are mutually interwoven."[63] Djurić is justified in concluding that motifs are more important than persons in epic poetry, but they are expressed through epic persons who are very different from each other.[64] Motifs were gathered and accumulated which transcend the bounds of the actual person and/or historical event. As motifs gathered around the historical person of Marko, his real personality was eventually pushed into the background, and he became generalized and abstracted from reality. Nevertheless, Marko's real or epic appearances were depicted within a factual framework of geographic places. With time the historical elements weakened and became vague, as the result of displacement by the process of typification. Once Prince Marko evolved into a type or symbol, he became the object of further popular appreciation and fascination, attracting motifs such as dragon-slayer, wedding with obstacles, killing in ignorance, etc. The myths and legends, the ethical and religious concepts of the Balkan people—all focussed on the generalized type, Prince Marko. Growing in stature, Prince Marko exerted a powerful magnetism which drew together most of the major heroes of the South Slavs: Miloš Obilić, Relya the Winged, Yanko of Sibin, and Bogdan the Perilous. Their stories and Prince Marko's become intricately intertwined.

Whole historical epochs were extricated from their chronological place in time and attributed, or sometimes even subordinated, to the epic figure of Prince Marko. Thus Prince Marko stretches from before the times of Emperor Dušan to the end of the Outlaw period in the eighteenth century. Perhaps it is due to such complexity that the epic figure of Prince Marko, as created by the faith and imagination of the Balkan people, may sometimes appear distorted or incomprehensible.

The earliest songs about Prince Marko had to have been chronicle-songs, which appeared quite spontaneously and often described an important event right after it had taken place.[65] Although the original versions of such chronicle-songs were not preserved, some recollections surface in the later epic songs, such as the real name of King Vukašin, his actual battle and death at Marica River, and other elements of local value. Chronicle-songs of those days supplied epic bards with information about King Marko to be used in the composition of new motif-songs.[66] Ordinarily motif-songs appeared when the link with the actual events had been weakened. Typical motifs were introduced to describe the traditional heroic way of life. (For more about motifs see Boris Tomashevskii.[67]) Generalized themes were ascribed interchangeably to other epic characters, including the person of Prince Marko. Some of the motif-songs about Prince Marko deal with the universal motifs which appear in many other literatures, both oral and written.

The reason that Prince Marko attracted and stimulated epic interest to such extent is because he managed to succeed in his ventures with outstanding bravery, wisdom, strength, nobility, and above all, a sense of justice.

Epic poems about Prince Marko were very dynamic, never in their final form. Contemporary versions will, in turn, be modified by future bards. Prince Marko's epic poems became enriched with their migration from one region to another. Historical events which triggered the forming of a chronicle-song gradually blurred, and the songs adapted to new places and circumstances. Such was the epic poem, "Marko Kralyević and His Brother Andriyaš," which was found far from King Marko's homeland, in the Adriatic area.

The maturation of Prince Marko's songs was characterized by the disappearance of specific historical elements about him. A less inhibited expression of a more generalized nature took place, giving the impetus for the creation of the truly beautiful heroic poems. Over the centuries bards forgot feudal fights and historical precision, and from being mere "history in verse" the songs became composed around interesting motifs. Detached from his historical context Prince Marko became a legendary giant who was a carrier of universal motifs, such as husband on the wedding of wife, matricide, parricide, fratricide, etc. The very best epic poems were those which creatively integrated the full epic figure of Prince Marko with some of those universal motifs. This could only be accomplished by a bard of great epic vision.

Popularity of Prince Marko

> Prince Marko is "a rough counterpart of the Greek Hercules, of the Persian Rustan, but of course in a Scythian and most barbaric way."[68]

The overall role of Prince Marko was created through a drastic departure from historical truth. Indeed, had bards confined themselves to historical facts only, Prince Marko might never have been elevated to the status of a hero. It remained a matter of scholarly debate, as to how the South Slavic people could embody their ideals in a relatively minor historical person such as Prince Marko. It is evident that Prince Marko had become so close to the South Slavs that the epic bards attributed major folk motifs to him. These include defender of people from injustice and enslavement, rescuer of princesses from dragons and black Moors, and avenger of his father's death.

Once it became obvious that Marko's extraordinary popularity could not be explained through his historical accomplishments, a group of scholars tried to find a reason for Marko's alleged unusual physical strength. Among such scholars were Tomo Maretić, Vatroslav Yagić, and the Serbian pioneer of folk literature, Vuk Stefanović Karadžić, who said, "If he [Marko] had not been an exceptional man certainly his name would not have been glorified."[69]

Tomo Maretić shared the same view and believed that Marko "must have been a man of quite unusual strength and possibly already during his life, or a short time after his death, the rumor of the feats by which he proved his strength must have circulated from mouth to mouth."[70]

The legendary strength of Prince Marko which transformed him into a South Slavic Hercules was insufficient to explain or justify his popularity. Sreten Stoykovic believed that when the things went downhill with the Turkish rule, people needed courageous men to protect and defend them from the variety of taxation the corrupt Turkish administration tried to impose. Prince Marko's outstanding moral qualities, combined with his unique physical prowess, were decisive factors in the affirmation of Prince Marko's popularity and legend. Stoykovic notes: "Unusual strength could provoke admiration and wonder, but it was the sense of noble virtue as applied . . . to the protection of honor and life . . . which deeply influenced the heart and soul of a poor and suffering people."[71]

Corovic agrees with Stoykovic that Prince Marko's physical and moral qualities appealed to the people, as well as his role as the protector from the Turks.[72] Corovic also felt that Prince Marko's contemporaries were grateful to him in many ways since bards began to praise him during his own lifetime. Stoykovic also suggested that King Marko's soldiers and mercenaries loved and respected him, and spread his fame through singing the heroic songs.

Mikhail Khalanskii expresses a similar opinion by assuming that songs dealing with Marko appeared during his own lifetime. He notes several possible reasons for Marko's widespread and early popularity. Marko was less egotistic than other noblemen of his time and he had the people's sympathy for having to serve as a Turkish vassal.

> In a time of great national calamity there are certain individuals whose misfortunes more clearly and vividly reflect the general misery and suffering. Prince Marko was the conspicuous guiltless sufferer, an ill-fated ruler punished for the errors and crimes of others. . . . Sympathy toward Marko's fate and possibly toward his person was, perhaps, the main reason for his popularity and for the spreading of tales about him throughout Serbia and Bulgaria.[73]

According to Khalanskii, Marko suffered for the crimes of his father, King Vukašin, whose greed and lust for power weakened his country in the face of the Turkish crisis. The German historian, Leopold von Ranke, also sought the reason for Marko's popularity in his relationship with his father, who had become a symbol of evil in the eyes of his people:

> . . . . The Merlyavčeviċes—allied with demons and with the Vili—and whom we find, immediately after Dušan's death, possessing themselves of the highest authority. According to the testimony of history, this is to be ascribed to the incapacity of the weak Uroš; whom the song represents as a child of forty-days' old [sic] at the murder of his father: an act of violence that did not, however, gratify all the members of that race [Mrnyav-čeviċes]. From the Merlyavčeviċes was descended the hero of the nation, Marko Kralyeviċ, who feared no one but the true God. He declared that the kingdom should be given up by his father and his uncles, and restored to him, to whom it belonged. Could a hero be introduced under more favourable circumstances.[74]

Kostiċ attributes Marko's popularity to the bards with whom Marko associated and who in turn preserved his name and fame for posterity: "Because of his [Marko's] cordial relations with popular singers, whom he gathered around himself, he may have become their most popular hero appearing in a poetic role even as early as his own lifetime, remaining famous through the centuries."[75]

Maretiċ expressed a negative opinion concerning Prince Marko and believed that Marko's popularity was transferred from other heroes.

> It is certainly well known that he was a Turkish minion who brought nothing but misfortune on the Serbian people . . . but a few scores of years after his death, when his relationship with the Turks as well as with the Serbs had become forgotten, stories of other heroes began to be transferred to Marko, and later on just as many other tales which in Marko's time the people would have considered a hoax.[76]

The French scholar André Vaillant explains Marko's popularity primarily on the basis of historical events.[77] Vaillant concluded that Marko emerged as the representative of those Balkan Slavs who were under Turkish occupation and were becoming more or less reconciled to Turkish domination. Under such conditions, King Marko was supposedly accepted not only as a loyal vassal but also as an ally of the Turks. Because of the complex circumstances surrounding his death, however, which was climaxed by a state of near martyrdom resulting from the tragic conflict between his knightly honor and Christian faith, Marko became a hero of the South Slavic population. Furthermore, according to Vaillant, those who continued their fight against the Turks selected as their hero Miloš Obilić, who had killed Sultan Murad I during the Battle of Kossovo. Conversely, those who did not regret the demise of the feudal order and who had not yet come to resent Turkish rule accepted Marko. In the face of growing Turkish power the legend of Miloš Obilić became submerged. Bards and poets might have feared to eulogize as champion a man who had assassinated the Sultan.

Nikola Banašević explained Prince Marko's epic popularity with cultural influences from Western Europe. Banašević pointed to clear analogies between the Prince Marko legend and romances in *chanson de geste,* a genre of old French epic poems celebrating the deeds of heroic or historical figures.[78] These influences seem to have come to the Balkans by way of Italy and the Dalmatian coast, from where they apparently spread all over the Balkan Peninsula. Banašević's comparative research of Western European epic poetry resulted in the conclusion that the figure of Prince Marko is very similar to French epic hero, Guillaume d'Orange from the *chanson de geste.* The wicked role of Marko's father, King Vukašin, who is traditionally charged with killing the legitimate ruler Uroš, is countered by Marko's role as the defender of justice. The legend of *Le Couronnement de Louis* deals with much the same issue: a nobleman, Arneïs d'Orléans tries to cheat the young King Louis, who is in turn protected through the intervention of the knight Guillaume d'Orange.[79]

The basic similarities in motifs regarding Prince Marko and Guillaume d'Orange have been, according to Kravtsov, the result of similarity of local and historical conditions, thus excluding the possibility of any foreign influence on the formation of Marko's popularity. Kravtsov believed that the poems about Prince Marko blossomed from a historical nucleus in which social conditions closely corresponded to those in France.[80]

None of the above-mentioned interpretations supplies a complete answer for Prince Marko's extraordinary popularity. Taken all together, however, they offer a complex answer. First, epic singers chose Prince Marko as their central hero because he was king in troubled times, and, although he did not participate in any spectacular battles, he remained well-known as a brave and able warrior. His physical strength, although overstated, probably had some foundation. His role as protector of the common people in times when other noblemen capriciously fought each other must have found expression in quite a number of songs. Marko's buoyant nature, his association with friends, warriors, and especially epic singers, could have triggered a process which led to his poetic fame. The historical role of Marko's father King Vukašin, whom the epic bards loathed, served only to emphasize Marko's own popularity. It seems plausible that he was singled out by his people in contrast to his own greedy family and its moral degeneracy which is even today referred to as "Mrnyavčevščina."[81] All these elements became interwoven into a fabric of Prince Marko's popularity. The dominant determinant of Prince Marko's heroic value lies in his being a tragic hero who is bound by conflicting vows to act as both a Turkish minion and an avenger of his enslaved people.

Tracing the later development of Prince Marko's legend is a far easier task than deciphering its origin. The historical nucleus surrounding the person of Prince Marko proved dynamic enough to absorb various associated themes, breaking out of the bounds of a local region and ultimately spreading throughout the entire Balkans.

Population Migrations and the Marko Legend

A major change in the status of epic poetry in the Balkans occurred during the Great Serbian Migration which took place at the end of the seventeenth century. The exodus began in 1688, after the Turkish victory over Austria, which had been supported by Serbs. After the Austrian withdrawal, those Serbs who had been prominent in the fighting dared not remain in their homes for fear of Turkish revenge. About 60,000 families, under the leadership of the head of the Serbian Church, Patriarch Arseniye Čarnoyević III,[82] left their homeland in 1690 and, moving from southeastern Serbia to the north, crossed the Danube and Sava rivers, finally entering southern Hungary. Many similar movements took place after that time, and one can observe a slow but relentless wave of migrations taking place in the general direction of the north and northwest, a process which occupied subsequent years until the early nineteenth century.[83]

These migrations, especially the major one in 1690, had a decisive influence on the epic poetry of the South Slavs, the Prince Marko legend in particular. Because of the large-scale shifts in the population and changes in its composition, a massive displacement involving ethnic and other groups took place, particularly prominent in the area of southern Serbia which remained at the time almost entirely unpopulated.[84] These shifts had a far-reaching impact on the development of epic poetry in relation to Prince Marko. While the first songs about Prince Marko sprang from the Prilep area in Macedonia, where he as a historical person actually lived, the people carried such songs with them to new areas in the north during the migrations in the seventeenth century. Those who came to live in the abandoned areas of southern Serbia as a result of migrations were ignorant or vaguely aware of the historical facts relating to Prince Marko. Epic songs dealing with Marko began to take on new shape and meaning for both the people who had migrated and those who replaced them. The arrival of the newcomers, most of them Albanians, introduced new elements into the already formulated epic poems about Prince Marko. This can be observed in the song, "Doičin the Hero, Sirak Ianko and King Marko, Protectors of Salonica," in Brothers Miladinov, No. 156. Northbound emigrating Serbs also encountered new views and attitudes which came to be reflected in their oral poetry, as shown in the songs, "German Queen and Marko," in Brothers Miladinov, No. 126 and in "Giuro of Temišvar, Prince Marko, Duke Iankula, and Child Golomeše," in Brothers Miladinov, No. 173. New names and places were introduced, such as Salonica (Greece), Temišvar (Romania), Slankamen (Srem), and the German Queen. This eventually produced a situation in which all parallelism between historical events and the epic songs were scrambled. Only in this way can we account for those songs about Prince Marko which show him in various geographical locations, in Sarayevo (Bosnia) drinking in a tavern with Muyo Sarayliya, and in Udbina (Western Croatia).

Population migrations contributed to the extensive spreading of the legend of Prince Marko. The old Macedonian and South Serbian epic tradition dealing with Prince Marko assimilated the new sub-motifs, places, situations, and persons, retaining at its core only second-hand reminiscences of the early Prince Marko.

The old tradition concerning Prince Marko had little meaning for the bards and audiences in new areas and cultures. The evolution of the Prince Marko cycle from this point in the seventeenth century was not linear but scattered in many directions. In many cases new historical and other events were added to, or deleted from, the epic songs about Prince Marko. The motifs which originally belonged to the Prince Marko cycle of songs frequently faded under the influence of later additions.

As time passed and distances increased between the precise era and location where Prince Marko's legend originated and the new regions to which his legend was introduced, Marko blossomed into the central figure of epic poetry. He began to embody ideals and aspirations of South Slavic peoples ranging from the highly heroic to the raiding of Turkish manors. While on the surface the epic poetry appeared well regulated by rigid rules not easily prone to change, the central core slowly altered under the diverse internal pressures, intricate undercurrents, and inevitable transformations. The main characters shifted, and sometimes even leaped, from one song to another. There is a long list of songs which have only taken on Prince Marko's name as a label for what are generally mediocre plots, originally related to other, sometimes obscure, characters.

In the Slovenian song, "Young Marko Sold to the Turks," in Matica Slovenska, No. 47, events and details are forgotten and replaced. The motif of vassalage to the Sultan is substituted by the motif of selling the outlaw Marko to the Sultan. The act of deception of Sultan by Prince Marko is introduced, then the division of spoil, and above all the cruelty of Marko which is far from his usual heroic stance. Another song, "Yankula," in Brothers Miladinov, No. 96, exemplifies the mechanical use of Prince Marko's name unrelated to plot or action. The only mention of Prince Marko is when the surrounded Yankula asks his adversaries whether they want him or Prince Marko.

Divinities, saints, strange creatures and peripheral characters gradually or sometimes even suddenly enter the repertoire of poems on Prince Marko.[85] Even the Almighty Lord is challenged by Prince Marko's conceited arrogance in the song, "Marko Lost Strength," in Laktinski collection, p. 67–73. In this Macedonian song Prince Marko brags that no one is equal to him, not even dragons, serpents (*lamia*), or fairies. Only when God made him feeble, Prince Marko realizes his sacrilegious words:

> Let Him from the Heaven,
> Come down and fight me.

Deprived of his heroic prowess, Prince Marko is stricken by the horror of his insolence only to receive the forgiveness:

> Now, I want to bless thee,
> Hero above heroes, thou shall be.

Prince Marko in Popular Lore

> *And men think of Prince Marko,*
> *As of a lucky day in the year.*[86]

The popularity of Prince Marko, which was best expressed in the heroic poetry, was not limited to any particular folk genre. This most favored son of all South Slavic people permeated not only people's lives, but also the many facets of popular lore such as beliefs, customs, tales, proverbs, riddles, sayings, and puns. Some popular beliefs found their way into epic poetry about Prince Marko and vice versa. Reflections of wisdom were extracted from epic poetry to stand on their own.

People were so identified with Prince Marko and his legend that they surrounded themselves with tokens of Marko's presence. That is why there is a large number of geographic terms or landmarks which are named after, or are derived from, Prince Marko. Corović made an inventory of such terms with particular regard to topography. He noted the huge rock, possibly a glacial moraine, which folk tradition explained as having been moved by Marko himself. Also described was a row of deep holes known as the track of Prince Marko's footprints and those of his magic horse, Šarac.

In the Hercegovina region in the village of Gnoynice, near the town of Mostar, there is a giant stone named *Markovac* (Marko Stone). Tradition relates the name of the stone to Prince Marko who is alleged to have proven his strength by lifting and throwing it. On the border between Srem and Slavoniya in Croatia, near the village of Gaboš, there stands a lonely hill which tradition and folk tales ascribe to Marko. One day he cleaned the mud from his moccasins (*opanci*) and left this hill.[87]

Tradition about Prince Marko is alive as far as the northern Croatian Coastland. According to Ivan Fillipović, in Vrbovsko county, between Bosilyevo and Lešce villages, there is a small glen called "Prince Marko hoof" which was made by the horse Šarac when Marko rode there.[88] In the village of Begovići is another big stone slab with an unintelligible inscription. The popular explanation is that Marko once fought on this spot with Musa the Robber, his perennial adversary, and that the tracings on the slab were made by Marko's fingers and feet. *Demir Kapiya*, an impressive Vardar river gorge in Yugoslav Macedonia, is still believed to have been created by a stroke of Prince Marko's sword.

In Croatia and along the Adriatic coast and peripheral islands are numerous caves, rivers, rocks, and other objects which are also associated with Prince Marko and are often named after him. All these examples are strong evidence that Marko has remained in the popular mind and that the people, especially villagers, continue to be proud of him, wanting to believe that at some point in time Marko really lived and fought in their area. Thus we have the Mountain Klek in western Croatia which, when observed from a distance, gives the vague impression of a large silhouette of a man lying along the ridge of the mountain, his face turned upward. According to popular tradition this is Prince Marko asleep on the mountain awaiting the call to rise.

Professor Mikhail Arnaudov of Sofia University enumerated several landmarks in Bulgaria which are related to Prince Marko. On the Harman

Peak of Stara Planina (Old Mountain) in Bulgaria Prince Marko is believed to have had his threshing floor. In Vidin, in northwestern Bulgaria, Marko's teeth are visible on Stambol Gate! Huge rocks thrown by Marko are found near Kukuš (Albania), and in Kičevo and Prilep (Macedonia). Near the town of Ohrid was Marko's winery where a barrel broke, spilling red wine and, as it was told, turning the whole mountain red. South Slavs do not easily forget. There is a proliferation of Marko's burial mounds, Marko's cliffs, Marko's towers, Marko's swaths, Marko's groves, Marko's grottoes, etc. As Arnaudov concludes, "Whatever is huge and extraordinary, whatever is marvellous is all Marko's."[89]

Although oral lore of Prince Marko tended to attach itself to topology, it also existed and circulated among the people via compact proverbs and sayings which best expressed their moods and character. Such proverbial expressions are numerous. Popular reminiscences on Prince Marko are many—as shown in the Vuk Karadžić collection *Serbian Popular Proverbs and Riddles*. Some of them are critical, such as "Bungled like Marko on Kossovo," which reproaches Prince Marko for not participating in the Battle of Kossovo against the Turks (1389). Another proverb relates to Prince Marko's insolence and spitefulness, "Just for spite (*inat*), Marko would turn even Moslem." For the impatient people the proverb is, "Even to Marko it is difficult to wait when he is hard pressed." For those who complain about obstacles the advice is, "Whereever Marko comes to water, there are bridges." For poor people Marko means abundance, "Until Christmas as with Marko, after Christmas, woe to me, my mother." A general admonishment to be cautious, "Only a blind man baits Prince Marko." If one wants something for nothing the saying goes, "When facing enemy all complain: Where is Prince Marko? When spoils are divided, all ask Marko: Where from are you, O Unknown knight?"

These examples represent only a small segment of the vast richness of the popular proverbs, sayings, and maxims. Epic poetry became a repository of the national ethos and popular wisdom became an ingredient in the epic narrative. For the sake of illustration, Marko's agility and temper are shown in the verse, "And Marko's anger blazed like living fire. With one leg he stepped, with other he leapt." Prince Marko proves his remarkable strength by squeezing nine years dry cornel-wood: "And there sprang forth two drops of water." Marko's common sense is proverbial as in, "And if he should take the head from my shoulders, of what avail were three charges of gold?" Therefore he understands the despairing maiden when she responds in the similar way, "Why do you ask, when you cannot help?" Marko's superiority in duels is intended to downgrade his adversary, "There will still be time for fighting." In the same vein Prince Marko despised an unworthy opponent, "Dear God, a mighty marvel! Good steel for an evil knight." Since it is not enough to be right, Prince Marko knows that he ought to be strong. The moral is, "Obey me, or get out of my way." According to the chivalric rules, Prince Marko is bound to destroy his adversary, but he is ready to recognize a good fighter, "God of Mercy," quoth he, "woe is me! For I have slain a better than myself." The classical verse about Prince Marko's impartial justice supported by his mother became widely proverbial: "Do not thou bear false witness, To pleasure either thy father or thy uncles, But speak according to the judgment of the true God." Indeed, according to the popular trust in Prince Marko, it could not be otherwise, but: "Marko will speak forth the truth For Marko feareth none, Save only the one true god."

The abundance of phrases about Prince Marko shows a rich treasure of popular lore which is highly diversified. We have touched upon popular perceptions of Prince Marko which represent different moods, attitudes and expectations. Some are entertaining or humorous, others are educational or practical, yet all of them contain the morally-laden popular wisdom which relies on the Prince Marko legend.

One of the dimensions of the epic spirit is people's identification with epic heroes—in this case with Prince Marko. Thus the popular interest in contests, duels, and verbal bets, even to death, found an outlet in Prince Marko's life. The folk tale "Justice never loses" as well as three comparable folk songs deal with Prince Marko's betting over the faithfulness of his wife. Marko boasts: "My wife is very tough, Very tough, but a wise wife; No one can seduce her." Marko's wife is both faithful and wise. She helps Prince Marko to win the bet by making the other contestant seem ridiculous.[90]

Many facets of the Marko legend were expressed and formulated through oral tradition. By being told and retold, they were kept fresh and alive. Epic poems were the most powerful among them because they were the vehicle which best expressed the ideal of heroism.

3

Interplay of Legend and History in Epic Songs about Prince Marko

Marko Kralyević . . . a sort of burly brawling Viking of the land, with just a touch in his composition of Roland and the Cid, but with more about him of Gargantua.[1]

THE BIRTH OF A HERO

The birth of a hero is a rare and exceptional event, anticipating the child's future significance. The epic poetry dealing with Prince Marko's birth describes it in several different ways. Sometimes Prince Marko is born of a fairy or he is the son of a dragon. In most instances his birth is removed from the realm of the supernatural and brought down to the world of mortals with King Vukašin and Queen Yevrosima as his parents.

As a descendant of a fairy, Prince Marko was established as a hero who inherited extraordinary qualities from his fairy mother. King Vukašin had succeeded by treachery to ensnare the fairy while she was asleep at a mountain lake, and to steal her wings. This motif is briefly described in the song, "King Vukašin Caught a Fairy and Married Her," in Bogišić, No. 85. Much better and more informative is the song, "King Vukašin and Fairy Mandalina," in Matica Hrvatska, 1, No. 51, in which King Vukašin stole the fairy's crown and tunic. In this way the fairy was forced to become King Vukašin's wife:

> King Vukašin married the fairy,
> Two sons she bore to him,
> The first was Prince Marko,
> And the second was the young Andriya.   (45)*

Fairies are supernatural creatures who treasure their freedom. They may marry now and then, but they do not spend their lives with mortals. Thus fairy Mandalina waited for her opportunity:

> King Vukašin marries off his son Marko,
> Merry reel dance goes on in the Court.   (52)

Fairy Mandalina lures King Vukašin to give her crown and tunic, to join Marko's wedding merry dance. Lightly King Vukašin agrees:

> Fairy went to lead the dance,
> Two times she danced around,
> And third time she leapt into clouds,
> From the cloud called the fairy:
> "Fare with God, King Vukašin!
> Hear me you will, but see never."   (59)

Prince Marko was not only born of a fairy but he appears in epic poetry as a son of a dragon. Mikhail Khalanskii noted that the Slavs had two concepts of dragons: some with the features of oppressors and others as popular heroes or fathers of heroes.[2] In the Petranović collection 3, the song No. 24 explicitly states the relationship between heroes and supernatural beings:

> Whatever heroes are among the Serbs,
> Each one of them is raised by fairies,
> And many are born of dragons.

In this song the heroes who were born of dragons are enumerated, including: Miloš Obilić, Vuk the Fiery Dragon, Relya the Winged, Banović Sekula and Banović Strahinya, as well as Lyutica Bogdan:

---

*Numbers in parentheses refer to line numbers of songs in collections cited. Line numbers are not given for song fragments.

> And the seventh is Prince Marko,
> His Sire was also a dragon.
> Each one of them has his dragon-mark;
> ....
>
> On the brawn of his right arm,
> A plait of wolf's hair is there;
> On the leg is the second dragon-mark,
> And on the hip is a sabre brand.[3]

Even when Prince Marko was born of human parents, as son of a king and a queen, elements of supernatural kind were subsequently introduced. One such element is in the form of a prophetic dream of King Vukašin's wife, as shown in a song from the Filipović collection, "The Birth and Youth of Prince Marko," No. 2. In the opening lines of the song it is foretold that King Vukašin's wife, "Lyuba Mrnyavića," will give birth to a dragon-hero who will grow up to be an avenger against the Turks:

> A dream dreamt the good wife of Mrnyavić
> In the white city of Prizren,
> She dreamt a dream, in which she saw,
> That a fierce dragon she had borne,
> Who cutteth off Turkish heads.

According to Filipović, this variant was recorded and printed for the first time in 1856, in the Serbian periodical "Neven."[4] Characteristically, the bard provided two supernatural powers for Prince Marko. In addition to being a dragon, as a young boy Prince Marko was bestowed an enormous strength by the Mountain Fairy.

The most widespread interpretation of Prince Marko's epic birth is found in the song, "The Marriage of King Vukašin," in Vuk 2, No. 24. Vuk Karadžić selected this song from the singer Stoyan the Outlaw as the best of five other variants. According to the *Notes* by Svetozar Matić,[5] Vuk mentioned that the singer Stoyan told him "he had killed an old woman believing that she as a witch had eaten (*izela*) his child." The case shows the cultural level of the singer of this song.[6]

In his collection Vuk Karadžić included the song, "The Marriage of King Vukašin," as his choice concerning the birth of Prince Marko. With a talent for selecting the very best in folk poetry, Vuk censored and discarded those songs which included popular beliefs and superstitions about dragons and fairies as Prince Marko's parents. The song in question actually contains two motifs side by side, which could otherwise constitute separate songs. Prince Marko's birth in this song has been connected with the universal motif of the unfaithful wife as well as the motif of King Vukašin's wedding.

The epic bards started with the historical fact that King Vukašin was Marko's father. However, the way in which King Vukašin married Marko's mother Yevrosima was a product of popular imagination. The epic singers connected Yevrosima with Duke Momčilo by making them sister and brother. The historical Momčilo, a Bulgarian, who was somewhere between an outlaw and a lord, developed into a great hero in epic poetry and became the epic uncle of Prince Marko.

The epic poets used the archetypal motif of the unfaithful wife in describing Duke Momčilo's wife Vidosava's liaison with King Vukašin. As a counterpart to the "treacherous" Vidosava, the bards selected Momčilo's sister, the sincere and devoted Yevrosima, who tried everything to save her brother from King Vukašin. Eventually the bards succeeded in procuring an anticlimactic but fascinating transposition from Vidosava to Yevrosima in the song, "The Marriage of King Vukašin." In this song they wed King Vukašin to Yevrosima. In order to emphasize the dramatic change in tone, the bards managed to create a situation in which the dying Momčilo gives his sister Yevrosima to the victorious King Vukašin, blessing them both. Historically, Duke Momčilo was killed in 1345.

In this impressive and beautiful poem King Vukašin is depicted as a schemer who used any means to achieve his goals. He lures Momčilo's wife into betraying her husband and delivering him to the mighty fortress of Pirlitor. King Vukašin breaks all rules of honor and violates those virtues which constitute the fundamental core of ethics within epic poetry. He is treated with contemptuous mockery, especially when he tries to dress himself in Duke Momčilo's garments and armor which the unfaithful wife Vidosava brought to him. The bards made a parody of the rule that all spoils go to the victor by saying in an anticlimax:

> That which had reached to Momčilo's knees
> Trailed on the ground behind Vukašin;
> What for Momčilo had been a fitting helmet
> Came down on the shoulders of Vukašin;
> What had been a fitting boot for Momčilo
> Therein Vukašin could put both his legs;   (279)
> ....
>
> What had been a proper sword for Momčilo
> Trailed on the ground an ell's-length behind Vukašin.

What had been a coat of mail for Momčilo
Beneath its weight the King cannot bear him up.[7]   (285)

Low, No. 1

In these scenes the audience saw the victor Vukašin dwarfed in contrast to
the vanquished Momčilo, who looms even greater in his death. Vukašin realized then that Vidosava betrayed a better hero than he and that she could
not be trusted. Therefore he punishes her cruelly by ordering her to be
quartered by horses. The poem, "Wedding of Prince Marko's Father," Filipović, No. 1, relates the story as follows:

> "All-powerfull God, thou art great! Woe is me!
> Behold that minx, Vidosava the bitch!
> A hero better than any in the world today,
> Him she snared and heinously did betray!
> Nay! Nay! And again nay! Me too, she shall not betray!"
> So growled Vukašin to his crafty henchmen,
> Vidosava the bitch, they briskly jumped,
> To horsetails they made her fast,
> Four horses agile, quartered her alive.[8]

Filipović, No. 1

The historically inaccurate unfaithfulness of Momčilo's wife construed
in epic songs emphasized King Vukašin's baseness and Duke Momčilo's no-
bleness. The epic bard implicated that Duke Momčilo was such a hero that
he could never have been defeated except through treachery. Variants of this
song appear in Bogišić's collection, No. 97, "The German Ruler and Momčilo's Wife," in which King Vukašin's role is taken by a German magnate
and Duke Momčilo's sister goes by the name of Andjeliya. Still other variants of the same song can be found in Milutinović, No. 147, and a series of
Bulgarian variants, as in the song "Duke Momčilo," in Brothers Miladinov,
No. 105, where Duke Momčilo's wife was jealous of her husband who had
many love affairs. Seeking revenge, she invites "the Emperor Kostadin of
Stambul," who is mentioned here in place of King Vukašin, although the
rest of the song corresponds closely to the song, "The Marriage of King
Vukašin," in Vuk 2, No. 24.[9]

Khalanskii established a parallel between the songs dealing with Duke
Momčilo's death and the French *chanson de geste* concerning Beuves de
Haumtone.[10] He found that translations relating to Beuves de Haumtone
from the Italian codex, *I Reali di Francia*, were probably available in Serbia,
and travelled to Russia where they surfaced in the story of Bova Korole-
vich.[11]

The Beuves motif found its way into the theme of Duke Momčilo and King Vukašin. Blandoia betrays her husband Guidon, and Vidosava does the same to Duke Momčilo. Dodon attacks Guidon during a hunt, while King Vukašin ambushes Duke Momčilo under the same circumstances. After Dodon and King Vukašin kill their rivals, each enters the city of his victim.

The South Slavic epic bards make it unequivocally clear that King Vukašin's offspring Marko did not inherit the negative traits of his father. Instead, Marko was eventually extolled as a great hero, taking after his mother Yevrosima and his epic "uncle" Duke Momčilo. The poet tells that message as follows:

> The King laid waste Momčilo's stronghold,
> And took to him Momčilo's sister,
> Called Dilber—Yevrosima—the Fair Yevrosima;
> He carried her off to Skadar on Boyana,
> And took her to be his wife;
> And by her he begat fair offspring,
> She bare him Marko and Andrea,
> And Marko followed in his uncle's footsteps,
> In the footsteps of his uncle Voyvoda Momčilo. (305)
>
> Low, No. 1

As we have seen, the epic poems about the birth of Prince Marko represent a wide spectrum of possibilities regarding the roles of his parents. Whether his parents are human (a king and a queen), or superhuman (dragons or fairies), Prince Marko is of heroic stock. Upon him are bestowed the qualities of an extraordinary man. Sometimes his greatness is related to a dragon-hero father, or a fairy-mother, but even when he is born by human parents there appears a fairy to reward him with superhuman strength.

People needed to have a hero like Prince Marko and they transferred all conceivable powers to him. Endowed with the strength of a giant, Prince Marko's mission was to take people's dreams and test them in the epic world. He was flanked by his noble mother, his valiant uncle, and many companions-at-arms. His wicked father, the king, was also present as Prince Marko's shadow—a dark shadow needed to emphasize the bright image of a hero.

FATHER-SON CONFLICT

> *Son Marko, may God slay thee,*
> *Mayst thou have neither grave nor posterity,*
> *And may thy soul not leave thee,*
> *Until thou hast served the Turkish Sultan!*[12]

The birth of Prince Marko was sometimes connected with the universal parricide motif which is found in different forms around the world. Scholars, among them Cecil Bowra, relate parricide to a certain fundamental element in human nature, the rivalry between father and son. Bowra also provides a comparative survey of parricide cases in various national heroic poetries:

> In Greece the son, Oedipus, kills the father, and discovers later what he has done. Among the Ossetes Uryzmag kills a boy by accident and discovers later that it is his son. In Persia Sohrab has already delivered the fatal blow when he sees who his opponent, not yet dead, is. When Hildebrand fights Hadubrand, he knows the truth, but Hadubrand does not, and in some versions the fight ends with the son's death. In Ireland Cuchulainn kills his son without knowing who he is, and when he finds out, goes mad and dies fighting the waves. In Russia Ilya of Murom first fights his son in ignorance, then discovers his identity, and spares his life, only to kill him later when, at his mother's instigation, he returns to murder his father. In Armenia David fights Mher the Younger without either knowing who the other is, but the fight is stopped, and all ends happily.[13]

It was through the Medieval Byzantine literature that the parricide and the incest motifs found their way into the South Slavic oral tradition. The legend about the Byzantine saint from the sixth century, Paul of Kesaria (Caesarea), was very popular on the Balkans. It elaborates the mythological story about King Oedipus, and Christianized the incest motif for the medieval audiences. Although preserved only in a manuscript from the seventeenth century, this Byzantine legend had to have been translated much earlier into the Bulgarian and Serbian.[14] Priests and monks used the legend of Paul of Kesaria for their sermons, and there the legend entered the oral tradition.[15]

The influence of the Saint Paul legend with the incest motif is reflected in the folk song, "Simeon the Foundling," Vuk 2, Nos. 13 and 14. The poem No. 13 describes how the Old Abbot discovered a baby boy in a trunk cast on the river's bank. The Abbot took the boy, named him Simeon, and raised him as his own. Once grown, Simeon set off to find his parents. In the city of Budim, he met the Queen. She liked Simeon, but in the morning she recognized in him her son. Learning the truth, Simeon returned to the Old Abbot and confessed his sin. The Abbot locked Simeon in a dungeon, full of snakes and scorpions. Throwing the keys into the Danube River, the Old Abbot whispered:

> As the keys come out of the Danube River,
> So let Simeon's sin be forgiven. (184)
>
> Vuk 2, No. 13

There is a direct parallel between the Saint Paul legend and the song, "Simeon the Foundling." Although committed out of ignorance, the incest results in severe punishment—imprisonment for many years. In both the legend and the song, fishermen eventually found the keys in fish. Paul and Simeon were found, forgiven, and sanctified in the end.

One could argue that the incest motif was universal in nature. Still, such motifs survived only when the local conditions favored their absorption, mirroring their own likeness. Themes of incest may have also entered South Slavic epic poetry directly from life. Incest could have occurred in ignorance in the Balkans during the Turkish enslavement from the fourteenth century on. There was a widespread practice of collecting Christian children for Turkish military service, the so-called blood-tax. Furthermore, women were abducted and slaves taken and sold. Some of these people were converted to Islam and lost contact with members of their original families. Epic singers could not openly sing about these cases because they did not fit into the ethical code of a strict patriarchal society. Nevertheless, the strain somehow found its way into the epic poetry as an unavoidable reflection of real life conditions. Such is the song, "Dušan Wants to Marry His Sister," Vuk 2, No. 26, in which the incest motif involved the historical Emperor Dušan.

The birth of Prince Marko was also connected with the parricide motif in a pattern that is similar to the Delphic oracle. King Vukašin's son was prophesied to become a hero and as such to "break all the bones of his father."

The parricide motif surfaced clearly in the Macedonian songs, "Marko in a Prophecy Delivered by the Fates," in the Iordanov collection, and, "Marko the King and His Father Volkašin," in Laktinski, p. 5–11.[16] These songs describe Marko's baptism. The christening is followed by a feast. During the night the three Fates deliver their prophecy and, according to Laktinski, they are overheard by King Vukašin [Volkašin]:

The hours were on the midnight,
On the midnight, the dead of the night,
When there came the three Fates,
To set the child's destiny, his *kismet*.
. . . .

The Third said: Marko to be a hero,
When he becomes a young man,
His father's bones he will break.

In fear of his son, King Vukašin decides to abandon the child:

Grasps [Volkašin] firmly the wee Marko,
And put him in a beehive,
Greased it with heavy pitch,
Let it float on white Vardar river,
To drown and to get rid of him.

The baby does not drown but is found by a shepherd who raises the boy as
one of his own children. As a young man, Marko happens to participate in
a wedding party. There he encounters a beast and cuts off its three heads,
saving the bride. Marko beats those in the wedding party with his mace for
not protecting the bride and for considering him dead when they drank a
toast to his soul. Marko's father King Vukašin is also among those present
at the wedding, and in ignorance Marko beats his father just as predicted by
the prophecy:

Shouted Marko to old Volkašin,
Hit him ten times with the mace,
And all his ribs were broken.[17]

The recognition comes during the continued wedding merry-making, when
King Vukašin asks Marko for his parents. Marko answers:

Lo and behold, you old Volkašin,
Vardar river is my Mother, Vardar is my Father,
Of sand my home is made.
When King Volkašin heard,
What Marko had just said,
He remembered: This one is my Marko.

Unlike Oedipus, Prince Marko does not kill his father but instead, in the spirit of patriarchal respect, asks for and receives the old man's forgiveness:

> When Prince Marko heard!
> What Volkašin the old, him just told,
> He leaps on his young legs,
> Three times he deeply bows,
> And he kisses his father's hand,
> He begs his father for forgiveness,
> For having broken his bones with a mace.

There are a number of songs with the same motif, each with its own variations. In one of these songs, "The Birth and Youth of Prince Marko," Filipović, No. 2, one can find a prophetic dream of Marko's mother, King Vukašin's neglect of the child, and the child's exile from the parental castle:

> Sorrowful, Marko hovers across the mountain,
> Very hungry and even more thirsty,
> Bewailing like a lost bird,
> Howling like a young she-wolf.

The shepherds chased the boy away and he wandered to the castle of his godfather, Emperor Dušan. All are unfriendly toward the young boy, whose troubles are eventually resolved when he is befriended by a mountain fairy.

Epic poetry does not supply much information about Prince Marko's troubled childhood. The acquisition of his enormous strength was a decisive factor in enabling Prince Marko to face his own father, when the time came. The prophecy of parricide in connection with Prince Marko did not occur in the majority of epic songs. Prince Marko usually remains fully aware of his identity and of his kinship to his father and mother. There is not a single instance in South Slavic poetry in which epic bards have Prince Marko marry Yevrosima and ascend to the throne in the style of the original Oedipal myth. In Prince Marko's case, the father is already dead when Marko ascends to the throne. Consequently, there could not have been any rivalry historically or in epic poetry between King Vukašin and Marko over the royal throne.

Epic bards openly avoided involving Prince Marko with overt or covert parricide. Occasionally Prince Marko is depicted in the songs as being hostile to King Vukašin. One such song, in the Veliko Iordanov collection, No.

3, we find Prince Marko boasting before a large assembly of dignitaries and kings that he is a better hero than his father. King Vukašin hears Prince Marko's bragging and attempts to kill him, but Prince Marko saves himself by fleeing.[18] The majority of epic songs clearly show Prince Marko avoiding his father who persistently persecutes and even tries to kill him.

The opportunities for Prince Marko to commit parricide were certainly many, some perhaps justified since King Vukašin in the epic poetry either deserved punishment or tried, in his aggressiveness, to murder his son. Parricide, however, was generally considered so horrible that the bards had to use another alternative: instead of the real father, the son could kill a "substitute" father, i.e., the father image in the guise of someone else. The antagonism between father and son in South Slavic epic poetry is thus resolved by the slaying of a monster, alien king, or aggressor, who is, in essence, the father-surrogate. In the case of Prince Marko, he does not commit parricide against his father, but rather upon a giant who stands for his father. This presents only one ramification of the Oedipal myth. That giant and father-surrogate is known as Nedo Djidovina.[19]

Among several songs about the giant who encounters Prince Marko, there is one variant called, "The Fiery Dragon and Nedo Djidovina," in Petranović collection, No. 43, in which the original conflict is further modified. Nedo Djidovina is known as Nedo Djidović and he is made into a Turk. His duel is with Prince Marko's friend and proxy, the Fiery Dragon. The slaying of the father-surrogate is accomplished by Prince Marko's friend who becomes the son-surrogate. Both the giant and the Fiery Dragon possess supernatural qualities. That the giant is indeed Prince Marko's father-surrogate is shown in Prince Marko's praise of the giant as a hero better than himself, as well as in the descriptions immediately following the arrival of the terrifying hero:

> With screens of fog the air was damp,
> Along the sea, from the dismal swamp,
> Behold! A warrior appeared in a rattle,
> Sitting upright on a chestnut steed of battle,
> With a lance around him, he tarried,
> And terror he raised, may God strike him down!   (39)

A more direct approach to parricide appears in a song on the same theme, "Prince Marko and Neda Djidovina," in Nikolić collection, No. 5, in which the giant openly boasts before the lords of the city of Budim that Prince Marko is his bastard son:

Do you know, fool, who sired you?
Hearken, bastard, it was I who fathered you!
When the Serbs sacked Budim and shook,
Then in dishonor your mother I took.[20]

Prince Marko, of course, could not stand for such an insult, especially since it was directed at his mother. He does not immediately react. He first goes home to ask his mother Yevrosima whether his true father is indeed King Vukašin, or the giant Neda Djidovina:

Tell me, Mother, who is my father:
Is he, Mother, Neda the Giant,
Or he is, Mother, King Vukašin?

Prince Marko's decision to delay the fight indicates that he had some doubts with regard to his origin. Epic poets add to the suspense by having Yevrosima give a vague answer. She denies that the giant is her son's true father, yet she concedes that at the time she was only sixteen years old and that both the giant Neda Djidovina and King Vukašin competed for her hand in marriage.

He wanted to rape me
For his woman took me,
Your father is Vukašin the King.

This explanation seems to satisfy Prince Marko. He returns to Neda Djidovina and cuts his head off:

Took the head Prince Marko,
Tied the head on Neda's horse,
Took the head to the kingly tavern.
All the lords walked out to look,
From the large kingly tavern,
And to weigh Djidovina's head,
Weigh they full hundred of pounds
Wondered all the lords to one,
To Prince Marko they say:
Hail to thee young Prince Marko,
Healthy be your parents
When you killed such a hero,
Such a hero as was Neda Djidovina.

This duel between two great warriors is of high importance, because Prince Marko defeated not only a hero and a giant, but someone who, after all, may have been his father, and who was at least an image of his father. Khalanskii concludes "that the negative implies the affirmative," referring to the fact that although the giant's assertions concerning his relationship to Prince Marko's mother were refuted by Yevrosima herself, they thus represented only a possibility, not an accomplished act. Nevertheless, in this variant, Prince Marko symbolically fought his father over his mother and eventually killed him.[21] Prince Marko becomes an outward projection of this omnipresent theme. Whenever Marko does fight his father, overtly or covertly, the epic bards stand behind him all the way.

Songs with the parricide motif are significant documents concerning family relations. Nevertheless, talented epic bards generally avoided employing the theme of parricide in relation to Prince Marko because it did not agree with the ethical views of the patriarchal society. Therefore, rather than belonging to the mainstream of South Slavic epic poetry, parricide and incest motifs generally appear in the peripheral areas of the Balkans, such as northwestern Croatia, Slovenia, northeastern Serbia, and eastern Bulgaria. These songs did not circulate sufficiently among the people to become fully assimilated as forceful motif songs in the larger tradition.[22]

If such local songs had had the opportunity to orally circulate long enough, they would have lost more of their individual features and would have absorbed more of the accepted generalizations. On the other hand, a few of the more ingenious collectors of folk poetry, among them Vuk Stefanović Karadžić, edited the collected songs to such an extent that many of controversial themes and events, such as incest and parricide, were ignored.

In the mainstream of epic poetry the father-son conflict between King Vukašin and Prince Marko was fueled by ethical issues of paramount importance in the heroic world. Numerous poems are based on poetic confrontations between good son and the evil father. Myth-makers succeeded in building a magnificent and consistently logical legend about the father-son struggle in which historical data became not only irrelevant but reversed.

The issue of succession to the throne was belabored in such a way by the epic bards that the father-son conflict was brought to a climax in the song, "Uroš and the Mrnyavčevićes," Vuk 2, No. 33. The dispute between the father and son did not relate to the rivalry over the rule of their small kingdom in Prilep. Instead, the epic theme of succession to the imperial crown was at stake. The popular view embodied by Prince Marko considered the preservation of state unity most important, and therefore Prince Marko was made by the bards to support the legitimate heir Uroš. On the

other hand, King Vukašin stood for the interests of feudal lords and tried to
seize the empire from the legitimate but weak emperor.

The time of feudal despotism is well preserved in the above-mentioned
song, reflecting the extent to which folk tradition mirrored the actual arrogance and lawlessness of the nobility of that time. This is illustrated in a
scene in which King Vukašin's heralds stormed the holy place where Archpriest Nedelyko is conducting a church service:

> So fierce were those fierce heralds,
>   so keen the strong of the strong,
> That they came not down from the chargers,
>   but through the door did dash,
> And the good Archpriest Nedelyko they smote
>   with the woven lash.
>
> Noyes, p. 112

Recoiling from the insolent feudal wielders of power, the common people endeavored to place themselves beneath the protective shield of their epic
protagonist Prince Marko. Epic bards had faith in Prince Marko's ability to
resist King Vukašin's demands for power, something which Archpriest Nedelyko had not been able to do. The hierarch was the keeper of "the ancient
and sacred books," in which, according to tradition, the successor to the
throne was named.[23] Yet in fear, the hierarch Nedelyko directs King Vukašin
to ask his son Prince Marko for a decision about the heir:

> For Marko was my pupil to read in charactery;
> And the good Marko Kralyevič was a scribe before
>   the Tsar.
> And the books of yore with their ancient lore,
>   this day with him they are;
> And who shall have the kingdom, Prince Marko
>   shall make known.
> He speaketh the truth, for he feareth none save
>   the true God alone.
>
> Noyes, p. 113

At this moment the issue of succession to the throne became the very
core of the father-son epic conflict. How could Prince Marko ever betray the
people who built him into a legend? He was, after all, the conscience and the
spokesman of his people. Thus Prince Marko's decision as evident in the

song, could never be anything less than justice itself, even if he had to turn against his father and kin.

Prince Marko's decision is reinforced by his wise mother Yevrosima:

> Marko—only son of thy mother, (126)
>
> . . . .
>
> Do not thou bear false witness,
> To pleasure either thy father or thy uncles,
> But speak according to the judgment of the true God;
> Lose not thy soul, my son;
> Better it is to lose thy head,
> Than to sin against thy soul. (133)
>
> Lord, No. 3

Prince Marko is now prepared to stand for justice, even at the price of challenging his father and uncles. Prince Marko reproaches his father with bitter words:

> O King Vukašin, my father!
> Is thy kingdom too small for thee?
> Is it too small? May it become a desert!
> Ye dispute now an empire that is another's. (197)
>
> Low, No. 3

Then Prince Marko pronounces his judgment which is so just and final:

> Look ye now, else may God not regard you!
> The record saith that the empire goeth to Uroš,
> From the father it descendeth to the son,
> To the child the empire belongeth by heritage,
> To him the Tsar bequeathed it,
> When he died and went to his rest. (211)
>
> Low, No. 3

Prince Marko's decision that Uroš should be the emperor enraged King Vukašin so that he tried to slay his son. Prince Marko fled to the church where an angel protected him. In the end King Vukašin laid a curse upon Marko:

> Son Marko, may God slay thee,
> Mayst thou have neither grave nor posterity,
> And may thy soul not leave thee,
> Until thou hast served the Turkish Sultan!   (249)
>
>   Low, No. 3

Emperor Uroš extolled him as the greatest hero:

> Marko, my godfather, may God be thy stay!
> May thy face shine in the council-chamber!
> May thy sword be sharp in the battle!
> May no knight be found to put thee to the worse!
> Be thy name renowned everywhere,
> Whilst sun and moon endure!   (256)
>
>   Low, No. 3

Both the paternal curse and the imperial blessing came true. This paradox epitomizes the complexity of the issues and the solutions. Prince Marko's whole epic life consisted in fulfilling both.

The theme of succession to the throne found its way into a number of songs which do not address the inheritance of the empire. Instead, it is taken for granted that Uroš is the only heir. The dying Emperor Stefan Dušan the Mighty wanted to ensure that young Uroš would be protected until he came of age.

King Vukašin's wicked character and his resentment of his son Marko (which is historically unfounded), can be observed in the epic fragment song, "The Death of Dušan," in Vuk 2, No. 32. The Emperor gathered the high lords of the state and among them entrusted King Vukašin with his minor son Uroš. Vukašin was to reign for seven years and "on the eighth give over to my son Uroš."

In a surprising speech King Vukašin excuses himself from such an honorable duty, complaining about his son Marko whom he labelled as an obstacle because of his bad habits:

> Dear godfather, Tsar Stepan,
> Not for me thine Empire,
> Not for me to play the ruler,
> Since myself have a wayward son,
> Mine own son, Kralyević Marko;

He goeth whither him listeth, asking leave of none,
And ever at his down-sitting he drinketh wine out of measure,
And ever he stirreth up brawl and conflict.   (50)

                                                        Low, No. 2

Despite King Vukašin's refusal to accept the responsibility for the young
Uroš, Dušan decided to appoint him to reign. Cunning King Vukašin ruled
for over sixteen years, preventing Uroš from taking over the empire. It is remarkable that the duration of King Vukašin's rule was quoted in the song
as "sixteen years he reigned," which is exactly the time between historical
deaths of Emperor Stefan Dušan the Mighty (1355) and of King Vukašin
(1371).

In this song, the epic singer impressively pictured the reign of King Vukašin as very difficult and repressive for the people:

And did so oppress the people
That what they had of fine raiment,
What they wore of silk apparel
They must change for rough homespun.   (71)

                                                        Low, No. 2

Here is also a third song from the Petranović collection, No. 17, "Death
of Dušan and Uroš," which combines motifs from the songs, "Uroš and
Mrnyavčevićes" and "The Death of Dušan." It takes the motif of the competition for the throne from the first song and from the second the dying
Emperor's decision regarding the care of his minor son.

In Petranović's song the motif of the competition for the throne is modified to throwing the crown into the air by the "trial of one's faith," the
so-called "Judgment of God." The other motif in which the dying Emperor
entrusts the care for his minor son is the same in both songs, except that
Petranović's song has Prince Marko as the caretaker of Uroš instead of his
father, King Vukašin.

The reaction of Prince Marko to the request of the dying emperor is hes-
itant. He is afraid to accept the honor, noting his family's interference as the
obstacle:

O Glorious Emperor Stefan, Sire!
Do not leave the empire on me,
Cursed is our breed,
We are the Mrnyavčevićes,
I have my dear father,

> Dear father, Vukašin the King,
> There are two uncles of mine,
> One is Goyko, another is Uglyeša,
> When they learn that you died,
> They will quarrel among themselves,
> Whom of them will come the empire?
> One will say: "to me," the other: "to me,"
> The third will say: "To neither of you, but to me."   (49)

It is of interest to compare Prince Marko's comments about his family with the words of his father who blamed Marko as a troublemaker in the fragment song, "The Death of Dušan."

In these songs the epic singers expressed the concern of the dying emperor and emphasized the discord among the noblemen. In Petranović's song, emperor Dušan decides to entrust the empire to Prince Marko:

> My liegeman, Prince Marko!
> Death comes to me tomorrow,
> To you I give my blessing,
> Care for my empire in Prizren,
> Care for seven years, my Prince,
> Until child Uroš grows up.   (60)

The struggle for succession to a throne was a very common motif in medieval times. The descriptive details of the crowning of Uroš are similar to reports found in French legends, particularly in the Guillaume cycle of the *chansons de geste* and in the *Couronnement de Louis* which deal with the succession of Charlemagne by the weak Louis.[24] Emperor Dušan corresponds to Charlemagne, Uroš to Louis, King Vukašin to the nobleman Arneïs d'Orléans, and Prince Marko to Guillaume d'Orange.

The Petranović song No. 17 "Death of Dušan and Uroš," describes King Vukašin's intimidation of his son. He pressured Prince Marko to reveal to whom Dušan's empire was bequeathed:

> Behold, how terrifying is Vukašin, the King!
> He hugs the heavy spiked mace,
> He braggs with sharp shining saber,
> Helmet is down to his brow,
> Underneath glare his black eyes,
> Stares he with threat and across,
> Angrily to his son he spoke,

> To his son Prince Marko:
> My son, my Prince Marko!
> Talk true and be well!
> Before he died, to you the Emperor spoke,
> Who will take the empire?
> I myself, or a brother of mine? (184)

Prince Marko is caught in a difficult dilemma:

> O my God, what do I do? How?
> If I do right, I am afraid of my Father,
> Because of God, I cannot do wrong. (110)

The only acceptable resolution for all involved is to invoke God's judgment by throwing a crown in the air to see to whom it will fall:

> Here we have the crown of Stefan,
> Throw it high under the clouds,
> To see, what the right is.
> Heard it Vukašin the King,
> With anger he was mad,
> He took the crown in his white hands,
> Threw it high under the clouds,
> Streaked the crown high into the sky,
> Falls the crown to Uroš the Child,
> To the right arm, into the white hand.
> The King does not believe it,
> Three times threw it the King again,
> Three times the crown comes to Uroš.
> Saw it, Vukašin the King. (282)

Banašević notes that the main difference between the South Slavic and the French legends is that, while Prince Marko comes into conflict with his own father, protecting the legitimate heir Uroš, the French counterparts Arneïs and Guillaume are never mentioned as being blood relatives.[25]

The father-son conflict progressed as they both grew more firm in their respective stands. The issue of the succession to the throne deepened the differences between Prince Marko and his father. The climax of their opposing stances was reached in the Petranović song No. 17, when King Vukašin schemed and eventually succeeded in murdering the young emperor Uroš, who was under the protection of Prince Marko. (Historically, however, Uroš

died three months after King Vukašin, in December, 1371).[26] This lengthy
epic work can be considered as a song within a song, with the murder of
Uroš superimposed on the throne succession sequence.

The epic bard in this rare song dramatically approaches the tragic end
of emperor Uroš by introducing the hunting scene with King Vukašin:

> Vukašin took Uroš to the mountain lake,
> To hunt ducks of six golden wings,
> They let go their impatient falcons,
> Shrilly sounded raucous calls.
> Crooned softly, Vukašin the King:
> "Look, my son, Uroš the Child!
> Look sharply into water of the lake,
> There will leap up a beaky falcon
> With fish wriggling and wiggling!"
> Behold Vukašin, a snake bit him,
> With heavy mace he hits Uroš,
> He hits him between dark eyes,
> Burst Uroš head, eyes jumped out,
> And dropped Uroš into mountain lake.
> It was God's will, as foretold.

In Petranović song No. 17, Prince Marko casts his filial curse for the
murder of his father by the Turks, although it is well known from other epic
songs that it was Vukašin who cursed Prince Marko. The Petranović song
reflects historical reminiscences of King Vukašin's death, but the bard's accusation of King Vukašin expressed in the line: "Because you have destroyed our empire" (311) is certainly without historical foundation.

The epic bards presented the popular version of why the empire was
lost, by blaming villains like King Vukašin, who were obsessed with their
ambitions and greed. Bards sang of Prince Marko as a popular champion
fighting against the very same feudal lords to whom he historically belonged. Epic poetry depicted such conflict of issues by narrowing it down to
an epic confrontation between father and son. That is why Prince Marko
does not carry personal hatred against his father, but stands as a protagonist for national unity and justice. Prince Marko was the voice of the people.
He grew to become the people themselves.

AVENGING THE FATHER

> *Ask me not, Sultan, my adopted father!*
> *I have recognized my dead father's sabre.*
> *If God himself had given it to you,*
> *I would be that angry with you too!*[27]

Despite the deep conflict between epic Prince Marko and King Vukašin, based on principles each held, their actual relations were formal and patriarchal in nature. Exposed to his father's authority and wrath, heroic Prince Marko sought refuge in escape, thus avoiding personal confrontation. He did not want to break the rules of filial respect.

The defeat and death of King Vukašin at the Marica River battle in Bulgaria (1371) are mentioned in the text of the chronicle *Tronoša Genealogy*. The battle's importance justified its inclusion in the realm of epic poetry through such songs as, "Marko Recognizes His Father's Sword," in Vuk 2, Nos. 56 and 57, and Matica Hrvatska, 2, pt. 1, Nos. 4, 5, and 6, which tell how Prince Marko avenged his father's death.

Although relations between father and son were strained, there remained an essential family bond which had to be honored. These frictions were implied in the chronicle of Patriarch Paysiy and amply stated by epic poets. Even when their conflict was reaching its peak, Prince Marko's demeanor towards his father was respectful, conforming with the generally accepted conventions and formulaic terms in addressing parents. Thus in the previously mentioned song, "Death of Dušan and Uroš," Petranović No. 17, Prince Marko tells his father:

> Be yourself, my merciful Sire!
> Dear Sire, Lo Vukašin the King! (306)

Or, when Prince Marko talks to emperor Dušan he alludes to his father:

> I have my dear Father,
> Dear Father, Vukašin the King. (42)

When King Vukašin was killed, Prince Marko's filial obligation to his dead father became paramount, overriding all other considerations. Low's variant No. 12 and Matica Hrvatska, 2, pt. 1, No. 4, both correctly cite the geographic area of the battle and identify it as being near the Marica River. Variant No. 6 of Matica Hrvatska, however, shifts the location to the Boyana River in the border region of Montenegro and Albania, near Skadar. It is interesting that two songs, the Low No. 13 variant and Matica Hrvatska, No. 5, change the battlefield to Kossovo. The bards placed King Vukašin at this battle in 1389, but the actual battle of Kossovo Field took place eighteen years after his death. Here are good examples of misdating (anachronism) and misplacing (anachorism). According to the epic songs, King Vukašin was wounded and then killed at Kossovo Field by a Turk who took away Vukašin's sword with the royal monograms:

> What time Marko looked well at the Damascus blade,
> And lo, upon the blade three Christian words!
> The first was the name of Saint Demetrius,
> The second was the name of the holy archangel,
> The third was the name of King Vukašin.   (41)
>   Low, No. 13

Fascination with all kinds of weapons was one of the features of medieval life, particularly in the Balkans. Epic bards and audiences were most impressed with the Damascene steel sabres which were made by outstanding craftsmen. King Vukašin's sabre was described in great detail in several songs. One of the best descriptions of the sabre is found in Vuk 2, No. 56 in Low translation No. 12, which Vuk recorded in 1815 from the well-known singer Tešan Podrugović. In this variant of the song the royal monograms appeared in the following combination:

> When Marko examined the sabre,
> Lo, thereon were three Christian words!
> The first was the name of Novak, the smith,
> The second was the name of Vukašin the King,
> The third was the name of Kralyević Marko!   (90)

In addition to the beauty of its craftsmanship, King Vukašin's sabre was a very special one:

> Great and small examined the sabre,
> But none might draw it from its scabbard.
> The sabre went from hand to hand,
> It came into the hands of Marko Kralyević,
> And for him the sabre left the scabbard of its own accord.   (84)

Miraculously, Prince Marko, like King Arthur, drew out the sabre without the slightest effort.

In most songs the sabre motif was firmly connected with King Vukašin and Prince Marko. There are a few songs found in Bulgaria and Macedonia in which the sabre motif became separated from the rest of the story. The song, "The Sword," No. 124, from the Bulgarian collection and "Marko Purchases the Sabre," p. 21, from the Macedonian collection by Laktinski, appear to be fragments of the main song. Their only preserved part deals with the heralds of Constantinople who announce the sale of a sword which seems to be miraculously sharp. A fairy, Gjurgja Samovila, brings Prince Marko the news that the sword belonged to his dead father. She arrives accompanied by supernatural creatures:

> Gjurgja Samovila is fast,
> She takes a gray stag,
> Gray stag is her speedy horse,
> Two vipers serve her as stirrups,
> Yellow smoke is her whip,
> Now and then her stag she presses,
> Three full hours downwind she ran,
> All way down to the town of Prilep,
> Krale Marko tidings to bring. (15)

The fragment ends with Prince Marko's trip from Prilep to Constantinople although there is no direct mention of Prince Marko avenging the death of his father.

Mustapha-Aga, the murderer of King Vukašin, is not a historical person, although in the epic poem he found King Vukašin wounded near the Marica River in which Vukašin had historically disappeared.

The song goes on, with Prince Marko recognizing his father's sabre and inquiring further:

> Body of me, thou youthful Turk!
> Whence hast thou this sharp sabre?
> Hast thou bought it for gold?
> Or hast thou won it in battle?
> Was it bequeathed thee by thy father?
> Or did thy wife bring it thee?
> Did thy wife bring it as dowry? (98)
>
> Low, No. 12

The Turk tells Prince Marko the story of his sister's discovery of a
wounded knight half submerged in the Marica River, who asked her to be
his "sister-in-God," and offered her "three purses of gold" to help him heal
his wounds. The Turk, Mustapha-Aga, broke the patriarchal custom which
obliged everyone addressed as "brother or sister-in-God" to render help.
The Turk liked the "rich-wrought sabre" so much that he killed the
wounded knight with it and threw him in the river.

At this point, Prince Marko and the epic audience knew something that
the Turk did not know, namely that he had killed a king and the father of
Prince Marko. In an atmosphere of suspense, Prince Marko is still re-
strained:

> God do so unto thee, Turk, and more also!
> Wherefore didst thou not heal his wounds?
> I should have caused thee to receive favour
> At the hands of our illustrious Sultan.   (107)
>
> Low, No. 12

Mustapha-Aga adds more fuel to the fire by sneeringly calling Prince Marko
a "Giaour Marko," meaning an infidel, an insult considered obscene by the
Serbs. In addition, Aga condescendingly says:

> If thou couldst in sooth command favour,
> Thou wouldst grasp it for thyself first.
> So give back to me the rich-wrought sabre.   (111)
>
> Low, No. 12

In a Homeric epic construction, the narrative has been brought to the
boiling point and Prince Marko's action leads to resolution of the tragic
conflict. The lines which follow from the song in Vuk, No. 57 (Low, No. 13)
are powerful:

> "O Turk, may God do so unto thee and more also!
> Him thou slewest was my own dear father,
> My father, King Vukašin!
> Hadst thou waited for his soul to pass,
> Hadst thou buried him yonder,
> I would have given thee better burial."
> Right so he drew the damascened blade,
> And strake off the Turk's head.

> He took him by the hand,
> And cast him into Sitnica river.
> "Go, Turk," quoth he, "seek my father!" (102)
>
> Low, No. 13

The news of Mustapha's death spread all over the Turkish bivouac and the Sultan sent his summonses to Prince Marko who first ignored them and when he became wearied:

> He donned his wolf-cloak of hide reversed,
> He took his heavy mace,
> And went and entered into the Sultan's tent. (123)
>
> Low, No. 12

Prince Marko was very angry, "and tears of blood stood in his eyes." The Sultan understood and became worried for his own life. Epic bards made it clear that the mighty Sultan was deeply frightened by their Marko. They described the Sultan as understanding and generous, giving Prince Marko loads of gold.

The epic bards were apparently so enthused with Prince Marko's success with the Sultan that they sent him to Kossovo Field to take vengeance for the defeat of his people. This was stated in the song, "Marko Kralyević Recognizes His Father's Sword," in Matica Hrvatska, 2, pt. 1, No. 4:

> Marko took six loads of gold,
> He then goes to Kossovo plain,
> There he mows down hosts of Turks.
> A few Turks Marko cuts there:
> Three thousand and three hundred hundreds,
> Thus Marko avenged his father. (186)
>
> Matica Hrvatska, 2, pt. 1, No. 4

According to the epic poets who have become keepers of the national ethos, Prince Marko is the avenger of his people as well as of his father. The fact that Prince Marko and King Vukašin were adversaries in the epic world did not change Prince Marko's filial duty to avenge. Justice had been done. A father's death had been avenged. Both epic singers and their audiences awaited eagerly to see Prince Marko fulfill the sacred and inevitable duty a son owes to his dead father and to his people. No matter how much a father erred, the duty of a son is to avenge him. This is an absolute requisite in the epic code of honor.

MOTHER AND SON

Rather lose life than that the soul should have stain thereon.[28]

Major heroes in epic poetry are, as a matter of course, entitled to heroic mothers. The bond between them, which is based on the heroic tradition, holds them together in a union which is closer than that between ordinary mother and son. While these mother-son relationships are basically human in nature, they do function in a heroic realm and are elevated above ordinary life into a world of heroes.

Prince Marko's mother, Queen Yevrosima, historically known as Yelena, stands alongside her son in folk literature as a protagonist of noble ideals, justice, and generosity.[29] As the mother of a great hero, she can best be understood as the embodiment of goodness which guides Prince Marko through all his heroic deeds and adventures. Prince Marko is a brave warrior, and Queen Yevrosima is his lodestar who firmly leads him toward the good and steers him away from the evil.

There is very little information about relations between Queen Yevrosima and her epic husband King Vukašin in the epic poetry. A screen of silence covers the period after Yevrosima's traumatic wedding to King Vukašin. Bards sang forcefully of how King Vukašin took Yevrosima over the dead body of her brother Duke Momčilo, surrounded by flames and smoke of the burning fortress of Pirlitor. In the song, "The Marriage of King Vukašin," Vuk 2, No. 24, Yevrosima is depicted as a loving and compassionate sister who attempted to save her brother Momčilo by throwing "down from the Castle wall a length of linen cloth" for him to climb. Yet, Momčilo's unfaithful wife, who was torturing Yevrosima by binding her arms and hair to a pole, severed the linen sheet with a sharp sword:

> Momčilo fell down from the Castle wall,
> The King's henchmen await him,
> And on swords and war-spears he fell,
> On clubs and battle-maces,
> At the feet of King Vukašin;
> The King thrust at him with a war-spear,
> And pierced him through the living heart.

(247)

Low, No. 1

4. Yevrosima, Prince Marko's mother, drawing by Alexander Key. From Clarence A. Manning, *Marko, the King's Son* (New York: McBride, 1932).

Duke Momčilo, nevertheless, was able to cry to King Vukašin:

> do thou take my dear sister,
> Mine own dear sister Yevrosima,

> She will be faithful to thee ever,
> And will bear thee a hero like unto myself.   (258)
>
> Low, No. 1

So much for King Vukašin's wedding to noble Yevrosima. One could speculate on their marital life but with Yevrosima's character, which was consistently sincere and loyal, it could be assumed that she would not be different toward the father of her son Marko. Her tragedy was that King Vukašin
had been, at the same time, the killer of her brother.

An epic silence also covers the childhood of Yevrosima's son Marko after he was abandoned by his father, King Vukašin. From epic bards' meager
descriptions we learn that Marko was befriended by a fairy who bestowed
the powers of a hero upon him and raised him above other men. With the
goodness of his heart, Marko protected the sleeping fairy from the strong
sun:

> He made a cool shade to fairy,
> Lest her face be sunburnt
> Lest her beauty be stolen.
> A shade he made of pretty forest flowers,
> Of briar and of lilacs.
> When the fairy opened her eyes,
> She saw Marko bringing cool water.
>
> Matica Hrvatska, 2, pt. 1, No. 1

The fairy was touched and generous. Out of her gratitude she asked Marko
to wish for anything and she would fulfill it:

> "What do you want me to do for you?
> Do you need a treasure, or the strength of sabre,
> Or you crave for a maiden, or a piebald horse?"
> Marko follows up fast:
> "What is right, is also sound!
> No gold, but a sharp sabre,
> No woman, but a piebald horse,
> That I join the imperial host,
> That I free my captive mother
> And to become a hero in combat,
> In combat standing up to all heroes."
>
> Matica Hrvatska, 2, pt. 1, No. 1, p. 322

With rare balladic exceptions, King Vukašin and Queen Yevrosima do not appear together in epic poetry after their dramatic wedding, which is described in great detail. There are only a few instances in which bards have husband and wife as co-participants in the epic narrative. When Marko was called upon to declare the recipient of the empire (Song "Uroš and the Mrnjavčevićes," Vuk 2, No. 33), he encountered his father who was demanding the empire for himself:

> King Vukašin cried:
> "Good fortune is mine, by the dear God!
> Behold my son Marko!"   (141)

On the other hand, Mother Yevrosima indirectly disputes her husband's demand, advising her son Prince Marko, who had become a recognized hero:

> Better it is to lose thy head,
> Than to sin against thy soul.   (133)
>   Low, No. 3

What had happened to the family life of King Vukašin, Queen Yevrosima, and Prince Marko in the intervening years between the wedding and the confrontation over the loyalty of their heroic son? Epic bards never exposed the contention between the wife and husband. Instead, bards addressed each one separately: King Vukašin as a villain and schemer in his own right, and Queen Yevrosima as a supporter of her son's moral conduct. Vukašin and Yevrosima are opposites in their ethical stances and there is a profound abyss between their respective moral judgments.

History also fails to indicate what kind of relationship existed between King Vukašin and his wife Yelena (or Alena).[30] It cannot be ascertained whether or not Vukašin exiled her, or if she was indeed abandoned and later joined Marko. While historically the issue is not clear, folk literature pictures this royal family as consisting solely of mother and son; Yevrosima is queen of a court in which there is no king.

In the epics it was unheard of that a wife could openly disagree with her husband. In a world where a wife was to remain unconditionally loyal to her husband, no matter how much he was in the wrong, Queen Yevrosima must have had a compelling cause to defy King Vukašin. Yevrosima's stand against her husband was motivated not so much by personal feelings as by

ВУКАШИН

пофресци из Псаче - 1358 г.

Король Вукашин

По фреске из монастыря Псача (1358 г.). Рис. А. Дероко

5. Sketch of King Vukašin from the fresco in the Monastery of St. Nicholas in Psača, painted ca. 1358, drawn by Aleksandar Deroko in the 1920s. Reprinted by permission of the Academy of Sciences of USSR, from Golenishchev-Kutuzov, *Epos serbskogo naroda* (Moskva: Akademiia Nauk SSSR, 1963).

the moral code by which she raised her son. Queen Yevrosima embodied the generalized principle of heroic motherhood, providing a moral anchor for her son in which he finds ultimate security and fulfillment. Yevrosima's wisdom matched Prince Marko's heroism and inspired him to deeds which were as daring in bravery as they were great in generosity.

Prince Marko found his mother an enthusiastic but critical observer of his heroic adventures. Hearing about her son's successful duels and noble actions was always like a rebirth to Queen Yevrosima. The song, "Prince Marko Abolishes the Marriage-Tax," collected in Matica Hrvatska, 2, pt. 1, p. 339, describes a Moor building a tower at Kossovo Field and imposing a new levy on marriages. The epic singer from whom this song was recorded was called Nikola Rudan from the village Bogomolye on the island of Hvar. This fragment song vividly portrays how Prince Marko takes leave of his mother when going to meet the Moor in combat. In the exchange of toasts Prince Marko gives his mother precedence and conveys a very deep respect by saying:

> By God, my dear old mother!
> Much higher, my dear old mother,
> Much higher is Sun than Moon,
> Thus mother is higher than son.

Despite her motherly tears, Yevrosima bravely encourages Prince Marko before a heroic encounter:

> Go on, my son, time is right!
> Crush your enemies underneath,
> Like nails under a horseshoe.
> Let your blade cut and cut,
> Let your steed do a good work,
> Off now, by a hundred lucky hours.

As mother and woman, Queen Yevrosima feels compassion for and understands Prince Marko's weaknesses. When he confessed to sins committed in the heat of his perennially quick temper, Queen Yevrosima forgave him. One example is the song, "Prince Marko Deceived the Arab Maiden," which was recited by Živan Antun and collected by Luka Ilić from Mitrovica in Srem and published in Matica Hrvatska 2, pt. 1, as the supplement to songs Nos. 13 and 14.

The opening lines of this fragment song depict the familiar scene of Prince Marko and Yevrosima chatting around supper time. It is clear that they are very poor and their food is typically peasant:

> With his mother Marko dines
> Dry bread and a bit of sheep cheese,
> With water they soaked it,
> Since there is no wine or its like.

Yevrosima notes in conversation that wrongdoing makes her son's arm wither. Prince Marko confesses that it was a punishment for falsely swearing to the Arab king's daughter that he would marry her if she rescued him from her father's dungeon:

> But, alas, my dear mother
> I did perjure myself
> I broke my word of honor,
> I trampled on my given oath,
> This is why, my dear mother,
> This is why my right arm shrivels.

An emotional scene with Prince Marko's tears follows (heroes do cry). Marko confessed that he abandoned the Arab maiden and left her with the old shepherd Milovan in the mountain. His mother rebukes him "for staining his soul." In the final episode, Prince Marko's wife Andjeliya resolved the situation. According to the patriarchal customs, she was not supposed to take part in mother-son conversation but she eavesdropped. She went to the shepherd in the mountain, took the Arab maiden, and had her married to Prince Marko's brother Andriya. As a result, Prince Marko's arm was restored and healed.

It is of interest to note the popular superstitions shown in this song when the worried mother Yevrosima enumerates dangers which may have caused her son's ailment:

> O my child, Prince Marko!
> Why is your arm withering?
> Did you, by chance, falsely swear, my hero,
> And trample on your oath?
> Did you spill the innocent blood
> Which you, my son, should have protected?

> Or did you annoy the fairies
> So that they bewitched you?
> Did the witches catch you in their hands,
> The witches or the werewolves?

Whenever possible, Yevrosima guided her son toward penitence and led him along the path of moral betterment. This was the influence of the Church and the sacred written literature. The people themselves were deeply religious and devout. Christianity gave them support in their suffering and strength in their stand against the Turks. This is evident in "Marko's Confession," No. 54, *Bulgarian Folk Songs* by Brothers Miladinov. This song's subjects are Prince Marko's sins, the confession to nine priests who were brought by his mother Yevrosima, and the absolution of his sins. Again the motif is the deception of the Arab maiden:

> Come on Marko, come on my dear son!
> You are not sick because of God, my son,
> You are sick because of your sins, my son.
> Let me call priests and clergy,
> And my dear son, you will confess neatly,
> You will tell all your sins.

The rites of confession were long and solemn, and Prince Marko was cured after three ailing, bedridden years:

> Nine priests are standing there,
> They chanted the Holy Gospel,
> They invoked absolution prayers,
> They sang to him days three and three nights;
> Light slumber took Marko to sleep.
> When he woke up there,
> So little time he needed to sit up;
> Was all he needed to get well.

Protected by a son like Prince Marko, Queen Yevrosima did not need to enter into open conflict with her abominable husband, King Vukašin. This would have certainly concerned the patriarchal public. Queen Yevrosima appears on the epic scene already as an elderly woman. She has a grown son with the noble stature of a hero and protector of the weak. Here one finds Queen Yevrosima as a woman deeply proud of her motherhood.

Many of the epic songs open the narrative with a stereotyped dialogue between Prince Marko and his mother, a kind of epic protocol to introduce the coming of a story. One of these routine *loci communes* is in the song, "Marko's Ploughing," which goes as follows:

> Kralyević Marko sat at wine,
> With the aged Yevrosima his mother,
> And when they had enough drunken,
> Marko's mother spake to him, saying: (4)
> ....
>
> Low, No. 28

This is a very typical situation which was known and expected by epic audiences. Most of the talk centers around Prince Marko's numerous adventures, duels, and enemies. He relates the problems and she suggests the usually wise solutions. In the song, "Prince Marko and Ban Svilayin," in Matica Hrvatska 2, pt. 1, No. 44, after the usual opening:

> Last night Marko dined with his mother
> Dried bread and cold water ...

Prince Marko tells his mother that he has to make a difficult decision. He received three letters requesting his immediate presence:

> When she heard, mother Yevrosima,
> When she heard what Marko spake,
> Marko nicely she advised,
> She advised, and to him spake:
> "My child, Prince Marko!
> It is good to be the King's godfather,
> Since the king is of our line.
> It is good to join the Emperor's host,
> Since we live in the Emperor's land, my Marko.
> Do not go, Marko, to duel Ban,
> Ban has fairies, sisters-in-God,
> Marko has fairies, sisters-in-God.
> Mighty fairies will start to fight,
> Many will fight with all their might,
> And the black mountain they will break.
> My faith is harder than stone,
> One of you will lose his head."   (65)

Prince Marko feels sorely offended by Ban and has to fight him to defend his honor:

> If I do not come there to fight him,
> He will send me distaff and spindle,
> And five pounds of white Egypt flax,
> To knit his pants and tunic,
> To keep spinning and giving to him,
> To sew and tailor for him.
> What remains to put in treasure chest.   (82)

According to the epic code of honor, Prince Marko did not have any choice but to kill Ban Svilayin after such insults. It is interesting that, in this song, Prince Marko eventually kills the Turkish emperor himself:

> O emperor, be it known to you, infidel!
> My mother swore me often,
> Never to take out my sabre for naught,
> And Marko swung his damascene blade
> And he cut off the red imperial head.   (302)

Prince Marko listened very carefully to his mother's advice such as when and where he should go to war, which side he should join, and how he could avoid getting into fights on holidays and Sundays so as to refrain from spilling blood and committing a sin.

It is hard to select any one South Slavic song which would best characterize this warm mother-son relationship because the number of such songs is so great. Here we mention only a few which are remarkable in this respect: "Uroš and the Mrnjavčevićes" (Low, No. 3), "The Marriage of Prince Marko" (Low, No. 11), "Marko and Mina of Kostura" (Low, No. 17), "Marko and Djemo the Mountaineer" (Low, No. 23), "The Turks Come to Marko's Slava" (Low, No. 27), "Marko's Ploughing" (Low, No. 28), "Repentance and Confession of Prince Marko" (Vuk 6, No. 21), and "Marko with Mother" (Vuk 6, No. 22), etc.

Epic singers made Yevrosima the guardian of Prince Marko's religious faith and practice. She always made sure that her son observed the family Holy Day (*Slava*) and that he never spilled blood on that day, even when harassed.[31] In the poem, "The Turks Come to Marko's Slava" (Low, No. 27), the Janissaries crash into Prince Marko's house and interrupt the festivity. Prince Marko begins to swear:

> Hearken my lords and guests,
> I am not the son of my mother,
> The illustrious queen,
> If I garnish not Prilep,
> Not with basil nor yet with red roses,
> But with a row of Turkish heads.   (78)
>
> Low, No. 27

These words are pronounced solemnly in heroic style, and promise a serious encounter with the intruders. Prince Marko's tone contains suppressed yet boiling wrath against his adversaries, and suggests the punishment which the Turks would have to suffer. Moreover, Prince Marko irrevocably pledges himself to his mother by invoking a fitting punishment for the Turks, severe enough to justify his heroism in the eyes of Queen Yevrosima and the world. Prince Marko's personal character urges him to kill those who dared insult him during the observance of his Holy Day. Prince Marko's prospect of "a row of Turkish heads" adorning the walls of his capital instead of "basil and red roses" suggests that no one would be able to prevent him from realizing his threat. To this list of reasons, each of which has certainly enough justification for due punishment, one should add Prince Marko's well-known fierce nature which has often been compared in the literature to the onrush of a thunderstorm.

After such a forceful pledge, there is only one person in the world, Prince Marko's mother Yevrosima, who has the power to make him relent from his resolution to spill blood. It would be a miracle if even Queen Yevrosima could prevent Prince Marko from fighting, since Prince Marko had already publicly and irrevocably committed himself. Not only is his word of honor at stake, but Prince Marko is actually sworn to the act by the name of his own mother. Consequently, it is only she who could influence him to reconsider. The key to the hero's heart is a dramatic counterattack by the mother, after which Prince Marko concedes. The magic formula which is repeatedly used by Queen Yevrosima to prevent Prince Marko from doing wrong in haste is as follows:

> "Stay thee, Marko, my dear child!"
> And right so the mother made bare her breast, saying:
> "Lest thy mother's milk slay thee,
> Do no deed of blood this day,
> This day is glorious Slava."   (85)
>
> Low, No. 27

These words have a magic impact on Prince Marko. The "mother's curse" was a widespread phenomenon in the South Slavic folk tradition. It was the firm weapon of a mother. If her authority was denied, a mother could always avail herself of this extreme and terrible curse, effected by revealing her naked breasts which were viewed as the source and symbol of life. And now, this magic weapon could be used by Queen Yevrosima to appease her son's anger by invoking memories of early childhood. The spell is deep, its impact even deeper. Prince Marko is tamed by the fragile hand of an old woman. Only in this manner does she succeed where the mightiest would have failed.

Queen Yevrosima conveys to Prince Marko the Christian message of mercy according to which he must leave his door open on the Holy Day and welcome all the people, friends and enemies. This was the day of humility on which Queen Yevrosima wanted her son to feed the hungry, give drink to the thirsty, offer wine to all, and in particular, to not use weapons against anyone. Thus, Prince Marko had to do all his mother's bidding on that day.

Prince Marko would not have been himself if he had allowed the arrogant Turks to escape without punishment for their insults. If he had to heed the ban on spilling blood on the Holy Day, which was also a day of truce, he did not have to restrain from intimidating the Turks into paying his servant a tip, which consisted of all the gold the Turks had. Prince Marko finishes his party in jovial spirits because he was able to bring the Turks down from their initial state of haughty arrogance to a level of fear and humbleness, while still obeying his mother. Prince Marko gives her all the Turkish gold accompanied by the following words:

> Yevrosima, mine aged mother,
> I took not gold from the Turks,
> I took not gold because I had no gold,
> But I took gold from the Turks,
> That it should be said and sung,
> How Marko dealt with the Turks.

(152)

Low, No. 27

In this song, Prince Marko is both obedient and disobedient, since he succeeds in fulfilling his duties toward his mother but also his obligation toward his people whose enemies were the Turks. Prince Marko's relationship with his mother is presented as being tender, but he ultimately outwits her by complying while still punishing the arrogant enemies. During the course of the epic narrative Queen Yevrosima is revealed as a demanding mother, while Prince Marko emerges as a dutiful son even under strained conditions. A mighty hero in full control of his enemies, he is, at the same time, guided by a mother who insists on high ethical standards because she believes it is the only way he can achieve great honors and heroic glory.

One can speculate as to whether Prince Marko ever tried to disengage himself from his mother's influence. From time to time it appears as though the bards themselves became a bit resentful of Queen Yevrosima's common sense and sided more with Prince Marko who tended to act impulsively, to attack without premeditation, and to kill without sufficient justification. Perhaps this is why certain epic singers tried on occasion to twist Queen Yevrosima's righteous advice into foolish prattle which could have led to tragic outcomes for Prince Marko.

In the song, "Marko and Djemo the Mountaineer" (Low, No. 23), Prince Marko is ill advised by his mother to go without arms to get fish for his guests on Holy Day. Queen Yevrosima's words are crucial:

> After him hasted his aged mother,
> And spake [soft] words unto him:
> "Ah, my son, Kralyević Marko,
> Take not any weapon with thee,
> Else—so used to blood art thou—
> Thou wilt surely shed blood on thy festal day!"   (26)
>
> Low, No. 23

The mother's misguided advice manages to get Prince Marko captured and almost hung by the Turk Djemo the Mountaineer.

In another instance, Queen Yevrosima gives well-intended but nevertheless bad advice which, fortunately, turns out well in the end. In the song, "Marko's Ploughing," the theme of the mother's wish surfaces again when Prince Marko abandons a life of violence because of Queen Yevrosima's statement that she has become tired of having to "wash his bloody garments." Instead, she asks Prince Marko to pursue a new way of life as a farmer to "plough hill and valley." Prince Marko outwits his mother by apparently obeying her while actually doing just the opposite. He challenges the Turkish Janissaries by going to plough "the Sultan's highways." Unarmed, as in the previous song, Prince Marko kills his adversaries who attempt to prevent him from destroying the highway by swinging over it a plough and oxen. In a merry mood, Prince Marko brings his mother the booty of three charges of gold and jokingly says: "Behold ... what I have ploughed for thee this day."

6. Head of Kralyević Marko, Ivan Meštrović, plaster study, 1910 (National Museum, Belgrade). Reprinted from *The Sculpture of Ivan Meštrović* (Syracuse, N.Y.: Syracuse University Press, 1948).

Some of Queen Yevrosima's unsound advice occurs in the song "The Marriage of Marko" (Low, No. 11). It is not clear why Queen Yevrosima insists that Prince Marko selects as his best man the Doge of Venice, whose reputation with women was bad. Prince Marko's mother either wrongly evaluated the situation or nurtures hidden hostility toward Prince Marko's bride. In any case, Prince Marko is depicted as obedient son and when the best man attempts to seduce his bride, Marko does not hesitate to cut off the Doge's head:

> Then he returned back to his tent,
> He made ready himself and Šarac horse,
> The well-beseen wedding-guests set out,
> And in peace they journeyed to white Prilep.   (291)
>
> Low, No. 11

Unwise advice given by the mother Queen Yevrosima to her son is rather an exception. In the folk tradition, Queen Yevrosima occupies a distinguished role as the head of the family. It seems obvious that people craved for a heroine in the role of a mother as much as they did for a hero, the dutiful son. The people created idealized versions of the two mother and son prototypes, Queen Yevrosima and Prince Marko.

The negative portrayal of mother-son relations in South Slavic folklore culminated in the motif of matricide. The theme of matricide emerged from real-life situations on the Balkans and represented the dark side of living within large extended families. Tragic conflicts in the patriarchal family found their main reflection in the ballad-type family songs which were reinforced through similar universal motifs, such as the conflict between a mother and her daughter-in-law.

Less-imaginative epic bards recorded without discrimination the diversified popular sentiments, thoughts, and latent desires concerning mother-son relationships. These were reflected in the heroic world. Nevertheless, negative relations between Prince Marko and Queen Yevrosima were not typical, and should be viewed as episodes isolated from the mainstream of genuine heroic poetry. The merit of this group of songs is that certain aspects of family life among the South Slavs are documented in popular lore.

A young woman's lot was to work hard. The mother of the family, however, is often depicted in full authority and her power recalled in vivid and almost frighteningly blunt details. During the frequent absences of the man, usually due to his participation in wars on either the side of the Austrian emperors or the Turkish sultans, the mother of the family took advantage of opportunities to mistreat, or in some instances even rid herself of a daughter-in-law. After a son's return from war a mother would sometimes defame

her daughter-in-law as having been unfaithful. Then the son either killed his
wife or, finding her innocent, would eventually punish the mother.

In the rare variant, "The Wedding of Prince Marko," which is found in
the collection, *Serbian Popular Songs* by Nikolić, patriarchal relations are
described with reference to the difficult status of daughters-in-law. In a
lengthy dialogue in the opening of the song, Prince Marko teaches his young
wife how to pay due respect to his mother during his absence. Such elaboration is rare and is thus quoted in its entirety:

> You are to be late to bed, and early to rise;
> Before to your lily-white bed, my dear, you retire,
> On the right hand kiss my mother,
> Lightly, softly you will say to her:
> "My dear mother, may your night be good,
> Night be good, with the help of God!"
> And in the morning, my dear wife,
> When from your lily-white bed you rise;
> Say: "Good morning to you, my mother old and wise!"
> Again you will kiss her right hand.
> Prepare to break the fast, and the fire to light.
> And when Sunday comes young and bright,
> And when my mother leaves for church,
> Alongside her you will go to the very gate of the church,
> On the right hand kiss my mother,
> Kiss the path where my mother's slippers tread.
>
> Nikolić 1, No. 38

As far as the mother-son relationship is concerned, we still find the familiar picture of perfect harmony. Although married, Prince Marko is more
concerned with how his mother will be treated in his absence than with the
well being of his young bride.

There are, nevertheless, a number of songs in which epic bards reduced
the noble Queen Yevrosima to an unfriendly and even hostile mother-in-law.
Thus the song No. 94 in Matica Hrvatska, 2, pt. 1, p. 422–23, recorded by
Yosip Banić from Dolnyi Dolac in Dalmatia, tells how mother Yevrosima
married off Prince Marko who was then called the next day to the Sultan's
service for nine long years. Before leaving, Prince Marko entrusts his young
wife to mother, saying:

> Thus spoke Marko to his mother:
> "O my aged, my old mother!
> My faithful wife to you I entrust,

> Don't send her to mountain for water,
> A stranger could grab her,
> Assault her, and dishonor her.
> Don't send her, mother, to the green forest,
> There are outlaws to seize her;
> Neither send her to sheep in the hills,
> Because Turks could abduct her."

When Prince Marko left, his resentful mother did exactly the opposite. She chased away her daughter-in-law to tend sheep and instructed her not to return until she could bring home one thousand new lambs. Prince Marko's wife was wise and she let her husband know how she was treated and that the Turkish Paša wanted her:

> "If you know God and care for me,
> Hurry to ask your honorable Sultan,
> To return to your white manor, now.
> By the first Monday past next week,
> Turkish Paša comes with his men
> And he wants to abduct me."
> She finds a swallow swift,
> A handwritten scroll she gives to the bird.
> Takes to flight the fast swallow bird,
> Straight across the world wide,
> On Marko's knee she came down.

With the Sultan's permission Prince Marko promptly returns home, punishes his mother, cuts off the Turks' heads, and brings the Paša's head to garnish the Sultan's ramparts.

The Slovenian version of the matricide motif is presented in the song, "Marko Severs His Mother's Head," in Matica Slovenska, No. 51, which had been recorded by Ivan Kukulyević in Croatian Zagorye (northwest of Zagreb). In this song, Prince Marko sets off on a long war campaign and pledges his mother Yevrosima to protect his young wife who is called Katica. The mother, however, locks Katica in a room where she dies and eventually decomposes. When Prince Marko returns home after seven years and asks for Katica, his mother sends him to the room in which Katica had supposedly gone to pack her trousseau and prepare to leave for good in order to marry another man. The poem goes on to describe how Prince Marko enters the room and finds the decomposed remains of his wife. At the end of this brief Slovenian song, Prince Marko kills his mother without much ado:

The small sabre Marko shook,
Mother's little head he took:
"The head after head, let them go,
Soul after soul, let them blow!"   (27)

Matica Slovenska, No. 51

    This song is devoid of noble feelings or subtlety of expression. Instead of dealing with the lofty epic themes of Prince Marko's adventurous life, it emphasizes the personal tragedy of distorted family relations. In local Slovenian lore the heroic son had been transformed into a man who commits matricide. Bardic tales belonging to various periods were preserved in diverse ways and thus account for the lack of uniformity regarding the matricide theme. The oral tradition was not strong enough to sift through the multiplicity of themes, motifs, historical events, and incidents from everyday life. As a consequence, the songs about the Prince Marko–Queen Yevrosima relationship were not adequately integrated. Prince Marko seems to have emerged from many layers of songs from various time periods, some of which are in direct opposition to others.

    Aside from the rather exceptional matricidal motif songs, the strong influential mother was by far a widespread phenomenon throughout the entire Balkan Peninsula. From this point of view, the Prince Marko–Queen Yevrosima relationship expressed typical behavioral conventions within the patriarchal society. For Prince Marko, the mother image was sacrosanct. Failure to obey one's mother was almost sacrilegious. In her dignified status as a great hero's mother, Queen Yevrosima developed into such a perfectly rounded epic figure that, in comparison, no other woman could have lived up to her standards. Thus, the image of the mother came to overshadow all the other women in Prince Marko's life, causing him to remain the faithful son throughout his whole epic life.

PRINCE MARKO AND WOMEN

I found her by the waters of the cistern,
And when I saw her, mother,
Meseemed the ground turned about me.[32]

There is no doubt that the most important woman in Prince Marko's life was his mother, Queen Yevrosima. Their relationship can be best understood when observed within the context of South Slavic patriarchal life which was governed by fixed village customs. The mother's prominent role in the extended family was instrumental in obtaining a wife for her son. Although this wife was actually chosen by the father, the mother was in charge of the execution of the wedding and observed the strict wedding customs and rituals.

In Prince Marko's case the epic King Vukašin does not participate in the crucial family decision of choosing a bride for his son. Epic bards do not mention him, so it is as if Prince Marko was fatherless.

Epic singers reversed historical truth by giving the mother the decisive role in selecting the bride for Prince Marko. Historically King Vukašin conducted the whole undertaking. According to the historian Constantin Jireček, King Vukašin very much wanted his son to marry a princess from the noble Croatian family of the Šubići. King Vukašin carefully planned and concentrated his diplomatic efforts on this match but the negotiations were thwarted because of Pope Urban V's opposition.[33]

In epic poetry Prince Marko considered his marriage an act of filial duty toward his mother. Conversely, Queen Yevrosima was wise and she wanted her son to be happy. In one of the major songs, "The Marriage of Prince Marko," in the Vuk Karadžić collection, 2, No. 55, Queen Yevrosima urges her son to marry:

> Marko sat at supper with his mother,
> And she began to speak with Marko:
> "O my son, Prince Marko,
> Thy mother is now well stricken in years,
> She cannot prepare thy supper,
> She cannot serve the dark wine,
> She cannot make light with the pine splinter,
> Take thee a wife, therefore, my dearest son,
> That so I may have a successor afore I die." (9)
>
> Low, No. 11

Because of her age, it was too difficult for Queen Yevrosima to manage domestic affairs, and Prince Marko's marriage thus became a necessity. Befitting the role of dutiful son, Prince Marko accepts the idea and tells his mother that he has already looked for a maiden in ten kingdoms:

> When I found a maiden for myself,
> There was no friend for thee,
> And when I found friend for thee,
> For me there was no maiden there. (17)
>
> Low, No. 11

It became evident that it was not easy to find a bride who would please both his mother and himself. Prince Marko confesses that he had fallen for a maiden who was a daughter of the Bulgarian King Šišman:

> I found her by the waters of the cistern,
> And when I saw her, mother,
> Meseemed the ground turned about me,
> Behold, mother, the maid for me,
> And for thee also a worthy friends.   (25)
>
> Low, No. 11

This passage is from the Vuk collection and in the Filipović song, No. 15. The father of the Bulgarian girl historically did exist as Jovan Šišman III who lived in the fourteenth century as the last King of Bulgaria and who eventually accepted the Turkish rule.[34] But he was not related to the historical King Marko by either blood or marriage. The introduction of the Bulgarian King Šišman as Prince Marko's father-in-law instead of the actual Duke Hlapen of Kastoria, represents yet another historical distortion as a result of the intervention of bards and folk imagination.

These two songs display the wedding customs in which both mother Yevrosima and Prince Marko participate. They set the wedding date, select presents, and decide who will be invited to the wedding party. Yevrosima has heard that the bride is very beautiful and realizes that there might be trouble unless Prince Marko brings his own brother as the best man:

> For the damsel is peerless of beauty,
> And of some great shame we are adread!   (89)
>
> Low, No. 11

Since Prince Marko does not have a brother in this song, Queen Yevrosima soothes him with five hundred wedding guests as protection.

In addition to her extraordinary beauty, the bride is faithful and possesses all noble qualities. The bride's virtue is demonstrated during the wedding when the Venetian Doge, Prince Marko's best man and leader of the wedding procession, tries to seduce her. Frightened and insulted, the bride-to-be "leapt past the wedding-guests" and ran to Prince Marko's tent for protection. He misunderstands her coming and, because of his patriarchal upbringing, he remonstrates:

> Ignoble Maid!
> Mayst thou not endure

> Until we come to my white manor,
> And until the Christian law is accomplished?   (244)
>
> Low, No. 11

These are the words of duty which reveal how important it was for epic audiences to witness the strict observance of traditional wedding conventions, disregarding personal sentiments in relations between husband and wife.

Both songs introduce a related universal motif of the bride's subterfuge in asking the Doge of Venice to shave off his beard. Through this she not only gains time to inform Prince Marko of the attempted seduction, but also succeeds in inducing the Doge to make fun of himself and to provide the proof of his malfeasance.[35]

> Godfather, Doge of Venice,
> My old mother hath adjured me
> Never to love a full-bearded hero,
> But only a knight smooth of chin
> Such as is Prince Marko.   (205)
>
> Low, No. 11

Prince Marko said to his failed best man: "No jest it was to shave off thy beard" (Low, No. 11, l. 279), and he cut off his head. This event entered into the popular proverbs: "It is not a joke to have the beard shaved," meaning that one is in trouble due to one's own wrongdoing.

Epic singers liked to portray Prince Marko as a faithful and devoted husband, while his wife appears faithful in some songs and unfaithful in others. Prince Marko's historical wife was named Yelena, while in the epic poems she is also called Andjeliya, Grozdanka, Yanya, Katica, or whatever other name might have momentarily caught the fancy of the bard. Historical facts that Yelena and King Marko were separated, and that her lover was Balša II Balšić[36] gave rise to a series of epic songs in which Yelena was accurately shown as unfaithful and cunning, collaborating with Prince Marko's enemies in order to destroy him.

Prince Marko was a very complex epic personality and consequently his relations with women vary in nature. He is everything from the successful lover or caring husband to the rejected suitor who is mocked and insulted. Prince Marko was romantically involved with young girls and widows, Christians, and even Moslems. He rescues maidens and is rescued by them. He tortures his unfaithful wife in cold blood, and breaks his word of honor to a maiden he had promised to marry. Yet above all, his sins and vices notwithstanding, he endeavors to live according to the customs of his people and the Christian canon. Despite everything Prince Marko is a man of honor.

The historically recorded unsuccessful attempts of King Vukašin to marry his son Marko to a princess in Bosnia, left their imprint in the song "How Marko Vukašinović Was Rejected by a Bosnian Girl around 1360," which is given in fragmentary form in the Bogišić collection, No. 3. The song is taken from Mauro Orbini (No. 278), who edited it, and can be found in the Dubrovnik Manuscript. It refers to a haughty Bosnian girl who flatly and contemptuously rejected Prince Marko's proposal:

> Through a green mountain Prince Marko rides,
> On his fine steed,
> In the mountain night caught him,
> In the green mountain he raises his tent;   (4)

In the morning Prince Marko met three Bosnian maidens with golden bands. Two of them respectfully bowed to him while the third was haughty and boastful:

> If the King of Bosnia Himself had come here,
> I would not have made my obeisance to him,
> Why should I bow to a scoundrel!   (18)

Prince Marko appeared more sad than angered, and tried gently to reason with her:

> If you are proud of being rosy cheeked and fair,
> Your beauty, o Maiden, will be welcome to black earth!
> You boast with your golden head band,
> Soon your two maidens will carry it by and away.   (25)

The song concurs with historical data concerning the location of these events, placing them in Bosnia and timing them only ten years earlier (1360 instead of the historical 1370). The poem is indeed old. It can be assumed that a chronicle-song was created at approximately the same time the historical events took place and, only later, was made into an epic song about the maiden who refused Prince Marko.[37]

The group of songs with the motif of rejected suitor contains one in particular called "The Sister of Leka Kapetan," in Vuk, 2, No. 39. Rosanda the beautiful sister of Leka Kapetan was very conceited and haughty—no suitor was good enough for her. When Prince Marko and his companions-at-arms Miloš Obilić and Relya the Winged saw her beauty they were stunned:

> God! How fair she is, may no ill befall her!
> In the four quarters of the earth,
> In all the lands of Turk and of Christian,
> There was not her like for beauty in the whole world,
> Neither white Turkish maid nor Vlach,
> Nor yet no damsel of slender Latin breed.
> They that had seen the mountain Fairy
> Said that the Fairy, brother, might not compare with her.   (14)
>
> Low, No. 6

In her arrogance Rosanda did not only refuse the three Serbian dukes (three brothers-in-God), but she threw venomous insults at each of them: she humiliated Miloš Obilić by calling him a son of a mare; she called Relya a bastard found in the market place, and she branded Prince Marko as a minion of the Sultan. This was too much, "and Marko's anger blazed like living fire." He gave Rosanda the Beautiful a horrible punishment almost without comparison in abject cruelty in the South Slavic epic poetry: "Now Marko," quoth she, "thou mayst look on Rosa!" (532). The haughty maiden continued to taunt him:

> Marko raged and was wroth out of wit,
> One step he made and a mighty spring,
> And by the hand he seized the damsel,
> He drew the sharp dagger from his girdle,
> And cut off her right arm;
> He cut off her arm at the shoulder,
> And gave the right arm into her left hand,
> And with the dagger he put out her eyes,
> And wrapped them in a silken kerchief,
> And thrust them into her bosom.   (542)
>
> Low, No. 6

The macabre scene over, Leka Kapetan, the brother, "is silent as were he a cold stone. Rosa, mutilated, kept wailing." Prince Marko lifted up his voice:

> Come, brothers . . .
> The time is come for us to depart.   (561)
>
> Low, No. 6

The tragic outcome in the song could be accepted as a release of the challenged honor, but as D. H. Low said, "it is the detail of the execution that shocks the modern mind."[38] Therese Albertine Louise von Jacob, pseudonym Talvj, started to translate Serbian folk poetry into German in 1825 and she disapproved of Prince Marko. Goethe also considered Prince Marko a rough hero.

There is a very witty song which also deals with an unsuccessful wooing of Prince Marko, but the rejection is not of an insulting nature. Titled "A Damsel Outwits Marko," in Vuk 2, No. 40, and also in Filipović, No. 13, "Prince Marko Outwitted by a Damsel," the songs display certain cruelty on the part of Prince Marko, but properly harnessed by the wise damsel they change into celebrations.

Epic bards favored the damsel and they describe her in the opening lines:

> There was a poor maid that was an orphan,
> When she dined then she supped not,
> If she dined and supped
> Then she had no clothing.   (4)
>
> Low, No. 7

But as in a fairy tale she was very lucky to be sought in marriage by three knights, one of them Prince Marko himself. Boisterous and bragging, Prince Marko turned to the other suitor, asking him:

> Wherefore hast thou troubled so many guests,
> And wearied so many horses,
> Since that the maid is not for thee,
> But for me, Prince Marko?   (20)
>
> Low, No. 7

The suitor kept silent and so did the next one, both knowing Prince Marko's impulsive nature. Prince Marko did not look like other wedding guests and his mien was threatening:

> Prince Marko arose
> And pulled out his damascened sabre,
> And laid it across his knees.   (45)
>
> Low, No. 7

With the sabre on his knees, Prince Marko essentially forced the damsel's choice:

> We shall set out three golden apples,
> And three golden rings;
> Let them bring forth the fair damsel,
> And let her choose whose apple she will,
> Or apple or golden ring.
> And he whose ring or apple she taketh,
> Shall himself take the fair damsel.   (56)
>
> Low, No. 7

Now, the only freedom left to the damsel was to say "yes" to Prince Marko. But the epic bards, who had their own sense of humor, bestowed upon her a wisdom to outwit Prince Marko by addressing him as her godfather:

> When the damsel understood these words
> (Though poor she was also prudent),
> She answered him again, and said:
> "Godfather, Prince Marko!"   (68)
>
> Low, No. 7

Long ago the damsel had made the choice of her heart and it was not Prince Marko. She wisely precluded Prince Marko's plan by proclaiming him her godfather. According to the unwritten protocol of patriarchal society in the Balkans, it was required that those who address another as the godfather (*Kum*) enter with them into a blood relation. Next, she bravely and wisely announced her choice of husband:

> An apple is a toy for children,
> But a ring is a knightly pledge.
> I will wed with Pavle Ustupčić.   (74)
>
> Low, No. 7

Struck by the damsel's verdict, "Marko roared like a beast of the forest." In the outburst of impotent fury he questioned her:

> Bitch that thou art!
> Someone hath taught thee this,
> But say now who hath taught thee!   (80)
>
> Low, No. 7

It was the popular wisdom what the damsel answered:

> Dear Godfather [Kum], Prince Marko,
> Thy sword instructed me.   (83)
>
> Low, No. 7

The damsel won Prince Marko's favor and just as he roared in passion and fury, he now "laughed loudly upon her." In the closing lines of the song he told her of his cruel intentions, had she not outwitted him:

> Well for thee, fair damsel,
> That thou tookest no apple,
> Nor apple nor golden ring!
> By the faith of my body,
> I should have cut off thy two hands,
> Nor wouldst thou have saved thy head,
> Nor ever on thy head have worn the green garland!   (92)
>
> Low, No. 7

This concludes Prince Marko's unsuccessful endeavor to marry. The outcome was satisfying for both him and the damsel. His dignity did not suffer. On the contrary, he gained in stature by his ability to accept the damsel's choice. This was not easy for Prince Marko.

There is a thematic affinity between the motifs relating to Prince Marko as an unsuccessful suitor and the song "How Marko Kissed the Bride and She Did Not Recognize Him," in Bogišić, No. 4. Prince Marko is represented as a young man who is rejected by the pretty maiden because she did not recognize him as her betrothed. The poem is a mixture of a maiden's shyness, some confusion about true identities, and a rare occasion when Prince Marko is described in an amorous venture.

Prince Marko has raised a silk tent on a meadow at Budim:

> Each maiden calls a good morning to the young Prince Marko,
> A beautiful one, very beautiful, the youngest was among them,
> She wished not good morning to Prince Marko;
> Her dark eyes she turned down to the ground.   (10)
>   Bogišić, No. 4

Proud of her royal family, the damsel refuses to talk with a stranger:

> Go away scoundrel! Do not talk to me.
> I am a dear sister of the young Pavle Banović,
> The Budim's exalted King is my cousin
> And I am betrothed to the young Prince Marko.   (23)

Without identifying himself Prince Marko made a pass at her:

> Marko caught the young maiden for her right arm,
> To his tent of silk he brought her in,
> And a kiss he placed on her rosy cheek.   (32)
>   Bogišić, No. 4

Insulted and ashamed, the damsel threatens that Prince Marko "will be hanged on the gate of Budim," but when she returns home, she is told that he was her betrothed.

> When the young damsel understood her brother,
> She could not utter a single word,
> But the young damsel was shy and blushing,
> And in modesty she turned her dark eyes down.   (73)
>   Bogišić, No. 4

There is another type of song in which Prince Marko's romantic endeavors and gallivanting paid off. The epic bards also depict Prince Marko as a man who liked merry-making and fun with tavern women and widows. In this respect, the song "A Widow from Sarayevo," in the Begović collection of *Serbian Folk Songs in Lika and Baniya*, No. 204, is characteristic. Prince Marko is lonely and he notices how even nature itself is full of life and joy. In a lyrical vein the song goes:

> Marko rambles from town to town,
> He seeks a pleasurable poplar shade.
> Nowhere can he find such a poplar shade;
> But there is one near Sarayevo.   (9)
>
> Begović, No. 204

He has to make his choice between a young widow and a young maiden:

> Under the poplar tree sits the young widow,
> And beside her a maiden fair.   (11)

Prince Marko eventually makes his selection:

> He reclines in a thick shade,
> And keeps kissing the young widow.   (16)

The unhappy maiden swears in jealousy:

> Burn in flames, O Sarayevo!
> Where widows are kissed,
> And maidens are missed.   (21)
>
> Begović, No. 204

Prince Marko concludes this song by an almost proverbial saying:

> Quoth Prince Marko:
> "Do not be foolish, pretty maiden!
> I would rather have used gold . . .
> Than mint silver."   (25)
>
> Begović, No. 204

In the same vein belongs an authentic folk tale taken from the medieval Balkan ballads and freely developed by a modern writer, Marguerite Yourcenar in her book *Oriental Tales*.[39] Titled "Marko's Smile," the story is about Paša of Scutari's widow who spends nights with young Prince Marko in her "wooden worm-eaten house" in the Bay of Kotor. This story is told in a lighter and more frivolous way than were the epic songs. It is hard to find descriptions like this one in heroic poetry: He [Prince Marko] resigned himself to her heavy breasts, to her thick legs, to her eyebrows that met in the middle of her forehead, to the voracious and suspicious love of an older woman.[40]

The widow was charmed by Prince Marko and wanted to gratify him— so she prepared fancy dishes he liked. But she was a wicked woman and eventually betrayed Marko to the Turkish soldiers when he wanted to swim across the bay to Dubrovnik and leave her. Prince Marko dove into the waves. "For two hours Marko swam, unable to advance a single stroke," tells the story, until the Turks caught him.[41] In order to save his life, Prince Marko pretended to be dead. He could not deceive the vindictive widow who told the Turks: "You need more than a storm to drown Marko. ... If you throw him into the sea, he will charm the waves as he charmed me, poor woman, and they will carry him back to his own country."[42] The widow suggested that they crucify Prince Marko, whom she wanted to see tortured—for she had once passionately loved him. At her instigation, the Turkish executioners first hammered nails in him and then put live coal on his chest. Prince Marko endured the pain and did not move or sigh. The evil widow did not believe that he was dead and she cried: "You need more than a thousand nails and a hundred hammers to crucify Marko Kralyevič."[43]

After all her cruel efforts, the jealous widow invented the sweetest torture. She proposed bringing in the young village girls to dance around Prince Marko "and we shall see whether love continues to torment him."[44] It is a rare occurrence when Prince Marko is unable to resist the temptation of the beautiful Turkish girl Haiša. It is also rather rare that a beautiful girl like Haiša would find Prince Marko so handsome. She saved his life by throwing her scarf over his face to hide his smile and proclaiming him as dead.

All but the wicked widow left. Prince Marko did not hesitate to take his revenge. He pulled out the nails from his body and hammered them into her. "When the executioners returned, they found on the beach the convulsed corpse of an old woman instead of the body of a naked hero."[45]

As always, Prince Marko was consistent in his cruelty and justice. He exchanged the evil widow for the Turkish beauty, Haiša, with whom he returned to his country. Marguerite Yourcenar concludes the folktale by peering into an unknown corner of Prince Marko's personality, into his admiration for beauty. As she said, "What moves me is ... the smile on the tortured man's lips for whom desire is the sweetest torment."[46]

In the life of an oral epic song the major elements are usually maintained but the epic singers use them interchangeably and in different combinations. In this respect the epic song, "Prince Marko Outwitted by a

Damsel," in Matica Hrvatska, 2, pt. 1, No. 17, is a fascinating document which contains several essential elements found in the folktale, "Marko's Smile," retold by Marguerite Yourcenar.

Comparing the song and tale, one finds that the maiden Yanica plays dead as Prince Marko did in the tale. The torturing here is performed by Prince Marko and the maiden endures just as Prince Marko did. The maiden Yanica loves Prince Marko as the widow of Scutari did before her feelings changed. The widow was bent on revenge, while the maiden Yanica hides her secret love. The torture of Yanica is as follows:

> Marko lights a fire on her young heart,
> And he puts a barrel on her young heart,
> Then he slides his hands along her young bosom.
> Then he leaves, sad and full of sorrow.   (55)
>
> Matica Hrvatska, 2, pt. 1, No. 17

The unifying element in both song and tale is subtly threaded. Both Prince Marko and Yanica the Maiden endured physical torture, but Prince Marko almost betrayed himself by a smile for beauty (Haiša), while Yanica almost smiled when touched by the loving hands of Prince Marko. At the end she confessed to her mother:

> My dear mother, my very dear mother!
> This torment was the worst,
> When he lighted fire on my small heart,
> Had it been a little more, I would have died, indeed.
> When he put that barrel on my small heart,
> I only felt more warm.
> But when he slid his hand into my bosom,
> Just a bit longer, and I would have smiled, indeed.   (65)
>
> Matica Hrvatska, 2, pt. 1, No. 17

Christians and Turks were sharply divided, but by living next to each other for centuries they sometimes mixed and Prince Marko's relations with Turkish women were evident in epic poetry. It is unusual to find a song like, "Prince Marko's Wedding," in *Bosanska Vila,* 1887, No. 18, p. 283–84. Here Prince Marko marries Fatima, a Turkish girl and a sister of Omer-Beg. The locale is the Turkish tavern where Omer-Beg extolls his sister's virtues. His friends laugh at him, saying that Prince Marko from "beyond the sea" is her lover. Omer-Beg promptly requests that Fatima drown herself in Sava river, and this she does. The river brings her to the sea and washes her in front of Prince Marko's manor. After her baptism Prince Marko marries Fatima:

> With her Marko lived his age,
> And they had many good children.
>
> Bosnian Vila, No. 18

According to Khalanskii, this song contains an old universal motif from the Elder Edda about the drowned girl who is brought to her loved one by the sea. After her husband Atli was killed, Gudrun throws herself into the sea, which washes her out to the land of King Yonakr, whom she then marries. Gudrun bears him three sons: Sortli, Erpr, and Hamdir.[47]

Prince Marko also saw Turkish women as part of the inimical world. He wanted to not only fight Turks on the battlefield but to also humiliate them. In the song "Prince Marko and Emperor Suleiman," in Matica Hrvatska 2, pt. 1, No. 11, which was taken from a blind singer in Smilyevo village near Gospić in Croatia, the Turkish Sultan is insulted. The opening lines begin with a pledge of Prince Marko:

> Keeps an eye Prince Marko on his sheep,
> On Kossovo, the field of the battle.
> Pledges to himself Prince Marko,
> That he, the hero, will not marry until
> He takes in kisses the imperial ladies
> And the beautiful wives of the Sultan.   (6)
>
> Matica Hrvatska, 2, pt. 1, No. 11

When Sultan Suleiman hears of the boasting, he summons Prince Marko and gives him the choice of hanging or decapitation. Prince Marko succeeds in obtaining combat with three hundred Janissaries. With the help of a fairy, Prince Marko killed them all, and then goes to the Sultan:

> Went Prince Marko to the Sultan's palace
> He sat himself on the bench next to the Sultan.
> Sultan moves off, Prince Marko moves on.   (68)

When there was no more space on the bench, the Sultan gives Prince Marko golden ducats:

Go, Marko, from my palace!
Let them be: God and Mohammed the Holy,
And that my eyes never see you again.   (75)
                                       Matica Hrvatska, 2, pt. 1, No. 11

Among the songs dealing with relations with women, the song, "Daughter of Novak the Old" in *Serbian Popular Songs in Srem*, Nikolič, 1888, 1, No. 55, deserves special attention. The song describes the adventures of Yanya who is disguised as a knight and serves the imperial host for nine years in lieu of her elderly father, Novak the Old. Prince Marko is suspicious and wonders:

> My dear God, what a strange warrior
> To stand in for Novak the Old!
>   Nikolič, No. 55

Prince Marko asks his mother how to establish whether a warrior is a man or a woman. Mother Yevrosima is wise and succinct in teaching her son which tests to undertake.

Even more interesting is a variant on the same theme, "Warring of Ružica the Maiden," also in Nikolič, No. 27, in which the characters are changed to maiden Ružica and the Emperor himself. The Emperor acts as Prince Marko and addresses his mother in respectful manner:

> By God, O my old mother,
> This is not Ružica the brave knight,
> But this is Rosie the maiden,
> I would like, my dear Mother, to wed her myself.
>   Nikolič, No. 55

The mother counsels her son in her usual way and the maiden leaves her nine years of war service. Before marrying the Emperor, the bards conclude this variant song with an unusually erotic description:

> The breasts swell, the dolman bursts,
> Fair face seeks kissing,
> Seductive eyes crave to be cherished.
>   Nikolič, No. 55

The universal motif of women warriors disguised as men was applied
to Prince Marko's wife and sister in the song, "Prince Marko Rescued by
His Wife and Sister," in Matica Hrvatska, 2, pt. 1, No. 64. Prince Marko's
wife Andjuša is an adventurous and brave knight in a role which is out of
line with her status in a traditional family. The poem was collected by Mih-
ovio Pavlinović in Šibenik in Dalmatia, and is characterized by features of
peasant life, indicating that it circulated in villages for some time.

One first sees Prince Marko walking unarmed and without the "moccasins" which were used by Balkan peasantry. He is captured and imprisoned by a Turkish Beg:

> For nine years of days,
> In dark dungeon languid is Marko,
> His long hair stretches under him,
> Nails are so long, he could walk on them,
> His beard he can tie as a belt,
> His pigtail is enough to cover him.   (48)
> > Matica Hrvatska, 2, pt. 1, No. 64

Prince Marko's faithful wife devised a scheme to deceive the Turkish Beg by
impersonating the Sultan's heralds who came to escort Prince Marko to
Constantinople. The Turkish Beg was fooled by Prince Marko's wife and
sister, and brought out the prisoner who was faring poorly:

> Beg orders the young barbers
> Agile tailors are summoned;
> One shapes Marko's beard, another moustache,
> Golden lining on dolman puts another,
> Like glaring sun brightens Prince Marko.   (113)
> > Matica Hrvatska, 2, pt. 1, No. 64

When the hero Marko smiled his wife warrior used the opportunity to warn
him:

> When the young Andjuša sees it,
> With a Tartar whip, Marko she hits,
> Where she hits, the skin cracks,
> Skin cracks, black blood gushes.   (118)
> > Matica Hrvatska, 2, pt. 1, No. 64

The rescue through trickery is accomplished and the Turkish Beg is captured by Prince Marko's disguised warrior wife:

> When young Andjuša sees it,
> Ties she Beg's hands in reverse,
> Takes off his garments in velvet and silk,
> She undresses Beg, and dresses up Prince Marko.   (149)
>
> Matica Hrvatska, 2, pt. 1, No. 64

The act of execution usually performed by Prince Marko is transferred by epic bards to Prince Marko's wife:

> Her sabre quickly she takes out of scabbard,
> She hits the Beg of Gabella,
> So lightly did she hit,
> That earth Beg embraced,
> On the black ground lies dead, the Beg.   (154)
>
> Matica Hrvatska, 2, pt. 1, No. 64

There were many women in Prince Marko's life. He was so popular that the epic bards could project their dreams, desires and even sins onto his character. Traditional wooing and marriage were prescribed but not always practiced. There was a fun to be had with tavern women or Turkish girls and widows. In this wide range of relations with women he was once brought close to incest with his sister. This poem, "Prince Marko's Bride-to-be Becomes His Sister," is in the A. Popović collection, *Various Heroic Folk Songs*. This song falls in the category of traditional weddings with Prince Marko's mother as participant and advisor. In this wedding, the bride was a daughter of the Wallachian Duke. As the wedding party departed, the fair weather suddenly changed and it began to rain and snow. It was in this terrible tempest that Prince Marko finally asked the maiden about her family. She related that she was an adopted daughter of the Wallachian Duke, who had bought her as a child from Turkish slavery. Her real parents were King Vukašin and Queen Yevrosima.

During the emotional recognition scene between brother and sister the weather turned fair again. Prince Marko promptly gave his sister in marriage to his best man, Vuk the Fiery Dragon. There are several variant songs with the same motif, some of them explicitly mentioning Prince Marko by name, such as "Prince Marko Finds His Sister," in Matica Hrvatska, 2, pt.

1, No. 35. Other songs have the same plot and action but the name of Prince Marko is substituted with others. Such are the songs in the Brothers Miladinov collection "Stoyan and Ganka the Bielkanka," No. 76, "Janissaries and Fair Dragana," No. 87, and "Pavel and Sister," No. 135.

Prince Marko was once brought in contact with a giantess who had supernatural qualities and was in many respects equal and even better than he. Epic bards placed their hero face to face with the giantess, a rather strange creature who appeared as a female warrior, an Amazon. She was seeking a husband who would be equal if not better and stronger than she. This Amazon goes by several names in South Slavic folklore, many of which are similar in nature and have the same basic Greek and Latin root *gig*, which under the influence of phonetic laws was transformed into the South Slavic *djid*. In the epic tradition the word was used in several variations to designate monsters, giants, and giantesses. Prince Marko is faced with a giantess, called *Djidovka* or the *Djid*-Maiden, who endeavors to conquer his heart.

There exist several Serbian, Croatian and Bulgarian variants of the song entitled, "Prince Marko and the Djid-Maiden," in Matica Hrvatska, 2, pt. 1, No. 49. The song involves three main participants: Prince Marko, his mother Yevrosima, and the Djid-Maiden. After the opening, Prince Marko told his mother about a magic ostrich feather which belonged to the Djid-Maiden:

> My mother, O my old mother!
> Never have I been stricken with fear that much,
> As I felt today, my dear old mother!
> Three of us, we three young knights rode today,
> We rode through the mountain green,
> To the end of the black mountain, we came,
> Then we found an ostrich feather,
> And we took to carry it:
> Relya pulled it up to his strong shoulder,
> Miloš took it up to his waist,
> Hardly to my knee I raised it, my mother.   (15)
>
> Matica Hrvatska, 2, pt. 1, No. 49

Prince Marko begins to tell of the greatest fright in his life when he and his companions-in-arms encountered the Djid-Maiden. Although he is a very brave hero, Prince Marko is also human and can sometimes be very much afraid, especially when he meets the Djid-Maiden who is unlike other women and possesses magical powers. Prince Marko's companions hide his identity from the Djid-Maiden when they realize that they cannot stand up to her:

> Spake, the Djid-Maiden:
> "God be with you, three warriors young!
> Do you, perchance, know Prince Marko?"
> All three of us sware falsely:
> "By God, O Djid-Maiden!
> We do not know Prince Marko."   (27)
>
> Matica Hrvatska, 2, pt. 1, No. 49

In a confession to his mother Yevrosima, Prince Marko describes how his friends Miloš and Relya angered the Djid-Maiden when they attempted to kill her. They called him for rescue, and he eventually succeeded in slaying the Djid-Maiden:

> Spake from the ground Maiden's dead head:
> "Thank you for the gift, my dear God!
> I did not seek Prince Marko today,
> To combat him in the duel,
> But I came to find Marko,
> His faithful wife to become."   (57)
>
> Matica Hrvatska, 2, pt. 1, No. 49

There are several variations on the theme of how Prince Marko kills the Djid-Maiden through trickery. As much as she desired a husband, Prince Marko did not wish to marry her because he suspected that she was a sorceress. In the song, "Prince Marko and Djid-Maiden," in the Maryanović collection of *Croatian Folk Songs,* No. 15, Prince Marko tells his mother that he hid in a church after he killed the Djid-Maiden by hitting her with an arrow. Related to the motif of ostrich feather or wing, a silver spindle appears in this song and makes the knights powerless.

Prince Marko's vague suspicions about the danger of the Djid-Maiden were confirmed after he killed her and found that she possessed three hearts:

> One heart was beating well,
> Another has just awakened,
> Asleep the third was unaware that we fought;
> On it there was a three-headed snake;
> Had the snake seen me,
> Strangled and dead I would be.
>
> Maryanović, No. 15

In the song "Arvatka Maiden and 30 Heroes: Marko Kills Her by Treachery," in *Collection of Folk Sayings and Wisdom*, 1, p. 62–64, the Djid-Maiden goes by name of Arvatka, which Khalanskii associates with the old name for Albania, Arbania.[48] He also finds that Prince Marko's relation to the Djid-Maiden–Arvatka is similar to that in the German legend of *Riesinnen* and *Waldfrauen*.[49]

The Djid-Maiden was incomprehensible and alien to Prince Marko and he could not accept her. He did not tolerate anyone being a better hero than he. In addition, epic bards reflected the traditional values which did not recognize women in the epic world, particularly if they were a threat to a hero.

THE HUSBAND ON HIS WIFE'S WEDDING

> *Buildeth the nest a little swallow bird,*
> *For nine long years the nest hold,*
> *This very dawn it began to unfold;*
> *But cometh to her a grey-green falcon,*
> *He cometh from service of honorable tsar,*
> *"Do not unfold our nest, my little swallow bird."*[50]

The epic figure of Prince Marko attracted a wide range of motifs in which other South Slavic heroes were absorbed as main characters at one time or another. Prince Marko became the nucleus and carrier of various sundry themes and ideas, a number of which presented him in a highly inconsistent light, as was the case of his relations with women.

The universal motif of a husband returning home on the wedding day of his wife was very widespread among the South Slavic people. The precursor of this motif can be traced as far back as Homer, with Odysseus' return to Ithaca to find the faithful wife Penelope being forced to marry one of her suitors. Scholars disagree over the way in which the motif became dispersed in different Slavic nations. In an effort to explain the relevance of the motif to the South Slavic peoples, Radosav Medenica quoted the German folklorist Felix Liebrecht who claimed in his work, *Zur Volkskunde* (1879), that the common source of the motif was to be found in Greek oral poetry and, possibly, even in the Greek written literature of the medieval times. This view was substantiated with three Greek epic songs in Liebrecht's translation which, according to Medenica, influenced Albanian, Bulgarian, and possibly Russian epic poetry.[51]

Once the motif of a husband on wife's wedding arrived on South Slavic soil it found favorable conditions for proliferation. From the seventeenth century on it was increasingly common for people to fall into prolonged Turkish captivity. At the same time it often happened that Christians had to serve Turkish sultans and Austrian emperors for many years. Last but not least, the growth of the outlaw movement and the activities of border raiders increased the incidence of long separations between husbands and wives.

The model song which served as a basis for Prince Marko's variants on the universal motif of a husband on his wife's wedding is "The Captivity of Yankovič Stoyan," in Vuk Karadžić, 3, No. 25. This remarkable poem is a well-balanced composition of a series of collateral motifs which can be traced in different combinations as found in Prince Marko's group of songs. The major hero in the principal song is Stoyan Yankovič, whose story represents an outstanding epic creation which far overshadows its predecessors and followers. In this respect Prince Marko is a lesser rounded character and his epic story is inferior in quality.

In order to understand the group of Prince Marko's songs dealing with the universal motif of husband on his wife's wedding, it is necessary to take a close look at the song about Stoyan Yankovič as recorded in the Vuk's collection. The relationship between history and legend is clear: Stoyan Yankovič was a historical person and according to Vuk Karadžić, the Venice Republic awarded him great honors for bravery in 1669. He was imprisoned in Constantinople, and escaped to his Ravni Kotari in northern Dalmatia. He was later killed fighting the Turks.[52]

The historically based captivity motif was combined with the motif of escape from the Sultan who made Stoyan Yankovič and his brother Iliya Smilyanič Moslems. In the Prince Marko's songs, instead of the motifs of captivity and escape there is usually "a service of nine years" to the sultan or to the emperor. Such are the songs: "Prince Marko and His Wife Andjeliya," in Lazar Nikolič collection, *Prince Marko in Eight Folk Songs*, No. 1; "Wedding of Prince Marko," in *Ivanišev MSS. Collection*, JAZU, 1, a, 110; "Prince Marko's Wife Remarries," in Vlad. Krasič *Serbian Folk Songs*, No. 5; "Remarriage of Fair Yela," in *Serbian Folk Songs in Srem*, No. 2.

All of these songs repeat some of the episodes from the major poem, "Captivity of Yankovič Stoyan," Vuk, 3, No. 25. Such is the dramatic scene of Stoyan's meeting with his mother who does not recognize him:

> Aged mother the hair cuteth,
> Cuteth hair and ties the wine,
> With tears the vineyard she waters
> And keeps calling her son Stoyan.   (52)
>
> Vuk, 3, No. 25

While Stoyan Yankovic̓ escaped from captivity in order to return to his
wife, Prince Marko asks the emperor for furlough since he had a dream:

> Blooms a rose in my white manor,
> Blooms a rose for all nine years,
> They came to pick my rose now.
>
> Nicolić, No. 1

Most of the Prince Marko songs employ the same message which was
originally delivered by Stoyan Yankovic̓ to his wife during the wedding festivities. The metaphor about a falcon and a little swallow is one of the most
touching descriptions in South Slavic epic poetry, and its hidden message of
love reached his wife in time. Dramatic events leading to the joy of reunion
between husband and wife were brought to an anticlimax when, returning
from the vineyard, Stoyan's mother lamented:

> O Stoyan, my apple of gold,
> Stoyan's memory already fades;
> But mother will not forget Yela, her daughter-in-law.
> O my dear Yela, my gold never worn,
> Who will greet the aged mother,
> Who will walk with me?   (137)
>
> Vuk, 3, No. 25

When the grieving mother saw her son standing there alive, her heart broke
and she died.

So far it has been shown that the epic songs about Prince Marko on the
wedding of his wife dealt with her remarrying. Since Prince Marko was ab-
sent for a long time, his wife either gave consent or in some cases still re-
sisted, waiting for his return. There is another large group of songs which
also deal with the same universal motif of wedding, however, here we find
that Prince Marko's wife is abducted by force.

The theme of the abduction of Prince Marko's wife by his adversaries is
represented in the song "Prince Marko and Mina of Kastoria," in Vuk, 2,
No. 6. The epic Marko-Mina pair supplies rich material for an analysis of
the strange ways in which history and legend interact. A large number of
epic songs associate Mina of Kastoria as the abductor of Prince Marko's
wife, while Prince Marko is connected with the universal motif of the husband who attends the wedding of his own wife to Mina.

The epic Mina of Kastoria was never verified as a historical person, although it is known that the town of Kastoria came into King Marko's pos-

session through his marriage to Yelena, a daughter of Duke Radoslav Hlapen. King Marko lost Kastoria when his wife surrendered Kastoria to her new husband Balša II Balšić, Duke of Durazzo. According to Jireček, this happened around 1380.[53]

Epic songs involving Mina of Kastoria and Prince Marko reflect these historical encounters between Balša II Balšić and King Marko. They indicate that the historical events which became connected with epic personalities were still fresh in folk memory. The universal motif of the disguised husband who attends the wedding of his own wife found ground in the historical conflict around Prince Marko's wife, Yelena. King Marko's historically accurate vassalage and the actual seizure of the town of Kastoria during his absence are reflected in the epic abduction of his wife by Mina of Kastoria.

In the song "Prince Marko and Mina of Kastoria," Prince Marko departs to join the Sultan's army to fight the Arabs abroad, and he admonishes mother Yevrosima:

> Hearken unto me, O mother!
> Shut the doors of the castle early,
> And in the morning open them late,
> For I am at feud, mother,
> With the accursed Mina of Kostura.   (44)
>
> Low, No. 17

The wise warning did not prevent the vile Mina of Kastoria from destroying Prince Marko's household. In the meantime, far from home, Prince Marko was fighting for the Sultan. In his absence the Arabs would attack:

> Charge, fierce Arabs!
> Departed is the terrible knight
> That rideth on the great piebald steed.   (151)
>
> Low, No. 17

and they would inflict heavy casualties upon the Sultan's host. When Prince Marko was present the Arab watchers would cry:

> Give back now, fierce Arabs!
> Behold he cometh, the terrible knight
> On the great piebald steed!   (165)
>
> Low, No. 17

One day bad news arrived from home:

> Therewithal came a letter to him,
> How that his manor was plundered,
> Yea, plundered and burnt up with fire.
> How that his old mother was trampled under of horses;
> How that his faithful wife was taken captive.   (198)
>
> Low, No. 17

Prince Marko was in a deep rage, but he stayed quiet and went to the Holy Mountain (Mount Athos) to take sacrament and to confess. The sub-motif of disguising is now introduced:

> He did on a monk's raiment,
> And let grow his black beard to his girdle,
> And on his head he set the priestly *kamilavka*.
> Then he sprang on the back of Šarac
> And straightway went to white Kostura.   (261)
>
> Low, No. 17

Prince Marko is not recognized when he arrives at the manor of Mina of Kastoria. He sees his abducted wife Yela (a nickname for Yelena) serving the men. He is accepted as a monk and tells the story of Prince Marko's death, whom he said he had buried personally. Mina was so happy to be able to now marry Marko's captive wife, that he asked the monk to officiate at the ceremony.

The motif of Prince Marko's actual presence at the wedding is made more specific through direct dramatic participation:

> Prince Marko took the book,
> The book he took and wedded Mina,
> And to whom but to his own wife!   (291)
>
> Low, No. 17

The flow of action has been deliberately slowed down by Prince Marko in order to create suspense and excitement in the audience and greater dramatic effect. Once Prince Marko marries Mina and Yelena, he soon puts an end to the whole farce, but only after he is granted the permission of the bridegroom to dance:

> And he spake to Mina of Kostura:
> "Wilt thou grant in this thy gladness
> That the monk may tread a merry measure?   (313)

Again the audience is thrilled but the excitement is intensified when:

> Marko leapt lightly to his feet,
> He turned him about two times and three times,
> And all the castle shook to its foundations.
> Then he pulled out his rusty sabre,
> From right to left he swung it,
> And hewed off Mina's head!   (322)
>   Low, No. 17

Variants in other South Slavic collections generally agree with those found in the Vuk 2, No. 61 song. The Bogišić collection contains three other versions of the same subject, these being, "Prince Marko and Minya of Kastoria," No. 7, "The Singing of Prince Marko When He Killed Mihna of Kastoria and Captured Kastoria," No. 86, and "Again About Marko and Minya but Differently," No. 87. Notwithstanding basic similarities with Vuk Karadžić 2, No. 61, the Bogišić song No. 7 displays a greater sense of national pride: here epic singers alter Prince Marko's attitude in his dialogue with the Sultan just after Prince Marko has heard the news that Mina of Kastoria abducted his wife and robbed his manor. Instead of having to ask the Sultan for 300 Janisseries to fight Mina, the bards reverse the roles and make the Sultan offer help freely: "And to you, I shall give my good knights." (88) Bogišić, No. 7. Then, with an almost condescending dignity of a man who fights his battles alone, Prince Marko answers proudly:

> Your forgiveness or blessing I do not want,
> Neither, my Sire, your good knights do I want,
>   Honorable Emperor!
> I, myself, will take my vengeance with Marko's own right hand. (94)
>   Bogišić, No. 7

In Bogišić song No. 87, the bards combined Prince Marko's revenge on Mina with his service to the Sultan, so that by storming Kastoria he was really fulfilling his duty as a vassal. This was symbolized by Prince Marko's delivery of the city keys to the Sultan. The ending of the song is as follows:

He takes the keys of Kastoria,
Brings them to the honorable Emperor:
"Behold and know, Honorable Sire!
As befits a hero, a dauntless assault I made,
For you, O Lord, I took Kastoria."   (114)
                                               Bogišič, No. 87

This attitude is markedly different from the one expressed in Bogišič song
No. 7, in which Prince Marko refuses the Sultan's offer of help and chooses
to fight alone. These examples show how the question of Prince Marko's
vassalage was a complex issue for epic singers. It was like handling a double
edged knife. Some bards sang of a dutiful Prince Marko while others emphasized his pride and independence.

Motifs of the bride's abduction and husband on wife's wedding appear
side by side in epic poetry. The song "The Wife of Prince Marko Remarries," in Matica Hrvatska, 2, pt. 1, No. 28, predominates the classical motif
of the husband on the wife's wedding with the substitution of persons. The
role of the main abductor Mina of Kastoria is taken here by Senyanin Ivo,
who was a famous hero belonging to the cycle of Outlaws and the Border
Raiders (*Hayduci* and *Uskoci*) since the beginning of the seventeenth century. The bards however, degraded Senyanin Ivo to the role of Prince Marko's servant. Contempt for Prince Marko's rival is clearly expressed by his
mother Yevrosima when she writes to her son:

But my Marko, my dear child!
Either you don't know, or you don't care,
That your wife is about to remarry,
If for somebody else, I would not mind,
But for Senyanin Ivo, your servant,
Who curried your horses.   (71)
                                     Matica Hrvatska, 2, pt. 1, No. 28

Prince Marko returns home just in time to witness the wedding, during
which there is a scene of mutual recognition (anagnorisis) between the hero
and his wife through the motif of two halves of their wedding ring. At this
point Prince Marko falls into a rage, kills Senyanin Ivo, and brings his head
to the Sultan, who in turn supplies Prince Marko with treasures in recognition of his faithful service.

The motif of wife abduction is emphasized in the Slovenian folk songs
which are more balladic than epic in their nature. The *Matica Slovenska
Collection* contains a few songs of this kind. One of these is "Prince Marko

Rescues His Wife," No. 48, much like the Croatian song, "Prince Marko and the Three Young Germans," in Rikardo Ferdin's collection, *Croatian Folk Songs and Tales,* p. 89.[54]

Both songs share the motif of a husband's departure for military service on the day after his wedding, and his request that the bride should wait for nine years for him to return. In each song the abductors are presented as three young Germans who arrive from the neighboring country in the northwest, and who abduct Prince Marko's wife by force. When Prince Marko returns home, his mother tells him of the abduction and he instantly sets off for Germany in search of his wife. The Slovenian version supplies some details of daily life (for example, the mother bakes special flat unleavened bread for Prince Marko's journey). Both the Croatian and Slovenian variants introduce a new element—when Prince Marko finds his wife, she is dancing a reel dance (*kolo*). Prince Marko cuts in beside her, and at first she does not recognize him. The motif of two halves of the wedding ring is forgotten here. In order to identify himself, Prince Marko pulls the slippers from her small feet. Then he pulls off her pearl necklace. When his wife still fails to recognize him, Prince Marko grabs her:

> For the third time, when the reel surged:
> He threw her on the horse in front of him,
> Home, to his old mother, he carried her.   (59)
>
> Matica Slovenska, No. 48

Slovenian and northwestern Croatian songs relating to the wife abduction motif tend to be less heroic and more realistic in their outlook. They reflect the actual conditions and traditional family relations which existed in these regions. The bards to the northwest modified the wife's status to some extent. She is returned and accepted by the first husband after her remarriage. The patriarchal order of the Balkan Slavic people required the preservation of a wife's faithfulness to her first husband. There is little doubt that these changes in attitude were a result of strong German influences in the northwest. Thus, in the German Wolfdietrich variant song, the abducted wife marries her abductor and is only later rescued by her first husband.[55]

Authorities in the field do not agree about the exact relation between the motifs of wife abduction and the husband on his wife's wedding. Khalanskii distinguishes the motif of the hero returning home on the wedding day of his wife from the related motif of the abduction of Prince Marko's wife. He treats them separately because he considers them to be of different origin.[56] Sumtsov, however, investigated both groups of motifs and came to the conclusion that they represent a single motif which reached Russia from medieval chivalric literature via northern versions from Britain and Scandinavia.[57] Banašević and Kostić advocate the view that these motifs are also found in the medieval romance of Beuves de Haumtone which reached South Slavs via the Adriatic coast. There people were familiar with the popular Italian version of *I Reali di Francia,* both in original and translation.[58] The parallelism appears quite clearly in the Croatian Prince Marko variant songs, especially in the liberation of the hero from captivity, his travel to a foreign country in order to free his beloved who had been abducted in the meantime, the rescue of the woman during the wedding, and finally the escape of the lovers.

In summing up, the epic songs from this category included universal motifs, remote historical reminiscences, and incidents of daily life. The interplay between history and legend was executed more or less successfully depending on the ability of the bards. Some songs are remarkable gems such as "Captivity of Yankovič Stoyan," and the poem "Prince Marko and Mina of Kastoria." Sometimes the bards were more conventional. Above all, they endeavored to entertain their epic audiences.

AN ANACHRONISTIC WEDDING

This is the custom of the Serbs,
For they use to drink their wine across their weapons,
And beside their weapons they seek sleep at night.[59]

Marko's historical visit to the city of Dubrovnik in 1361 left a trace in folk tradition and epic poetry. The song "The Wedding of Djuradj of Smederevo," from Vuk collection 2, No. 78, reveals a close interrelationship between history and legend. The song describes the adventures of the wedding party which went to Dubrovnik to receive the bride. Prince Marko's role was that of "best man," and he was in charge of the whole party. He warns the participants as they near Dubrovnik that "Latins are a treacherous lot" and that all should be alert to any schemes which might be perpetrated by the unreliable hosts. At the gates of Dubrovnik Prince Marko orders everyone in the wedding party to leave their horses with the servants, but not their weapons. He feared that the Dubrovnik hosts planned to entrap them in order to cancel the whole wedding.

It was an ancient Serbian custom to eat and drink while armed, the natural result of relentless warring and the need to have one's arms handy at all times. Therefore it is not surprising that Prince Marko should warn the wedding party and advise them to let him do all the explaining when questioned by the Dubrovnik noblemen. Indeed, as the song goes, the King of Dubrovnik (although Dubrovnik was always a republic) complained of such behavior, and Prince Marko gave him a piece of his mind:

> Fair sweet Sir, thou King of Dubrovnik!
> This is the custom of the Serbs,
> For they use to drink their wine across their weapons,
> And beside their weapons they seek sleep at night. (184)
>
> Low, No. 29

The song describes the entertainment that follows. The list of the heroes attending the celebration is impressive, including the most popular names in the Serbian epic. They belong to time periods ranging from the mid 1300s to the mid 1700s. We see mingling epic heroes from the Kossovo cycle, such as Miloš Obilić, Toplica Milan, Kosančić Ivan—to the Outlaw cycle with Debelić Novak, Novaković Gruyo and others—all led by Prince Marko.

The whole wedding was considered light heroic entertainment in the familiar and attractive setting of Dubrovnik. There were lavish dinners and much festivity and drinking. Games and contests were played and won. They had a good time, reflecting the words of Prince Marko's mother from another occasion:

> Bringing home the bride is pleasure,
> Christening is the law of God,
> But soldiering is hard necessity.
>
> Pennington, No. 6

Although it was pleasant, Prince Marko eventually became concerned by the hosts' procrastination in delivering the bride and apprehensive of their ulterior motives. He tried to hasten the events and obtain the bride. He is helped by the bride Yerina herself, who warns them of the wicked intentions of her father King Michael. Yerina also informs the wedding party where she is kept hidden.

In order to obtain the bride the wedding party had to select their own knights who would win three contests given by the "Latins" (Dubrovnik hosts). The first was a duel between two Latins and the young Gruyica, "that of the two Latins he made four." The second contest required jumping over "three valiant steeds with fixed war-spears upward to the sky," a feat which was promptly achieved by Relya the Winged. In addition, Relya easily killed twelve armed horse attendants. The third and final requirement set by the Latins was to shoot at the apple on the castle tower. Prince Marko had other ideas and decided to stop the contest, and do something to free the bride from the castle instead.

Since Prince Marko knew where Yerina was hidden, he found her quickly. In the meantime, the Latins shut "seven and seventy gates." This angered Marko.

> And when Marko was mounted on Šarac,
> He drew his heavy mace,
> And so did his anger rage,
> That each door as he smote it,
> Brast altogether in sunder,
> Till he was come to the gate of the citadel,
> A mighty gate it was, God's curse upon it!
> And when Marko smote it with his heavy mace,
> The whole castle shook to its foundations,
> And stones fell down from the walls.   (272)
>
>   Low, No. 29

A shaken King Michael, hoping to save Dubrovnik from destruction, offered the keys of the city to Prince Marko, who in turn hit the King with his mace. "And the wedding-guests departed thence."

The atmosphere of suspicion, secret plots, and violence which permeated the wedding preparations in Dubrovnik has a clear and known historical background. In addition to King Marko's historically confirmed visit to Dubrovnik, a number of other facts can be verified. In 1446, Djuradj Branković, Lord of Serbia, agreed with Thomas Palaeologus, Lord of Morea (Peloponnesus) in Greece, that Djuradj's son Lazarus would marry Helena Palaeologus, a daughter of Thomas. Lazarus was the bridegroom, although the epic poem selected his father instead.

The bride Helena travelled from Glarentza in Achaia in the Morea to Dubrovnik on a flotilla supplied by the Dubrovnik Republic.[60] A large Serbian wedding party consisting of numerous noblemen went to Dubrovnik to await the bride. They waited several months and the wedding party was lodged in a Dubrovnik suburb. When Helena Palaeologus arrived at Dubrovnik, she was lavishly entertained by the Dubrovnik Republic for several days.

Whenever any member of the party ventured into the city they had to check their weapons at the gate. Dubrovnik enforced the strict law prohibiting armed foreigners from entering the city. During that time several brawls took place between Serbian and Dubrovnik noblemen. According to the official Dubrovnik archives of the period, the City Senate investigated the incidents and censured several local noblemen, punishing some of them, a fact which indicates that they were probably the instigators of the fights.[61]

Prince Marko's epic participation in this wedding, however, is pure anachronism, since King Marko died fifty-two years before the actual wedding, and his historical visit to Dubrovnik took place eighty-five years earlier. Prince Marko's role in the epic weddings goes beyond the historical framework of this event. Epic poems are replete with descriptions of wedding contests and knightly tournaments in which Prince Marko participates, passing all the tests and winning all the prizes. In the end he always chose to cede the bride to another knight while usually assuming the role of best man. Prince Marko acts as savior of brides, princesses, and maidens from the evils of abductors, conquerors, brigands, or even dragons. Nevertheless, such exciting adventures pass without Prince Marko becoming romantically involved. In those cases where Prince Marko does not deliver the rescued maiden in marriage to his blood-brother or to a friend, he frequently returns her to her parents. Epic bards celebrated Prince Marko in the wedding festivities where he was assigned a role more prominent than that of the groom. While attending to all the duties of the best man, removing all obstacles, and making everybody happy, Prince Marko remained distant from women. He treated them with patriarchal respect as if they were his sisters, but they are not a part of his heroic world. Prince Marko the hero is alone.

FRATRICIDE

Grey falcon spake hissing:
"To me without my wing
Is like to brother without brother."[62]

The theme of fratricide belongs to the family of universal motifs. Liebrecht,[63] Maretić,[64] and Djurić[65] describe a parallelism between South Slavic and Greek poems. The fratricide motif applied to Prince Marko did not have historical foundations. Marko's historical relationship with his brother Andriya is reflected in the Poreč Charter, which was drafted by King Vukašin in 1370 and cites two of his sons, Marko and Andriya, by name.[66] Historically, Andriya was the younger brother of King Marko, and according to available data, there is nothing to indicate that relations were in any

7. Prince Andriya, brother of King Marko, fresco in the Monastery of St. Andriya near Treska, founded in 1389. Painted by Metropolitan Bishop Yovan, called Zographos. From Svetozar Radoyčić, *Geschichte der Serbischen Kunst* (Berlin: Walter de Gruyter, 1969). Reprinted by permission of Walter de Gruyter & Co.

way strained or hostile between the two brothers. In fact, there are several strong indications that Marko and Andriya maintained good and friendly brotherly ties. The two men even had a cordial agreement according to which they would donate a number of their villages to the Sušica and Treska monasteries.[67] Andriya survived King Marko, and according to Jireček, collected their respective inheritances with the third brother Dimitar.[68] According to legal records, it was proved in the Dubrovnik Court in 1399 that the late King Marko left no heir.

Two types of epic songs deal with the relationship between the brothers Marko and Andriya. In one group they are treated as friendly toward each other, while in the other they fight as ardent enemies. The latter group of songs provide a clear example of how the general motif of fratricide came to be superimposed on those chronicle-songs dealing with Marko and Andriya as principal subjects. As highborn princes, the two brothers managed to capture the spotlight of public interest, becoming fascinating subjects for epic poets and their audiences. One became a king, while the other founded various monasteries and churches. Consequently the large number of chronicle-songs about Marko and Andriya is not surprising. In the course of time such songs became a vehicle for ancient local and migrating foreign motifs.

In the Marko-Andriya fratricide motif, the causes for fratricide are based either on human relationships involving rivalry, competition, prestige in having a: better weapon, attire, horse, or beautiful girl, or they are determined by historical conditions of prolonged Turkish captivity and outlawry. We are looking at a time of protracted and interminable wars, foreign invasions, rebellions, combats and duels, domestic treason, displacement of populations, and acrid collisions of opposing religions. Families were suddenly ripped apart. One brother might have remained Christian, while the other might have become a zealous Moslem. It may not have been a coincidence that brothers were fighting each other, since they may have belonged to opposite warring sides. Real life situations frequently appeared wherein brothers failed to recognize each other, having been separated for a long time.

The tragic conflict of fratricide provided epic poetry with an abundance of variations on the same recurring motif. South Slavic bards could not avoid tying together the powerful fratricide motif with their cherished hero Prince Marko.

Khalanskii analyzed the motifs concerning Marko-Andriya relations and enumerated various patterns, such as rescue, rivalry, killing, and carelessness.[69] Banašević claimed that the fight between two brothers who fail to recognize each other was well known and prevalent in medieval chivalric literature. He considered the motif a haphazard adaptation of Western in-

8. Marko's Monastery, Sušica, near Skopye, dedicated to St. Demetrius, completed in 1372 by King Marko. Frescoes in the monastery are characterized by a mixture of courtly Byzantine style and elements of monastic rigidity and realism which approach naturalism. Reprinted by permission of V. Djurić, from *Recherches sur l'art* (Novi Sad: Matica Srpska, 1968).

fluences.[70] While the parallelism of motifs may have been partially due to external influences, South Slavic bards had the same motif at their own fin-gertips.

The fratricide motif was present on the entire Balkan area. Geographic distance notwithstanding the motif appeared from Bulgaria to Macedonia and Serbia. It surfaced further in the area of Mid-Dalmatia and northwestern Croatia, extending to Istria and to the north in the Slavic-speaking regions of Burgenland in present-day Austria.[71] This wide range of the fratricide as well as other major motifs was primarily due to the effect of massive population migrations during the sixteenth and seventeenth centuries.

The Marko-Andriya songs dealing with fraternal conflict were already widespread in the sixteenth century. Proof for this has been supplied by the Dalmatian poet Petar Hektorović who published a ballad about the Marko-Andriya conflict in his 1568 work, *Fishing and Fishermen's Conversations*.[72] A fisherman named Paskoye Debelya sang to Hektorović of the fight between Prince Marko and his brother over the division of booty and about Andriya's death. This song also appears in the Bogišić collection, No. 6. Among the side motifs of fratricide in this song, we find a conflict between Prince Marko and Andriya over a horse. Both brothers refuse to acquiesce, even at the risk of a duel.

> But once they captured three good horses,
>   The two poor men,
> Each took a horse, each took his share,
> They could not agree about the third horse,
> They flared up and swore, but they were not,
> My friends I tell you, they were not two poor men,
> But one of them was Sir Marko King's son,
> Sir Marko King's son and his brother Andriyaš,
>   The young knights.   (13)
>   Pennington, 2, No. 1

The motif of the quarrel about a horse was associated with life accounts of the outlaws (*hayduci*) and border raiders (*uskoci*) who, while fighting the Turks, often argued vehemently over the division of booty, and sometimes fought among themselves. It also reflected "some elements of the feudal social setting" according to Professor Svetozar Kolyević, who continues: "thus the 'good horse,' which is the cause of the quarrel, was a symbol of feudal power in Serbian medieval law."[73] Kolyević's observation about "creative merging of different times and social settings" is significant for better insight into this song.[74] In this and even more in other songs Prince Marko takes the role of an outlaw almost exclusively, with not one allusion to his former self as the ruler of Prilep. Only his title of "Prince" (*Kralyević*) remained, but this form is sometimes used as a family name and was kept by the people as such.

Conflict over a sword is introduced frequently in Macedonian and Bulgarian ballads. The quarrel between two brothers over the division of booty also takes place in the outlaw type of songs, but this time instead of a horse the subject of dispute is a sword which is claimed by both. The ballad is titled "Who Were the Two Brothers?" in the Brothers Miladinov collection, No. 252. The song does not identify the brothers by name and only explains that it is the younger who slays the elder. In the case of Prince Marko and Andriya, it is Marko who kills his younger brother, the pattern having been reversed in this song.

A beautiful damsel for whose hand or favor the knightly brothers vye is the motif of fraternal rivalry which eventually could lead to fratricide. This motif was applied to Prince Marko and his brother Andriya who is named Marinko in Iordanov song, No. 12.

> How two bright and dear brothers fight each other,
> Two brothers, Marko and Marinko,
> They fight because of a maiden.
>
> Stoykovič, p. 37[75]

The outcome in this song is happy:

> Marko takes the pretty maiden,
> And Marinko is his best man,
> They went to wed in the church.
>
> Stoykovič, p. 37

In many a song, however, the outcome is tragic, as in the Delorko manuscript 310, in the Institute for Folk Arts in Zagreb (INU), No. 95, from Žirye Island near Šibenik.[76] The song "Brother Killed Brother Then Himself in Sorrow," in Matica Hrvatska, *Narodne epske pyesme,* 1, No. 3, describes the fratricide which is caused by conflict over Prince Marko's wife. Andriya complained to his brother Prince Marko, blaming his wife for being disrespectful to their old mother. Andriya threatened to punish his sister-in-law. Angered, Prince Marko killed Andriya and, realizing what he had done, takes his own life:

> When Prince Marko saw his brother dead,
> He pulled knife from Andriya's heart,
> And with it he kills himself.   (68)
>
> Matica Hrvatska 1, No. 3

Fraternal rivalry in some instances is brought about by a fairy, who transforms herself into a beautiful damsel to set brothers against each other. A fratricide caused or influenced by the supernatural powers embodied in a fairy, became attributed to *fatum*, which is an external independent force in the face of which human beings are helpless victims. The songs which contain such tragic encounters between two brothers probably originated at a much earlier date.

The family, although the primary social unit of patriarchal society, was often depicted as being rife with strained personal relationships, gossip, rumors, a persecuting mother-in-law, or petty quarrels between sisters-in-law. Sisters-in-law who were considered dangerous obstacles to good relations between brothers were highlighted in epic poetry. There are, conversely, numerous poems about noble sisters-in-law who prevent brothers from quarrelling over an inheritance or who reconcile them after a fight.

The fratricide motif of brothers killing in ignorance is present in a series of epic poems. The motif involves a fight between the brothers that terminates a long search by one for the other. The usual pattern with Prince Marko is that he learns from his mother that he was not an only child and that a brother had been born before him who was taken as a child by the Turks. Prince Marko then goes off in search of his brother and he either succeeds in rescuing him or he discovers that the Turks have already killed him. Prince Marko would then slaughter the Turks in revenge. Thus in the song "Prince Marko and his Brother Andriya," in Vuk, 6, No. 16, Prince Marko seeks out his brother and after many hardships they happily return home. Similarly, in Milutinović, No. 36, Prince Marko rescues Andriya from the Turks and both return safely home to their happy mother.

This song introduces the side motif of the brothers arranging a contest to determine who is the stronger. When the contest finally flares into a duel, Prince Marko refuses to fight, challenging that they would better prove themselves by fighting the Turks. The fratricide motif weakened here and was substituted by the theme of a competition. The importance of the endurance contest which was very popular in the heroic world was expressed in numerous variants centering on hunger, thirst, running, throwing heavy stones, etc. This side motif appears in the song "The Brothers-Princes," in Filipović, No. 3. This song registers the birth of Marko and Andriya as twins, a rare occurrence in South Slavic oral poetry. In the poem, the father of the twins is simply referred to as "King of Prilip" and he is described as celebrating the baptism of sons Marko and Andriya. When the twins grow up, Andriya challenges his brother Marko to a duel in order to prove his manhood. Marko refuses but proposes a contest to determine which of the two can last longer without water. He advises Andriya to go to a nearby tav-

ern maintained by Yanya, the inn-keeper. Prince Andriya encounters a brig-
and named Rosa and his outlaw band (*hayduci*) at the inn. The outlaws are
introduced as adversaries in place of the Turks and they kill Andriya. Prince
Marko, worried as to what has delayed his brother, finds him dead:

> Brigands threw the dead head out,
> The dead head of Prince Andriya,
> To play with head they began,
> From hand to hand goes the dead head,
> Until it came to hands of Prince Marko.   (138)
>
> Filipović, No. 3

Prince Marko slaughters all the outlaws and the hostess Yanya who was
their accomplice. Prince Marko's bereavement in this song is expressed in
strong emotional terms:

> Left Marko for his manor,
> Wails bitterly Marko after his dead brother.   (154)
>
> Filipović, No. 3

Fratricide has been weakened in some songs to such an extent that the
Turks kill Andriya while the Prince Marko appears in the role of avenger.
Thus instead of killing a brother, Prince Marko punishes enemies, a point
very dear to the popular bards. Prominent songs in this series are "Prince
Marko Avenges His Brother Andriyaš Who Was Killed by the Turks," in
Bogišić, No. 89, and, "Prince Marko Avenges the Death of His Brother An-
driyaš," in Matica Hrvatska, 2, pt. 1, No. 33. In both songs Andriya en-
counters a group of revelling Turks who kill him. Sometime later, Prince
Marko arrives and in revenge kills all the Turks he finds there. In the Bogišić
version Prince Marko hears of his brother's murder from a fairy:

> Wake up Prince Marko!
> Dead is thy young brother Andriyaš,
> In stone tavern he was murdered.   (47)
>
> Bogišić, No. 89

The Matica Hrvatska variant has Prince Marko discovering Andriya's
death himself when he sees his brother's horse:

By the tavern, there is Andriya's horse,
His bay-horse, hitched at the orange tree.   (85)

Entering the tavern Prince Marko addressed the Janissaries:

What did my brother do to you, Turks,
That you cuteth his head off,
That you bathed in wine dead head?   (109)

The Turks threatened to kill Prince Marko as they had his brother, but Prince Marko finished them off:

In a single stroke Marko swung his sabre,
All Turks, full thirty of them he slew,
And with them three ells of ground he caught.   (117)

Matica Hrvatska, 2, pt. 1, No. 33

Those were cruel times, when no respect was lost on dead enemies whose corpses were mutilated and spiked heads publicly exhibited. So the popular bards evoked one of these horror scenes from common life and applied it to Prince Marko's dead brother. Such songs were most likely created at the time when Turkish oppression had reached unbearable heights, for it seems as though the bards were looking for the justification for their hero Prince Marko to retaliate in a savage way. The more brutal the revenge, the greater the justice.

One aspect of the fratricide motif is when Prince Marko appears in the role of rescuer, this time of his quarrelling friends. In the song "Two Yakšičs and Prince Marko," in Filipović, No. 5, we find the newly introduced pair of quarrelling brothers, Mitar and Styepan Yakšić. A fairy provoked a quarrel between the brothers and one killed the other. Prince Marko appears on the scene, and when he realizes what the fairy has done:

Marko let go his greyhounds and bloodhounds,
To catch fairy in the mountain,
Into the green lake escapes the fairy,
Green, deep, and icy.
Marko let go his grey falcon,
To fetch the fairy in the lake,

Fairy flees under the clouds to sky,
Marko takes his spiked mace,
He throws his mace high under the sky.   (74)

Filipović, No. 5

Prince Marko overpowers the fairy and forces her to use her supernatural abilities to revive his dead friend Styepan Yakšić.[77]

In this song, Prince Marko is noble and the bard depicts his heroic character. He had already become so deeply entrenched in the role of a rescuer in the popular tradition, that the bards portrayed him as such, leaving the roles of quarrelling brothers to be assumed by other epic characters. Although Prince Marko appears to have been displaced from the fratricide motif he is once again proven to be the best hero.

Prince Marko and his brother were frequently identified by various names which have no historical foundation. Epic singers had other pairs of brothers available in their repertoire, such as brothers Yakšićs, and Predrag and Nenad. Singers would avail themselves of each particular pair of brothers depending on popular interest and sentiment of the time.

During the entire course of their development fratricide songs managed to retain strong balladic overtones in motif elaboration and in the treatment of details, perhaps because this motif was deeply entrenched in family life. The vitality of the fratricide motif, combined with Prince Marko's outstanding popularity, added a definite vigor to the whole segment of songs which had already found a favorable climate within South Slavic epic poetry.

HEROIC DRINKING

Right so Marko drank a vessel of wine,
And threw the vessel down on the green grass.[78]

Epic songs reveal yet another, merrier side of Prince Marko's life. It is quite certain that the life of King Marko's court involved, as was customary in those times, many diversions: feasts, celebrations, games, and dances. According to the historian Constantin Jireček[79] and Dragutin Kostić,[80] King Marko's royal court was replete with popular entertainers and epic singers, as was the court of another contemporary, King Tvrtko of Bosnia. King Marko spent many pleasurable hours in the company of his friends. One of King Marko's subjects, the scribe (*diyak*) Dobre from Poreč, recorded in the Khludov Manuscript that he participated in many such parties, noting,

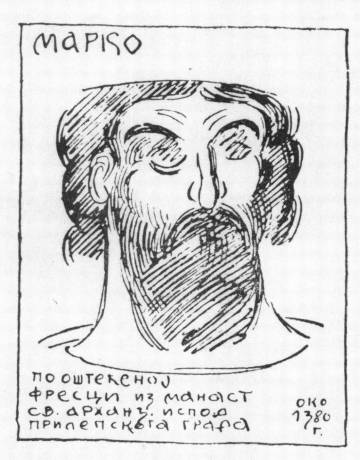

Король Марко

По фреске из монастыря св. Архангела близ г. Прилепа.
(около 1380 г.). Рис. А. Дероко

9. Sketch of King Marko from damaged fresco in the Monastery of St. Archangel Michael in Prilep, painted about 1380, and drawn by Aleksandar Deroko in the 1920s. Reprinted by permission of the Academy of Sciences of USSR, from Golenishchev-Kutuzov, *Epos serbskogo naroda* (Moskva: Akademiia Nauk SSSR, 1963).

"if they sin somewhere . . . or get drunk . . . do not condemn them."[81] Kostić
has gone so far as to consider the possibility that the scribe Dobre was a bit
inebriated at the time he made his annotations.[82] Dobre did not bother or
remember to date his annotation as it was customary at the time to at least
enter the year (since the creation of the world). Dobre also observes the exchange of women between "faithful King Marko" and his father-in-law,
Duke Hlapen.[83] The familiar tone of the writing, the allusion to frequent
drinking parties, and the fact that the scribe Dobre may have been intoxicated even while he was performing such a serious task indicate that drinking was not only customary but even admired.

Historical reminiscences of King Marko's drinking parties found their
expression in the epic songs. It would appear that the South Slavic peoples
were used to, or at least impressed by exorbitant drinking right before or
after making important decisions, as well as during wedding parties, before
battles, or on any other appropriate occasion. According to Vuk Karadžić,
the bards sang of the lavish hospitality of Leka Kapetan when he welcomed
Prince Marko and other suitors to his manor. This is seen in the song, "The
Sister of Leka Kapetan," Vuk 2, No. 39:

> And on the left side of the pavillion
> Was the well-garnished low round table,
> And along it wine had been poured out,
> And brimmed in golden beakers;
> And at the head therof stood a goblet
> That held full four okas[84] of wine,
> And was wrought of purest gold.
> It was the goblet of Leka Kapetan,
> And of that Marko had great marvel.   (264)
>   Low, No. 6

Such feasts in the heroic world are treated, as Cecil Bowra says, "with
style and dignity."[85] This attitude of the popular bards is explained further
by Cecil Bowra: "The heroes still conduct themselves with heroic propriety.
Indeed delight in drink and intoxication are often regarded as proper to a
hero, worthy of his physical strength and ebullient nature."[86]

The popular understanding of the South Slavs was that heavy drinking,
in addition to improving one's health, was a heroic feature. The bards
merely perpetuated this in Prince Marko's legend. The same consideration
was given to the pleasure of eating, elaborate dressing, and possessing an
exceptional horse and fancy weapons. These became necessary attributes of
a hero.

Scenes of wine drinking are very common in epic poetry, as shown in the first lines of the song, "Prince Marko and Philip the Hungarian," in Vuk 2, No. 58, which begins by describing a drinking party at which Philip the Hungarian[87] boasts of how he is going to kill Prince Marko:

> Thirty captains sat at wine together,
> In white Karlovci town.
> Amongst them Philip the Hungarian,
> And beside him Vuk the Fiery Dragon.
> And when they had well drunken,
> And were flown with wine,
> The thirty captains boasted themselves
> How many slaves each had taken,
> How many heads each had smitten off.   (9)
>
> Low, No. 14

Several scenes take place later in a tavern where Prince Marko is drinking. He greets Philip, but before starting a fight he invites him to have a drink:

> And to Philip the Hungarian he said:
> "Sit thee down in peace, thou Magyar bastard!
> Wake not the fleas on my skin,
> But light down from thy horse that we may drink wine.
> There will still be time for fighting."   (168)
>
> Low, No. 14

The avid audience for the heroic songs was impressed by the reckless and self-confident sense of courage Prince Marko displays. He does not even deem it necessary to interrupt his drinking in a tavern for the sake of a mortal fight. Prince Marko humiliates and condescends to Philip the Hungarian who is expected by the audience to act violently:

> But Philip smote Marko on the right hand,
> And brake his golden goblet,
> And spilled out the red wine.   (173)
>
> Low, No. 14

Popular fantasy embellished the impressive picture of Prince Marko as a rough Balkan warrior who swiftly assaults and punishes the haughty Philip:

He smote him on the right shoulder
And clave him in twain even on the saddle.
Through him went Marko's sword,
Even unto the door of marble stone,
And in twain it hewed him.

(182)

Low, No. 14

Another good example of a wine-drinking scene appears in the song "Prince Marko and Musa the Robber," in Vuk 2, No. 66. In the opening scene Musa is drinking wine at an inn and later in the same song, Musa's adversary Prince Marko is seen drinking and eating in order to gain strength for the fight:

The Sultan set Marko in the new inn,
And let serve him with wine and rakia,
With the flesh of fat rams,
And with loaves of white bread.
And there Marko tarried three months of days,
Until his life was a little returned to him.

(100)

Low, No. 22

After months of drinking and eating, Prince Marko feels that he is ready for a winning fight. It seems as though magical powers were elicited from indulging in wine and food, and it is thus that Prince Marko prepares himself for battles, gaining extraordinary strength. He passed the tests set for him by epic singers. He wanted to face Musa.

Prince Marko very often drinks in the company of his horse Šarac who shares heroic qualities with his master. They are the best of friends. They understand each other and are inseparable in decisive battles. Šarac's faithfulness is rewarded by Prince Marko's generosity and respect. They emerge together in a communion of heroic drinking, as can be seen from the song "Marko and the Moor," in Vuk 2, No. 65:

He drank not as men are wont to drink,
But he drank from a basin of twelve okas;
Himself drank half, and half he gave to Šarac.

Low, No. 21

The popular belief that wine is beneficial and helps wounds to heal is applied to Prince Marko who was ailing in the song, "Prince Marko and Mina of Kostur":

But Marko sought not a doctor; from inn to inn did he hie,
And ever sought Prince Marko where the best wine was to drain,
Scarce had he drunk his fill thereof, when his wounds were healed again.

Noyes, p. 159

Drinking was not only a part of dignified decorum, it was used by the epic bards as a suitable device for moving the epic narrative along.[88] Stereotyped openings are frequently utilized in which, for example, Prince Marko and his mother drink and eat together in a relaxed family atmosphere, as in the song "Marko's Ploughing":

Prince Marko sat at wine,
With the aged Yevrosima his mother.
And when they had enough drunken,
Marko's mother spake to him, saying. (4)

Low, No. 28

Heroic drinking functioned to emphasize Prince Marko's image as an epic hero with a drinking capacity no man could match. Prince Marko drinks from an ever-present colossal goblet containing four or more gallons of wine. Such capacity is shared with other epic heroes in the world, such as the Armenian hero David of Sasoun, who drinks from a cup as big as a basin. Epic singers used the hyperbole of heroic drinking to convince audiences of heroes' exceptional needs.

THE SULTAN'S VASSAL

Prince Marko's "patriotism has an ambiguous quality. At least, he is in the Sultan's service... The poets accept the fact and get over it as best they can by showing in what a jaunty, independent spirit Marko treats his master."[89]

Scholars have speculated a good deal about the apparent contradiction of making a hero of a Turkish vassal, which is what King Marko really was during the most critical and strained times of the Turkish conquest of the Balkans. Such an anomaly in the epic tradition resulted in the creation of two groups of epic songs dealing with Prince Marko's relationship with the Turks. One group presents Prince Marko as loyally fulfilling his vassalage to the Sultan, while the other group describes Prince Marko in the full glory of a relentless fighter against the Turks and protector of his people.

Prince Marko's status as a vassal has been commented on by scholars
in numerous and contradictory ways. Kostić set forth an eclectic summary.
He stated that such epic songs do not celebrate Prince Marko's vassalage but
explained it through his allegiance and chivalric fealty.

> [They] emphasize Marko's unhappiness because of this imposed and
> highly embarrassing service not only with regard to the Turks in general as
> oppressors and cruel rulers but especially with regard to the sultan him-
> self. In the latter case Marko is indeed a dutiful vassal . . . not by liking but
> out of necessity . . . since Marko had given his word of honor.[90]

As a vassal of the Sultan, King Marko lived at a time when the Turks
were stabilizing their gains (in the late 1300s). They were preparing for new
conquests and tried very hard not to antagonize neutral rulers. This was the
primary reason for their fairly accommodating attitude toward King
Marko. The historical necessity which rendered King Marko a Turkish vassal also indirectly contributed to his glory, although at first glance it might
seem paradoxical. An epic aura fully enveloped Prince Marko, placing him
among those knights whose epic stature was heightened through their service to a foreign, non-Christian ruler. In this respect Prince Marko shared
the poetic destiny of other folk heroes with whom medieval chivalric literature is replete. Such French Christian champions as Roland, Renaud, Olivier, Charlemagne, and Beuves de Haumtone pursued their thrilling adventures in the service of infidel Saracen lords and kings. A good example is
Dietrich von Bern in the *Nibelungenlied*, who served Etzel, King of the
Huns.

Medieval knights were frequently motivated by humiliation and personal anger to join the service of infidels. Banašević offers a comparison between King Marko and Charlemagne. The latter was exiled in his boyhood,
went to Toledo, Spain, and was knighted there by the Saracen ruler Galaf-
frus, an account of which appears in a twelfth-century codex, the *Codex
Calixtinus*.[91] The departure of Christian knights to the courts of infidel sov-
ereigns became a common feature (*locus communis*) of medieval chivalric
literature and *chansons de geste*.

Among those knights driven by anger into the service of infidels was
Beuves de Haumtone, who protected his Sultan from the onslaught of other
rulers and superhuman forces. Roland's adventures commence with his
quarrel with Charlemagne who slaps him in the face; Roland then leaves for
Barberia where he faithfully serves the Persian sultan. The champions Renaud and Olivier also rise up against Charlemagne for reasons of intrigue
and leave for a pagan land where they enter the service of infidels.[92]

The primary difference between Prince Marko and western Christian knights was that for a Western knight, service to a foreign king was an exciting adventure, while King Marko was forced to accept it out of sheer necessity. Krsto Lyumović notes this discrepancy and observes:

> The difference between the service of the French knights to infidel kings, and Marko's service to the Sultan is that the western knight after a certain time would return to his Christian ruler and to his homeland. Marko, however, although residing in Prilep continuously, remained a servant of the Sultan, or at least never severed that relation. In addition, Marko could not return to his Christian ruler and epic singers knew very well that after the death of the legitimate Emperor Uroš, there was no ruler to come back to.[93]

In contrast to Western knights, Marko's status was disadvantageous in several respects. He had no other choice but to accept his vassalage, no place to come back to as home, and, finally, this was not temporary service for him but a final choice. While in the West vassalage was considered almost fashionable, the Balkans of the fourteenth and fifteenth centuries regarded such service under the Turks as a disgrace. For these and other reasons the role of vassal has caused numerous complications and deviations in Marko's behavior in the epic. Despite anything the bards tried to suggest, King Marko did not join the Turks out of spite or due to a personal grudge. Nor did he join because he was slighted by his emperor, a common reason with many other great heroes, such as the proud Castillian warrior El Cid, who was exiled by King Alfonso VI (1072–1109).

It is believable that, after the loss of independence, King Marko had no alternative but to be loyal to his new master. Within the confines of his new duties toward the Sultan, King Marko succeeded in retaining relative freedom of action in his domestic affairs. Due to good relations with the Sultan, it is possible that he was able to intercede and ensure a certain degree of protection for his own countrymen.

While fighting for the Sultan, Prince Marko maintained a sincere Christian attitude, defending the Christians and his Church. He was always a dutiful observer of Christianity and faithfully celebrated all religious holidays. He is known to have gone to confession and he regularly took communion. The epic imagination transformed him into a man who was master of his capital in Prilep and, even though he fought for the Sultan whenever called, Prince Marko remained a Christian who feared and submitted to no one but God.

The Sultan–Prince Marko relationship varies in a series of songs, ranging from friendly comradeship to bitter enmity. An example of friendly vassal relations is found in the song "Prince Marko and Mina of Kostura," in Vuk 2, No. 61, in which Prince Marko conquers cities on behalf of the Sultan and arrives at the epic fortress of Kara-Okan:

> There they tarried three years of days,
> By Okan they tarried, nor might they take it.
> And Marko cut down the Arab knights,
> And brought their heads before the Sultan,
> And the Sultan gave gold therefor to Marko.   (91)
>
> Low, No. 17

Prince Marko was invaluable to the Sultan and even received "seventy wounds" after fighting with the Arabs. The Sultan was deeply concerned for Prince Marko's life:

> And the Lord Sultan asked him:
> "My son, Prince Marko,
> Are thy wounds to the death?
> Thinkest thou to be made whole of thy wounds?
> Shall I let bring salves and leeches?"   (79)
>
> Low, No. 17

This poem is characterized by a very warm personal relationship which goes beyond the formal vassal status. Thus the Sultan is described as "the Lord Sultan" who sympathizes with Prince Marko over the loss of his home which was ravaged by Mina of Kastoria while Prince Marko was fighting the Sultan's wars. The poem even provides a dialogue between the Sultan and Prince Marko, during which the Sultan offers to indemnify Prince Marko's loss in full and promises new and better substitutes for the town of Kastoria:

> Fear not, my son Marko!
> And if thy manor be burnt
> I shall build thee yet fairer dwelling,
> Hard by mine own, and like even unto mine.
> If thy gold be taken,
> I shall make thee collector of poll-tax,
> Thence shalt thou glean more gold than ever before.   (214)
>
> Low, No. 17

Prince Marko's answer is delicately elaborated. With a great deal of appreciation he nevertheless declines the Sultan's offer point by point:

> Thanks be to thee, my father the Sultan!
> But, and if thou build me a manor,
> The poor will curse me, saying:
> "See the whoreson Prince Marko!
> His old manor is burnt with fire,
> May his new one avail him naught!"
> And if thou make me collector of poll-tax,   (224)
> . . . .
>
> And the poor will curse me—
> "See the whoreson Prince Marko,
> The gold he had was ravished away,
> May this gold also do him naught of profit."   (230)
>
> Low, No. 17

Prince Marko manifests high ethical standards when he rejects estates, wealth, and honors, and especially when he refuses to collect taxes from his own people who were already very exploited by corrupt Turkish officials. The whole poem expresses what the epic bards and the audiences thought about the Sultan and their Prince Marko. The bards wished the mighty Sultan to behave in a fatherly and generous manner toward their hero. They also had faith in Prince Marko as their protector.

In other songs Prince Marko is cast as a vassal but he is very strong, fierce, and even dangerous to the Sultan. The bards bring him into dramatic situations where he emerges superior to his master, the Sultan. The pride with which Prince Marko is regarded in epic poetry is manifested in the song "Prince Marko Recognizes His Father's Sword," in Vuk 2, No. 56, which describes how the enraged Prince Marko frightened the Sultan after learning that a Turk had killed his wounded father merely to win a sword.

This epic song in the Vuk collection, as well as the Filipović variant No. 19, are well composed, and their beauty lies in conducting the narrative to a climax in the dramatic scene between the Sultan and Prince Marko:

> So fierce within him was Marko's anger,
> That booted as he was he sate him down on the carpet,
> He looked sideways at the Sultan,
> And tears of blood stood in his eyes.

> Now when the Sultan was ware of Marko,
> That he had with him his heavy mace,
> The Sultan went backwards and Marko followed after,
> Until he drave him even to the wall.   (131)
>
> Low, No. 12

The sultan is placed in a precarious situation where he must pacify Prince Marko's anger, and he eventually gives him a cask of gold to cheer him:

> Right so the Sultan put hand in pocket
> And drew forth an hundred ducats,
> And gave them to Prince Marko.
> "Go, Marko," quoth he, "drink thy fill of wine.
> What hath so sorely angered thee?"   (136)
>
> Low, No. 12

The bards expressed their rebellious feelings toward the Turkish Sultan through Prince Marko's anger. That is why they extolled the courage of a man who challenged a hated ruler, thus showing that even a slave could rise and become stronger than his master.

Prince Marko was frequently depicted as angering the Turks who would then complain to the Sultan. The Sultan would then summon Marko to Adrianople or in some songs to Constantinople to answer for his violence. The principal song in this group is "Marko Drinks Wine in Ramadan," in Vuk 2, No. 70, in which the most dramatic conflict between the two men takes place. Prince Marko refuses to obey the Moslem law prohibiting drinking, especially during the holiday of Ramadan:

> Sultan Suleiman let cry an order
> That none should drink wine in Ramadan,
> That none should wear green apparel,
> That none should bear a sword,
> That none should dance with women in the kolo.   (5)
>
> Low, No. 26

Prince Marko insolently violated this Islamic religious observance in such manner that the epic bards seem to be suggesting that he deliberately planned to do that which was prohibited and contrary to Moslem custom. Drinking or dancing were not as important for epic singers as was public disregard of, and opposition to, the authority of the Turkish system and religion.[94] That is why Prince Marko, when summoned, goes to challenge the Sultan:

> Father, Sultan Suleiman,
> If I drink wine in Ramadan,
> If indeed I drink, my faith alloweth it;
> If I put constraint on the hodžas and the hadžis
> It is that for very shame
> I may not drink while they do naught but look.
> Let them not come to me to the inn.
> And if I wear green apparel,
> I am young and it liketh me well.
> If I bear my rich-wrought sabre,
> With mine own gold I bought it,
> And if I dance with women in the kolo,
> It is that I have no wife of mine own,
> And thou too, Sultan, wert once unwed. (81)
>
> Low, No. 26

The epic singers confronted two opposing worlds—the Christian and the Moslem—making it clear, through Prince Marko, that their people live in accordance with patriarchal values which are not to be changed. Prince Marko's protest is carried further to the point of a threat to the Sultan himself:

> If I have pulled my kalpak over mine eyes,
> The forehead sweats when the Sultan frets,
> And I toy with my mace,
> And lay my sabre in my lap,
> Because I fear that strife may come of this;
> And if strife should come,
> Woe to him that is nearest Marko! (88)
>
> Low, No. 26

In an indirect way, this brilliant game of words foreshadows a deadly danger to the Sultan, who is already threatened by Prince Marko. With a keen sense of humor the bards designed the warning so the Sultan would easily understand his peril and become frightened. By humiliating the Sultan, the bards, conversely, extolled the valor of Prince Marko.

If in Vuk Karadžić's variant No. 70 the Sultan succeeded in placating Prince Marko, in the Matica Hrvatska song "Prince Marko Does not Fast on Ramadan," 2, pt. 1, No. 8, the outcome is fatal. On the Sultan's order, Prince Marko is trapped by the Janissaries, who try to hang him. Instead, after being delivered by his friends, Prince Marko is the one who hangs the Sultan:

> As Prince Marko hangs the emperor,
> Thus quoth Marko to him:
> "Thou, by God, O Sir the Emperor!
> Where is thy young wife, the Sultana,
> Where did you have coffee with her, this morn?"
> On the gibbet stayed the Emperor, hanging,
> To home departed Marko, singing.   (316)
>   Matica Hrvatska, 2, pt. 1, No. 8

The same Matica Hrvatska collection contains the variant song No. 10, in which the Sultan forgives Prince Marko for his stubbornness and disrespect for Turkish laws,[95] with the song ending on a friendly and happy note:

> When the Emperor heard Marko,
> Roared with laughter the Emperor
> Nice gifts to Marko he giveth:
> "Come along, my Marko, my grey falcon!
> And have your fill of wine."   (64)
>   Matica Hrvatska, 2, pt. 1, No. 10

Prince Marko's bravery and fierceness were dutifully recorded by the epic singers, but not always in a positive light. The Erlangen Manuscript of 1720 preserves an unusually negative portrayal of the epic Prince Marko,[96] in a series of epic songs which glorify the Sultan instead of Prince Marko. Song No. 87 emphasizes Prince Marko's tendency to be spiteful, impulsive, and disobedient toward the Sultan.[97] He was the only one among the lords who did not quickly heed the Sultan's summons. When he finally does present himself at court, Prince Marko refuses to pay the customary homage to the Sultan or to draw his sabre from its scabbard:

> The Emperor holds audience at his Divan.
> Whoever presents himself to the Emperor,
> Each Turk takes out his sabre.

> When Prince Marko made his entrance,
> Marko does not draw his sabre from the scabbard.   (117)
>
> Erlangen Manuscript, No. 87

When the Sultan asks him about his sabre, Prince Marko invokes his mother's advice "never to draw out a sabre for naught." Then the Sultan still insists on Marko's drawing his sabre and fight whom ever he wanted:

> Hissed Prince Marko like a viper,
> Lo, slays Marko, the Prince,
> He cut nine lords and nine dukes,
> Spake Sir Emperor to Marko, the Prince:
> It is enough, my son, Prince Marko.   (136)
>
> Erlangen Manuscript, No. 87

The Sultan recognized Prince Marko as a brave warrior, and in return, Marko snarled:

> Thanks to God, Sir Emperor,
> That my right arm turned tired,
> Otherwise you would be gone, too.   (140)
>
> Erlangen Manuscript, No. 87

Another instance of the bards' negativity because of Prince Marko's vassalage to the Sultan occurs in the song "The Sister of Leka Kapetan," in Vuk 2, No. 39. Marko is portrayed here as a rejected suitor and branded by the beautiful Rosanda for being a Turkish minion:

> Liever had I remain unwed,
> In this our realm of Prizren
> Than go to Prilep castle,
> And be called Marko's wife.
> For Marko holds of the Sultan,
> He fights and smites for the Turks.   (462)
>
> Low, No. 6

In most cases Prince Marko's vassalage was treated ambiguously, or if it happened to be explicitly mentioned, it was presented as something necessary, with no implication of the slightest weakness or humiliation. In this song, however, with embarrassing clarity and insulting frankness, the epic singer presents negative sentiments. We can assume that the words of the beautiful Rosanda haunted the minds of many:

Wherefore with all my beauty should I be wife to a Turkish minion?

The maiden's accusation wounded Prince Marko precisely where he was most sensitive, in his relationship with national enemies, the Sultan and the Turks. The nightmarish discrepancy of such a relationship hung heavily not only over Prince Marko but over the entire South Slavic epic tradition and its audience. Epic singers could not let the maiden go unpunished for having dared to utter the truth about their hero. All were eager for Prince Marko to punish the damsel for insulting him. After he blinded and maimed her:

Then spake Marko in this wise:
"Choose now, thou maid Rosanda,
Choose now which thou wilt,
Whether the Turkish minion,
Or Miloš the mare's son,
Or Relya the bastard!"   (548)
                                                      Low, No. 6

Prince Marko asserted himself in the most brutal manner possible, in order to stifle forever any potential future defamation.[98] The bards wanted to make it perfectly clear that the great Prince Marko would never allow his vassalage to be turned into servility. Cecil Bowra describes the complexity of a situation in which Prince Marko must be a slave to the enemy while simultaneously maintaining his devotion to national freedom and honor: He was "a man who accepted the real situation and was yet able to maintain his style and freedom. His life is not that of the singleminded, uncompromising hero, but in the mixed world of Turkish Serbia he shows that love of country still means something to the servant of an alien despot."[99]

In the oral tradition the Balkan people lived the imaginary heroic life of Prince Marko. As they changed him from a vassal in the Sultan's service into a fighter of the Turks, so they transmuted themselves from the reality of slavery to the spirit of active national resistance and the struggle for justice. As Cecil Bowra stated, "There are times when this resistance takes on a truly heroic character and every Serb becomes a hero."[100] This statement could be expanded to include all South Slavs.

KNIGHTLY ADVENTURES

Dear sister, damsel of Kossovo!
Speak not foolishly, leap not into the river,
Deal not death unto thyself.
But say me where is the Moor's manor?
I have words to speak with him.[101]

Motifs dealing with Prince Marko's campaigns in foreign lands during his service to the Sultan frequently parallel those found in the epic literature concerning Western Christian champions in the service of Saracen rulers. Such motifs probably existed before King Marko's time and eventually became associated with him, once his popularity had completely asserted itself in the minds of the people. Little historical information is available in these songs, except in the actual names of persons who are transposed into the fictional context of legend.

Most prominent among the universal motifs is the rescue of a princess who is about to be sacrificed to a monster-like creature. South Slavic bards cast Prince Marko in this honorable role, except that they denied him the pleasure of sentimental journeys and idyllic love affairs with the rescued maiden as was customary in Western chivalric lore. Prince Marko was never represented as a suitor. Banašević suggests that the lack of such behavior on the part of Prince Marko emerged as a consequence of the popularization of Prince Marko as a people's hero. The people in this case were peasants and shepherds rather than nobility or royalty. Banašević hypothetically assumes that songs about Prince Marko's sentimental adventures must have existed at an earlier time but that they were eventually forgotten.[102]

The rescuing of a princess was a typical motif in the accounts of chivalric adventures. According to Khalanskii, the motif began with the legend of St. George and a dragon which preyed upon young girls. Khalanskii carefully researched the dragon motif, tracing it back to the early Greek mythological stories of Perseus and Hercules.[103] He then followed its development in a tradition according to which an evil force, in the form of a dragon in association with demons, took the water away from the people and caused intense drought. According to a myth from India, the demon who took away the water was killed by Indra and the precious fluid restored to the people.[104] The primary characteristics of this ancient Indo-European myth describing the alternation between rain and drought evidently found their way into Slavic mythology where they surfaced in the form of a struggle between Perun, the God of Thunder, whose role was later taken over by Christian saints and heroes, and the Demon of Drought represented by a dragon. Khalanskii balanced the scales of good and evil by placing Indra, St. George, Ilia Muromets, Dobrynia, Olesha, and Prince Marko, among others, on one side and the dragon on the other.[105]

The motif of St. George and the dragon was assimilated into other Western chivalric romances of the fourteenth and fifteenth centuries. Christian champions such as Roland, Beuves de Haumtone, and Charlemagne, who were in the service of infidel sultans, frequently rescued a sultan's daughter or some other fair maiden from various alien predators and monsters. In South Slavic epic poetry this motif mainly involved Prince Marko, although at times other Christian champions (such as Miloš Obilić) assumed the role of rescuer.

In the series of songs about the battle between Prince Marko and the Black Moor or *Crni Arapin*,[106] we find a perfect illustration of two epic rules. The first is a substitution of names and the second a transplantation of a mythological motif to a Christian legend in which a Christian hero conquers all. Prince Marko could thus easily stand for St. George who slays the crafty dragon or, in this case, the Black Moor.[107]

Folk audiences enjoyed listening to songs which were the outgrowth of fantasy and imagination. As a knight in a foreign land, Prince Marko performed all those chivalric acts characteristic of his West European counterparts.

One of the primary songs in this particular chain is "Prince Marko and the Moor," in Vuk 2, No. 65, in which the Moor rebels against the Sultan, requesting the Sultan's daughter for his wife who would live in a castle built "by the wide blue sea." The Moor's proposal is followed by the threat that he will challenge the Sultan to a duel unless he is satisfied.

Many knights tried without success to vanquish the Moor, who in the meantime retaliates by occupying a stand before the main gates of Constantinople where he collects a frightening tax:

> That each night they should give him a barren sheep,
> A baking of white bread,
> A cask of strong rakia,
> Two casks of red wine,
> And a fair damsel.
> And she served him with red wine,
> And at night he kissed her fair face.   (62)
>
>   Low, No. 21

According to the epic song "the Sultan's Sultana Dreamed a Dream," the Sultana has been told who could save her daughter:

And in Prilep dwells Prince Marko,
And men praise him for a good knight of prowess.   (96)

Low, No. 21

Dreams have significant meaning in epic poetry. The Sultan wrote a firman, and the Sultana a letter carried by a royal messenger, but Prince Marko was reluctant to listen to their appeals to rescue the young damsel from the danger. The realistic attitude of South Slavic epic singers is expressed in Prince Marko's answer:

I dare not adventure me against the Moor.
The Moor is a full perilous knight,
He will take the head from off my shoulders,
And I prefer mine own head
Before all the treasure of the illustrious Sultan.   (140)

Low, No. 21

Only when sought by the desperate princess herself does Prince Marko feel a human urge to act on her behalf:

She struck the pen into her face,
She drew blood from her cheek,
And wrote a letter to Marko.   (148)

Low, No. 21

Coming unheralded, Prince Marko meets the Turkish princess herself, who is on the verge of committing suicide:

She bowed her down before the green lake.
"God aid thee, green lake," quoth she,
"God aid thee, my eternal home!
In thee I would be for ever!"   (212)

Low, No. 21

When Prince Marko hears this he introduces himself, telling the maiden that he has come to rescue her and to vanquish the Moor. He also advises her to proceed with the wedding to the Black Moor.

The song treats Prince Marko's defeat of the Black Moor in a highly poetic manner. After arriving in Constantinople Prince Marko stays in a tavern. He orders the innkeeper to keep it open while all others were shut down because of the terror of the Black Moor. In the meantime:

> The Arab communed with himself:
> "Dear God, what great marvel is this!
> All Stamboul hath closed its doors
> Because of the great terror of my name,
> Alone the door of the new inn is not closed."   (293)
>   Low, No. 21

Prince Marko personally dislikes the Moor and continues his drinking while the wedding procession passes by the inn. After the Moor took the princess from the Sultan, the wedding procession passed again by the open tavern. The horse Šarac prevents the Black Moor from entering the tavern where Prince Marko sits drinking:

> But Šarac tethered to the doorpost,
> Suffered him not to enter in,
> But kicked his mare in the ribs.   (317)
>   Low, No. 21

The next move comes from Prince Marko. The poem describes his actions step by step, including such epic details as the way in which he mounted Šarac. Prince Marko is becoming angry with the Black Moor and he expresses his fury by turning his cloak inside out:

> Then arose Prince Marko,
> He turned his wolf-skin cloak inside out,
> Inside out his cap of wolf-skin.   (322)
>   Low, No. 21

Prince Marko's real harassment of the wedding procession is about to begin. From the tavern, Prince Marko proceeds to Constantinople's main marketplace where he overtakes the wedding party and challenges each participant, promptly slaying the main witness and the best man. After everyone has been challenged and beaten, all that remains is for the Black Moor to fight Prince Marko face to face. Epic singers are particular in describing how Prince Marko's challenge passes through the entire wedding procession until it finally reaches the groom himself. The Black Moor regards the challenger as an exceptional man, a hero, with an even more exceptional horse:

His horse is not as other horses,
But piebald like as a cattle-beast;
Nor is the knight like as other knights,
He weareth a cloak of wolf-skin,
And on his head a cap of wolf-skin;
In his teeth is something black
That is as large as a lamb of half a year.   (344)
Low, No. 21

Following the bizarre description of Prince Marko's mustache, a conventional medieval duel is performed according to the rules of chivalry. The two men cry out at each other and the Black Moor challenges:

Art thou a witless churl that knowest naught of me?
Or art thou a knight of worship that hath lost his reason?
Or is life become a weariness to thee?   (356)
Low, No. 21

And Prince Marko responds:

Lie me no lies, black Arab!
If God and knightly fortune will it,
Thou shalt not leap so far as now I stand.   (365)
Low, No. 21

Then they begin to fight, trying all sorts of weapons. For a time no one wins, each being a great warrior. The epic song goes on:

Ah, had one been there to see,
How hero ran in upon hero,
The swarthy Moor upon Kralyević Marko!
But neither might the Moor slay Marko,
Nor yet might Marko slay the Moor.   (381)
Low, No. 21

After a display of forceful fighting between the two of them, Prince Marko finally frightens the Black Moor into retreat and after killing him, frees the princess.

The song contains much of the flavor typical of medieval knightly encounters. Although Prince Marko is portrayed as a knight who behaves precisely according to the set chivalric code, he is vastly different from other knights because in him is a primitive and almost terrifying power which completely and brutally annihilates his enemies. Perhaps because of the general brutality and suffering incurred at the hands of the Turks, Balkan bards of epic poetry and their audiences were not as excited by the prospect of romance between Prince Marko and the rescued princess and probably would have been embarrassed by it. But they were undoubtedly delighted when, by way of thanks, the Sultan addressed Prince Marko as "my son," and gave him "seven loads of gold" as a reward.

In some versions of this popular motif, the Sultan is replaced by the "Emperor Constantin" and the princess is[108] referred to as merely "the girl." Such is the song "The Future of Yesteryear," in *Pievaniia crnogorska i hercegovska* collected by Milutinović, No. 137, p. 249–52, in which Prince Marko arrives in Constantinople to rescue the girl who had written to him imploring for help and delivery from the Black Moor. In other songs on this theme, Prince Marko goes through similar episodes such as meeting the maiden at the lakeside, going to a tavern, intercepting the wedding procession, killing the groom-to-be, liberating the maiden, and being generously rewarded by the Emperor Constantin.

A second series of songs deals with Prince Marko's role as the rescuer of maidens from their slavery to the Black Moor. This segment of songs incorporates the tale of Prince Marko's abolition of the marriage tax levied by the Black Moor, who set the amount at such a high level that young people could never earn enough money to pay it and get married. Banašević correctly observes that this motif was kept alive through memories of the Turkish occupation when it was a common practice to capture Balkan women in particular and sell them at slave markets for profit. The imposition of a heavy marriage tax, so high that it could not be paid, is presented in epic poetry as another form of enslavement.[109]

The central song in this respect is "Prince Marko Abolishes the Marriage Tax," in Vuk, 2, No. 68, in which a Kossovo girl meets an unknown knight who, with patriarchal respect, addresses her as his "dear sister." He is kind and ready to listen to her troubles and he is, of course, Prince Marko. The poor fair maiden relates her grievances, explaining how she must pay thirty golden pieces for the marriage tax. Moreover,

> A greater shame the Moor hath put upon us,
> For each night he will have a young wife, and a maiden also,
> And the Moor embraceth the maiden,
> And his servants take the young wife.
> And all Kossovo must send him in appointed turn,

> Their young wives and their maidens also,
> And behold, wretched that I am, mine own turn is come,
> And this night I must thither to the Moor.   (53)
>
> Low, No. 24

Instead of a princess, the victim is now a poor village girl who is nevertheless so desperate about her fate that she considers drowning herself
rather than losing her honor. Whether it is a common girl or a princess,
dragon or Moor, the basic qualities underlying the two sets of legends remain the same.

Prince Marko behaves like a genuine knight. He is even polite to the
Black Moor when they meet, first offering to pay the maiden's marriage tax
himself. This is only a convention by which epic singers cleared their favorite
hero of all blame and paved the way for shifting full responsibility for the
coming bloodshed onto the evil Moor who is necessarily the guilty party. In
the meantime the audience knows full well that an act of good will on Prince
Marko's part only emphasizes the wickedness of the Black Moor, thus
bringing the hero nearer to his inevitable spiritual and physical victory over
the force of evil.

The manner in which Prince Marko approaches the Black Moor's tent
is recounted in the speech of the Moor's henchman:

> Lord and master, Moor from beyond the sea!
> A marvellous knight rideth down to Kossovo,
> On a passing great piebald horse,
> And he hath spurred him to fury,
> That living fire flasheth from his hoofs,
> And a blue flame goeth from his nostrils.   (129)
>
> Low, No. 24

There is no doubt in the Black Moor's mind of the serious threat posed
by such a fierce-looking hero on an equally impressive horse. Prince Marko
is the avenger for all the injuries inflicted upon his people by the oppressors.
Bards and audiences could never forget the 1389 defeat at Kossovo Field and
they bring Prince Marko to speak his mind in the song:

> In wrath rode Marko athwart Kossovo,
> Tears ran down the hero's face,
> And wrathful through his tears he spake:
> "Ah me! Thou Kossovo plain,

> What ills are come upon thee now,
> Since the days of our illustrious prince,
> That Moors should sit in judgment over thee!"   (114)
>
> Low, No. 24

Heroic tears are not only shed in sorrow, they also express Prince Marko's anger:

> But this shame I may not suffer,
> Nor endure the heaviness thereof,
> That the Moors do us this great despite,
> And lie with our brides and young maidens!   (118)
>
> Low, No. 24

The terrorizing of defenseless people at Kossovo by the Black Moor sets the stage for the final act of Prince Marko's revenge against the oppressor and the restoration of justice to the people of Kossovo:

> This day, my brethren, I shall revenge you,
> I shall revenge you, or I will perish!   (120)
>
> Low, No. 24

The world of the epic is an ideal universe where Evil is punished and Justice triumphs—but without great excitement as Prince Marko himself says at the end:

> "Dear God," quoth he, "thanks be to thee in all things!"
> As swiftly went this knight's head from him
> As if head he had never borne.   (221)
>
> Low, No. 24

Word of Prince Marko's victory had quickly spread, and in the closing lines the bard, speaking on behalf of all oppressed people, expresses his faith in Justice and Prince Marko:

> And all the people, both great and small, cried:
> "God keep Kralyević Marko,
> Who hath delivered the land from evil,
> Who hath utterly destroyed the oppressor:
> God save him, both soul and body!"   (251)
>
> Low, No. 24

Thus the idea of rescuing a princess is closely associated with the motif of freeing Christian girls from the Black Moor, and songs involving this theme place Prince Marko in the central role of protector of enslaved women and deliverer of Christians in general. One such song is "Marko and the Smoky Mountain," Brothers Miladinov, No. 148, in which Prince Marko attacks the Black Moor and frees three columns of slaves. One consists of brave men, another of betrothed maidens, and the third of children.

These songs mark the appearance of the motif of a conversation between the Forest and Prince Marko. According to these songs, the Forest was an animate being which possessed a soul, and a Bulgarian song about "Smoky Mountain" faithfully reproduces this ancient view. Prince Marko asks the Forest why it has become so dry and withered: was it perhaps burnt by flames or frost? The Forest then explains that it has withered because of all the injustice which was perpetrated upon Prince Marko's people without his knowledge. The Forest also informs Prince Marko that he can intercept the Arabs when they pass through with their many Christian slaves. In other songs, a friendly fairy comes to Prince Marko with tidings that Turks were driving Christian slaves through the forest.

Prince Marko's image, as shown in this type of epic poem, was one of a man predestined for the great and heroic adventures reserved only for those who occupied the highest rank in the people's esteem. However, in South Slavic epic poetry, Prince Marko was less romantic and glamorous than the knights of the Western European chivalric poetry. According to Cecil Bowra, there is more realism in South Slavic epic poetry, bringing "the story closer to life and [making] it more substantial."[110] Prince Marko had to face that in the real world his people were slaves, and he was bound to protect them in his heroic world.

RESCUE FROM CAPTIVITY

I will not let Marko forth of the dungeon,
But will hold him nine years,
Till the snakes have sucked his eyes,
And the scorpions have marred his visage.[111]

The central motif in this series of songs is the idea of freeing someone from imprisonment. Prince Marko's role is reversed, in that he is now a captive in Constantinople. His rescuers are various other persons, sometimes heroic and sometimes not, but always one of his own friends or the daughter of a Sultan.[112] The historical King Marko was never imprisoned by the Sultan, their relationship having actually been of a friendly nature. Historically,

Marko Viteazul of Wallachia, who lived and fought around two hundred
years after King Marko's death, was imprisoned by the Turks.[113] The fact
that the two historical Markos merged into one in epic poetry helps explain
inconsistencies in the Sultan's behavior when he imprisons Prince Marko as
one of his own vassals. Thus the central figure in the motif of rescue from
imprisonment is not modelled after King Marko Mrnyavčevič but rather after Marko Viteazul of Wallachia.

West European chivalric narratives have their own assortment of infidel
princesses rescuing young nobles or knights. In the *chansons de geste,* for
example, Saracen princesses fall in love with imprisoned Christian knights
and help them to escape at the price of marriage. Banaševič's comparative
study enumerates many examples in which Prince Marko and other South
Slavic epic heroes have adventures very similar to those of Western European knights. A particularly conspicuous parallel exists between Prince
Marko and Beuves de Haumtone, each of whom was imprisoned in the dungeon of a Moslem ruler whose daughter falls in love with him—the only difference being that Prince Marko escapes with the maiden, while Beuves de
Haumtone gets away by himself.[114]

Banaševič, the great advocate of Western influences as a major factor in
South Slavic epic poetry, combined his ideas with those of Khalanskii and
advanced the notion that the motif of escape was very much a result of joint
influences from the Western chivalric narrative and the Byzantine romance
of Digenis Akritas.[115]

Both Prince Marko and Digenis Akritas were imprisoned by the Sultan,
that is, the Emir of Syria.[116] The daughters of the two captors fell in love with
Prince Marko and Digenis. In both cases the maidens supplied the heroes
with horses and their fathers' treasures, and the two heroes ran away with
them. Both men failed to keep promises of marriage and eventually left the
maidens behind.

The Byzantine poem about Digenis Akritas exerted indisputable influence in Bulgaria, and this influence became widespread throughout the Balkans, making its way into oral folk poetry, becoming one of its basic com-
ponents. This was not a simple process, if one takes into account the
particular local circumstances which were ultimately of such decisive importance, for example, the slave trade which flourished under Turkish rule
and the existence of Marko Viteazul whose adventures overlapped those of
Prince Marko. Kostič was able to identify these issues, despite the complexity of local peculiarities and various influences from the East and, later,
from the West, particularly France and Italy.[117] All the motifs, however, regardless of whether they were an outgrowth of foreign influence or indepen-

dent local creations, reflected the individual set of circumstances which led to their rise in a specific ethnic region.

The motif of Prince Marko's deliverance from captivity appears in many epic songs which were scattered all over the Balkan Peninsula from Bulgaria in the southeast to Croatia in the northwest. Such epic songs have in common the central idea that, as a result of his long time in prison, Prince Marko is considerably weakened and in a perilous state of health. The opening lines of the fragment-song "Marko in the Dungeon of Azak," in Vuk 2, No. 64, gives a description of Prince Marko languishing in the prison:

> Dear God, to thee be praise in all things!
> What a knight of worship and hardiness was Marko!
> And see how he fareth this day in a dungeon,
> The accursed dungeon of Azak!   (4)
>
> Low, No. 20

The portrayal of the Azak dungeon is impressive:

> Therein the water came to his knees,
> And the bones of dead heroes reached to his middle.
> And there went to and fro snakes and scorpions;
> The snakes sought men's eyes for to suck;
> The scorpions sought faces for to mar them,
> The legs of heroes were loosed from their knees,
> And their arms fell from their shoulders.   (12)
>
> Low, No. 20

The epic bard conjures the profound nature of Prince Marko's anguish:

> In the dungeon Marko made dole and sorrow out of measure
> Such dole he made that God himself was ware of it.   (14)
>
> Low, No. 20

Finding himself in peril, Prince Marko was desperately determined to find a way out. Finally, he saw through the window of dungeon, a fair damsel who was a daughter of the King of Azak. Prince Marko called to her, "Sister-in-God, king's daughter." She talked to him and agreed to try to persuade her father to exchange Prince Marko for a ransom. The King of Azak's reaction is full of passionate hatred; he not only refused his daughter but also vowed that he would cripple Prince Marko:

> Until his legs fall from the knees,
> And his arms from his shoulders.
> When Marko has suffered these torments,
> I shall let forth the captive, without ransom,
> I shall turn him a cripple into the street.
> Let him beg for bread to nourish him!   (86)
>
>   Low, No. 20

When the princess heard her father she shuddered, and having a good heart, she wanted to alleviate Prince Marko's suffering. She consented to supply Prince Marko with inkhorn and paper to write home to his old mother and good wife. Prince Marko did not tell her the truth, and instead he sent the letter to his friend Doyčilo in Salonica (another South Slavic hero):

> O Doyčilo, brother-in-God,
> I am fallen on evil days,
> And suffer torment at the hands of the Arabs;
> Enslaved am I and in a dungeon,
> In Azak, in an accursed dungeon,
> And I may not long endure in the dungeon,
> For me a dungeon is an unwonted lodging;
> Deliver me if God thou knowest!   (117)
>
>   Low, No. 20

This fragment song is interrupted when Doyčilo, disguised as an Arab, comes to the Azak town to rescue Prince Marko.

This song deviates somewhat from the mainstream of poems relating to the motif of rescue by a princess. Thus, the princess does not fall in love with Prince Marko but is simply a nice person. She does not conduct the actual rescue, which is taken over by Prince Marko's friend Doyčilo. Finally, Prince Marko does not commit any transgression or breaking of a marriage promise since he did not propose to her, nor did the princess expect it.

In the other songs Prince Marko is noticed by the daughter of a Sultan or a Moorish King who then falls in love with him. He promises to marry the princess, but once freed, he abandons or even kills her. The main song in this group is "Prince Marko and the Daughter of the Moorish King," in Vuk 2, No. 63, in which Prince Marko tells his mother about his imprisonment by the Arabs, his liberation by the maiden, and his betrayal of her. The emphasis is on Prince Marko's penitence which he demonstrated by building churches and similar edifices for the sin he committed.

The song opens with a description of the cold dark dungeon in which Prince Marko was incarcerated. He saw nothing in the darkness but was able to hear sounds from the outside:

> The King cast me into the depths of a dungeon,
> Where for seven years I languished.
> I knew not when summer came,
> Nor knew I when came winter,
> Save by one token, mother.
> In winter the damsels as they played at snowballs,
> Would throw to me a snowball,
> By that I knew that winter was come.
> In summer they would throw me a spray of basil,
> By that I knew that it was summer.   (37)
>   Low, No. 19

The intolerable conditions of prison life convinced Prince Marko to accept the rescue offer by a Moorish maiden who had fallen in love with him:

> It was not the prison that tormented me,
> But a Moorish maiden,
> Dear daughter of the Moorish King.
> Morning and evening she would come,
> And call to me through the dungeon window:
> "Pine not away, unhappy Marko, in thy dungeon!
> But give me thy solemn oath
> That thou wilt take me to wife,
> And I shall deliver thee out of prison."   (47)
>   Low, No. 19

Prince Marko confesses to his mother that his oath to the Moorish maiden was a mockery:

> When I considered of my evil plight,
> I took of my cap and laid it on my knee,
> And swore to the cap on my knee, saying:

> "I take solemn oath I will not leave thee,
> I take solemn oath I will not deceive thee.
> The sun himself breaketh faith,
> And warmeth not the earth in winter as in summer,
> But never will I break mine oath!"   (58)
>
> Low, No. 19

Prince Marko's dishonorable action and breach of promise were not technically legal because his oath to the maiden was done over a cap on his knee, and not sworn by God and the Holy Cross.[118] Such deception represents the introduction of the sub-motif of an invalid oath.

Prince Marko continues the narrative by telling his mother how the Arab maiden trusted him and helped him to escape:

> We mounted our horses,
> And departed thence through the land of the Moors.   (69)
>
> Low, No. 19

But his grim awakening came during their escape:

> On a morning, as day dawned,
> I sate me down to rest,
> And the Moorish maiden took me,
> Encircling me with her black arms,
> And when I looked on her, mother,
> On her black face and white teeth,
> A loathing gat hold on me;
> I drew the rich-wrought sabre,
> And smote her on the silken girdle,
> That the sabre cut clean through her.   (79)
>
> Low, No. 19

Prince Marko's savage behavior is expressed in his brutal misdeed toward the Moorish maiden. In addition, the bard described Prince Marko as repelled by the maiden's dark color. The whole picture is a contrast to the customary portrayal of Prince Marko as a champion of justice and virtue.

In another song belonging to this series, "Marko's Confession," in the Brothers Miladinov, No. 54, Prince Marko experiences very definite feelings of guilt for having deceived the innocent princess who had been instrumental in obtaining his freedom. He sinned by leaving her helpless. The song's contents attests to the strong ethical influence of the medieval Church. The motif of Prince Marko's confession exemplifies the direct role of the monks in judging his action. We encounter an ailing Prince Marko who was bed-ridden for three full years after sinning against the Arab princess. One day he confesses to his mother, who in turn calls nine priests, all of whom hear Prince Marko's confession. The entire poetic narrative consists of the actual dialogue of confession and Prince Marko's penitence and eventual recovery.

Some Croatian songs also elaborate on Prince Marko's distaste for the Arab maiden whom he first promises to marry but later abandons. One such exposition is a short ballad, "Prince Marko Cheated the Arab Girl," in Matica Hrvatska 2, No. 13. The narrative consists of a dialogue between Prince Marko and his mother Yevrosima in which he relates the events of his escapade with the Arab girl. In this case Marko does not kill the girl, but abandons her on a mountainside. The mother reprimands Prince Marko for his action and tells him that he should have brought her home where she, Yevrosima, would have cared for her as long as she lived.

A second version of this song bears the same title as the first and is also found in the Matica Hrvatska collection, 2, No. 14, but it is much longer and introduces several changes in the motif. For one thing, the girl in question is not a daughter but rather a sister of the Black Moor. Prince Marko promises to marry her after his escape and her baptism, but in their passage through a mountain, they come upon the Boyana River, where they halt. The maiden washes her face to make it a lighter shade, like that of "young Italian girls":

> Washes her face, the maiden of the Moor,
> With her right and with her left, she rubs faster,
> But, as the maiden rubs and scrubs more,
> The dark face turns even blacker. (135)
>
> Matica Hrvatska 2, No. 14

Prince Marko watches her washing herself and imagines how embarrassed he would be in his "White Prilep" when all the local maidens would taunt him because of his black bride. Thus, we have our hero cowardly abandoning his bride. Alone on the mountain and desperate, the maiden throws herself into the river and drowns.

Prince Marko's mother appears in a few of these songs as the force of human conscience who awakens Prince Marko to the full realization of what he has done. His mother induces him to return to the mountain, find the maiden, and bring her home as his wife. This charming song has an overabundance of details concerning Prince Marko's discovery of the dead girl and his ensuing lamentations. The entire scene lacks credibility, since it is quite clear that he had never loved the maiden and is only returning for her out of a sense of duty. Although Prince Marko pulls the maiden from the river and gives her a proper burial, his penance is superficial. His tears, if any, are not for the maiden but for his own guilt and sin. The songs are generally average, lacking dramatic impact.

The social conventions of the seventeenth century were as obdurate as those of later times. South Slavic bards were against mixed marriages for practical reasons, yet condemned Prince Marko's behavior in principle. Perhaps it was for this reason that they chose a hero of Prince Marko's stature who could be made to err just like any other man, but who would also have the moral strength to recognize and censure his own wrongdoings.

MARKO AGAINST THE REBELS

> *Be not adread, my Lord Sultan!*
> *How hadst thou received him living,*
> *When his dead head maketh thee so to leap?*[119]

King Marko, who had basically accepted the Turkish Sultan as his Lord, was willing to serve him in the capacity of a loyal vassal and fight the Sultan's enemies. Prince Marko fights on the Sultan's behalf against the disloyal Janissaries, the Arabs, or other infidels. Although contradictory, enemies of Christians frequently appear as rebels against the Sultan himself. This apparent conflict of interests and loyalties is superficial when one considers that both the infidel Sultan and the Christian Prince Marko confront essentially the same adversaries. For this reason the Sultan seeks the service of a brave warrior like Prince Marko who will help introduce a sense of order into his vast and shaky empire.

One of Prince Marko's most prominent adversaries is Musa the Robber, who is at the same time a rebel against the Sultan. Songs about their encounters rank among the finest creations of South Slavic epic poetry. Both champions, Prince Marko and Musa the Robber were actual historical persons. The processes which gave rise to their epic personalities show several definite stages of development, involving the incorporation of and contamination by various and widely differing motifs. Musa the Robber underwent a process of merging several historical persons who lived and thrived at different times and places.[120] They include a member of the Albanian noble family of Musaki who was a contemporary of King Marko; Prince Musa, a son of Sultan Bayazet at the end of the fifteenth century; Musa (or Moysiye) the Albanian (*Arbanas*), one of the high commanders under Scanderbeg, ruler of Albania (1443–1468); and a lieutenant of Yegen Paša, a Turkish rebel of the late seventeenth century.

In the song "Prince Marko and Musa the Robber," in Vuk 2, No. 66, Musa appears as the personification of rebels against the Sultan and his grievances are set forth in the opening lines:

> Nine years already
> Have I served the Sultan in Stamboul,
> Nor have I gained by my service horse nor weapon,
> Nor a new cloak nor yet an old one.   (8)
>
> Low, No. 22

In rebellion, Musa entrenched himself in a tower he built by the sea. He blocked nearby highways and hung Moslem holy men (*hodže*) along with other devout Moslems, and *hadži* (those who had made a pilgrimage to Mecca). Musa is a kind of picaresque outlaw, impressing epic audiences with his courage and his rebellion against the hated Turkish ruler and the Moslem religion.

Musa the Robber's revolutionary stance appears in his parley with Prince Marko before they engage in combat. Musa emphasizes his low and poor origin and contrasts it in a poetic parable with the royal upbringing of Prince Marko:

> But I will not do obeisance before thee,
> Albeit a queen bore thee,
> In a manor amongst soft cushions,
> And wrapped thee in pure silk,
> And bound thee about with thread of gold,
> And nourished thee on honey and on sugar.
> But as for me—a wild Arnaut woman bore me,
> Amongst the sheep on the cold ground.
> In a rough black mantle she wrapped me,
> And bound me about with thorns,
> And nourished me on porridge.
> Oft did she make me swear,
> Never to give way to no man.   (193)
>
> Low, No. 22

The contradictory elements replete in epic poetry are easily discernible in this song. Musa is depicted as being of peasant stock (historically un-true), and therefore a representative of common men. Prince Marko is portrayed as protecting his own people against Musa, even though he was a feudal prince. Although the Sultan seeks Prince Marko's help to protect his royal treasures which are being appropriated by Musa, the South Slavic popular attitude turned in favor of the Sultan who is seen here as the lesser of two evils. The people were primarily concerned with legality and order, even if it was Turkish and dealt with various rebels and warlords who were in fact the most cruel oppressors.

This aspect of popular sentiment is exemplified by Prince Marko who is ready and willing to fight faithfully on behalf of the very same Sultan who incarcerated him for three years, greatly diminishing his once fabulous strength. His outward appearance is described as follows:

> The mould from the stone had gotten hold on him,
> And he was become the colour of a dark stone.   (70)
>
> Low, No. 22

Prince Marko fights Musa the Robber even though the two men have much in common. Both have suffered greatly at the hands of the Sultan. Musa had been exploited for his services without receiving payment, while Prince Marko had been thrown into a dungeon despite faithful vassalage to the Sultan. The Sultan remembers his subject only when danger threatens his life and even then refers to Prince Marko with the contemptuous remark, "His very bones must or now be rotted" (Low, No. 22). The encounter of the two heroes was narrated in detail. After they broke their maces and sabres, they wrestled on the grass:

> For hero met hero in very sooth,
> When Musa met Prince Marko!
> Nor might Musa overthrow Marko,
> Nor by Marko might he be overthrown.
> So they wrestled till noon of a summer's day;
> White foam fell from Musa,
> From Marko foam white and bloody.   (226)
>
> Low, No. 22

Eventually, with some help from a fairy who diverted Musa's attention, Prince Marko used his knife and killed Musa the Robber.

Prince Marko did not rejoice in his victory, even though he had won against a great hero. It was with contempt that Prince Marko went to the Sultan and cast down the dead Musa's head:

> Be not adread, my Lord Sultan!
> How hadst thou received him living,
> When his dead head maketh thee so to leap?   (277)
>
>   Low, No. 22

Why did a bitter Prince Marko help a Sultan who did not care about him? The answer is in the changing perceptions of epic singers who lived in different time periods. Generations of bards were modifying their interpretations of the contents of this song. It is not inconceivable that some singers might have been impressed with the epic personality of Musa the Robber, and placed in his mouth the daring words seen above, words which otherwise would have better suited Prince Marko's heroic profile. Musa has many of the qualities of a protagonist representing peasant pride and protest, a point which was clearly applauded by the bards who emphasized Musa's low social upbringing in contrast to Prince Marko's highborn status.

Epic poetry frequently presented another of Prince Marko's adversaries, Djemo the Mountaineer. In some songs Djemo is described as the brother of Musa the Robber, and the two characters are sometimes portrayed interchangeably. The historical identity of Djemo the Mountaineer can be traced to Turkish Yegen Paša, from the seventeenth century.[121] He was a high commander and used his troops to plunder and ravage the Balkans. He terrorized the population whether they were Christian or Moslem. Eventually, the new Sultan Suleiman II outlawed him. Yegen Paša became known as "Robber Paša," and attempted to escape to Albania and then to Asia. Pillaging along the way he passed through Serbia, arriving in Ohrid in Macedonia. There, in the spring of 1689, the Turks captured him, cut his head off, and sent it to the Sultan.

Like Prince Marko, Djemo the Mountaineer also evolved in South Slavic epic poetry from historical reminiscences. The epic descriptions of Djemo's activities coincide with the historical route of Yegen Paša's raids.[122] It was also in Ohrid where the epic Djemo the Mountaineer was hanged by Prince Marko.[123] In time the two heroes became generalized figures, each a representative of a certain ethical stance. Djemo the Mountaineer became the prototype of tyrants, while Prince Marko stood as a defender of the people.

In the group of motifs relating to Djemo the Mountaineer the basic song is "Prince Marko and Djemo the Mountaineer," in Vuk 2, No. 67. The poem begins as follows:

> Prince Marko celebrated his Slava,
> He kept his Slava that fell on St. George's day.
> And many invited guests were there—

> Two hundred priests, three hundred monks,
> Twelve Serbian bishops,
> Four patriarchs well stricken in years
> And others without number.   (7)
>
> Low, No. 23

An aged monk praises the feast but complains that there is no fish:

> Give thee thanks, Prince Marko!
> There had nothing lacked in thy white manor,
> And thou hadst fish from Ohrid!   (12)
>
> Low, No. 23

The universal motif of a hero's trip to bring fish for the guests was popular in chivalric medieval literature and is here applied to Prince Marko.[124] According to Banašević, the motif in which Prince Marko brings fish for his guests[125] is similar to the legend, "Le Moniage Guillaume," where before his ordination the novice Guillaume is asked by the monks to take a trip and bring back some fish. The monks are really trying to find an excuse to get rid of Guillaume because of his enormous propensity for eating and drinking. Guillaume eventually succeeds in returning with the fish as requested, and then kills several monks. The other monks now find it more expedient to absolve Guillaume of his sins, and together they all feast on the fish.[126] According to W. Cloetta, the story about a hero who brings fish for monks might have originated as a monastic tale.[127]

As Prince Marko is about to leave to catch fish from the Ohrid Lake, his mother advises him to go unarmed:

> After him hasted his aged mother,
> And spake soft words unto him:
> "Ah, my son, Prince Marko,
> Take not any weapon with thee,
> Else—so used to blood art thou—
> Thou wilt surely shed blood on thy festal day."   (26)
>
> Low, No. 23

At this point a new motif is employed in the structure of the narrative. It is the universal motif of the unarmed warrior attached to Prince Marko who is to be confronted by the dangerous outlaw Djemo the Mountaineer.

Banaševié saw in both motifs the influence of Western medieval literature on South Slavic epic poetry.[128] The narrative proceeds with the introduction of Djemo the Mountaineer:

> Lo, a knight was there,
> Seated cross-legged on a brown horse;
> And ever he threw his battle-mace to the clouds,
> And caught it again in his white hands.   (38)
>
> Low, No. 23

Not recognizing Prince Marko, Djemo the Mountaineer announces his threat:

> If God will and knightly fortune prevail,
> His table shall swim in blood,
> And by God, I will hang him,
> Even on the gate of white Prilep.
> For long since he slew my brother,
> Musa, the outlaw.   (60)
>
> Low, No. 23

When Djemo the Mountaineer realizes that he is speaking with Prince Marko, he succeeds in subduing him. Epic singers allow their hero Prince Marko to be temporarily captured by Djemo. Indeed, Prince Marko lost the match because he was without weapons, from restrictions imposed during the observance of a religious holiday. Prince Marko is led by his captor along the same route which the historical Yegen Paša followed in his raids against the Christian population. The citizens of each town to which Djemo brings Prince Marko for hanging, say:

> Brother-in-God, Djemo the Mountaineer,
> Hang not Marko here,
> Lest vine and wheat bear not any fruit.
> Lo, here be three charges of gold!   (101)
>
> Low, No. 23

They pay gold to avert Prince Marko's execution in any of their towns. The background for such behavior is clear, since Yegen Paša historically stopped in those same towns and collected contributions and ransom money from their citizens. In this way Prince Marko became the symbol of the people persecuted by Yegen Paša.

On their journey together Djemo the Mountaineer becomes so thirsty that he is about to kill Prince Marko and drink his blood. Intending to escape by a ruse, Prince Marko tells the thirsty Djemo that there is a nearby tavern kept by a fish-wife, Yanya, whom Prince Marko describes as an old enemy. Actually, he is the best of friends with the fish-wife, who frees him by getting Djemo drunk.

The culmination of the dramatic narrative takes place when Djemo wakes and finds himself in chains. The situation is reversed: Prince Marko leads the now-shackled Djemo behind him on the return trip to Ohrid.[129] The song describes the citizens' hatred of Djemo and their repeated insistence that Prince Marko honor their town by hanging the tyrant Djemo there:[130]

> Thence came forth to him Christian lords, saying:
> "Brother-in-God, Prince Marko,
> See that thou hang Djemo here.
> Lo, here be three charges of gold!"   (194)
>
> Low, No. 23

Prince Marko declines the offer and instead returns to the citizens of each city the gold they had paid earlier to stop Djemo from hanging Marko in their town:

> At Ohrid he builded a gallows,
> And hanged Djemo the Mountaineer.
> And he took fish from Ohrid lake,
> And straightway gat him to white Prilep,
> And there did honour to his patron saint.   (216)
>
> Low, No. 23

In the song, "Prince Marko and Djemo the Mountaineer," the ancient popular belief that a dead man buried in a foreign soil may bring calamity and destroy crops is found repeatedly. Scholars as Maretić[131] and Tomić[132] analyze the song, lines 100, 109 and 118, which contain "Lest vine and wheat bear not any fruit." They speculate that the ancient myth was related to buried dragons or monsters, and later was associated in the epic song with the villain Djemo the Mountaineer. However, the popular bards applied the myth freely according to their needs. When it was necessary to res-

cue Prince Marko in the course of the narrative, then the burying of a dead
man was represented as a calamity which should be prevented. But when
they wanted to destroy Djemo the Mountaineer, the myth about the dead
man was reversed into a blessing.

A MOSLEM COUNTERPART OF MARKO

Wine drinks Djerzelez Aliya,
In the lovely town of Sarayevo,
With him drink thirty squires of Sarayevo.
There is no better hero today
Than the Turk, Djerzelez Aliya.[133]

Djerzelez Aliya was a prominent epic hero among the Balkan Moslems.
While Prince Marko represented the Christians, Djerzelez Aliya was the
protagonist for Moslem Slavs living in the Balkans. He was actually the
Moslem counterpart to Prince Marko for people who, under Turkish pressure or persuasion, had relinquished the Christian faith of their ancestors.
They were, nevertheless, South Slavs by origin and spoke the same Serbo-
Croatian language as their neighbors. Their epic poetry retained definite af-
finities with that of the South Slavs, except, of course, that all Christian heroes were treated as enemies and the protagonists were Moslem.

The historians Stoyan Novaković and Milan Vukičević believed that
the historical person behind the epic figure of Djerzelez Aliya was Ali Beg
Mihal Oglu (1425–1507), who belonged to an Islamicized family of Slavic
origin.[134] Ali Beg, whose father and grandfather were also high Turkish military commanders, conducted campaigns into Hungary and Serbia during
the second half of the fifteenth century.[135] A. Olesnicki and Vido Latković[136]
introduce a second historical person, Gerz-Elyas, who originated in northern Bosnia and was also famous in the Turkish military inroads into Hungary by the end of the fifteenth century. In a battle at Krbava Field in Croatia, Gerz-Elyas was taken prisoner by Derenčin, Lord of Croatia, and was
executed, possibly in Buda (the capital of Hungary), in 1491 or 1492. Epic
bards mixed memories of these two Turkish historical figures, the most
likely prototypes, and the single legendary person of Djerzelez Aliya surfaced in Moslem epic poetry in the Balkans.[137]

Although Djerzelez Aliya is described as physically unattractive, no
other figure in South Slavic Moslem epic poetry can equal him in bravery
and generosity. The Yugoslav author and Nobel prize winner Ivo Andrić depicts Djerzelez Aliya in this way:

On a chestnut horse, his eyes bloodshot ... he carried the glory of many
combats, and his power impressed the people with fear ... unusually short
and heavy-set ... he moves slowly, his legs apart as with men not used to
being afoot ... his arms were excessively long ... and he spoke with the
Albanian intonation, his manner uncouth.[138]

A close comparison of epic songs about Djerzelez Aliya and Prince
Marko confirm that the poetic image of Djerzelez Aliya was modelled after
that of Prince Marko. The Moslems in Bosnia made him a hero who was
invested with extraordinary qualities similar to those of Prince Marko.
Djerzelez Aliya's epic horse is similar to Prince Marko's Šarac, and in some
Moslem songs is also called Šarac. Like Prince Marko, Djerzelez Aliya is
friendly with fairies, who help him in times of danger.

While Prince Marko's other adversaries were symbols of evil forces and
injustices and had to be destroyed, Djerzelez Aliya was modelled so much in
Prince Marko's own likeness that he evoked a deep respect even among the
Christians who portrayed him as an antagonist. Prince Marko himself is
said to have considered him an honorable opponent. Prince Marko was geographically connected with Prilep in Macedonia and Djerzelez Aliya with
Sarayevo in Bosnia. The epic Djerzelez Aliya is presented as an adventurous
knight who frequently travels to Constantinople, where he defends the Sultan and fights duels on his behalf, much as Prince Marko did.

There were obvious similarities in the respective relationships of Prince
Marko and Djerzelez Aliya with the Sultan. Both have an intrinsic distrust
of the courtiers who cluster around the Sultan. In one Moslem song entitled
"Djerzelez Aliya," in *Moslem Heroic Songs* by Frndić, p. 9–20, the Sultan
orders the death of Djerzelez Aliya in order to quell the demands and threats
of his enemies. Like Prince Marko in "Marko Drinks Wine in Ramadan,"
Low, No. 26, and "Prince Marko and Emperor Suleiman," Matica Hrvatska, 2, pt. 1, No. 11, Djerzelez Aliya remains alive thanks to the protection
of the Mullah Čuprilić who emerges as the figure of a statesman and who
corresponds to the historical Grand Vizier Mohammed Kiuprili (1583–
1661):

> Spaketh Čupriliya the Mullah:
> "O my trouble, my Djerzelez Aliya!
> Here I received your death order,
> To deliver the dead head,
> The dead head of Aliya,
> And to send your steed, your knightly steed,
> With the steed two small Brescia muskets,

Along with the steed, the sharp bladed sabre.
Get yourself, Aliya, to your white manor,
I am loath to have you killed,
Do not come here, Aliya,
Until a week of days passes by."   (59)

Moslem Collection, p. 10

Mullah Cuprilić delivers the head to the Sultan along with Aliya's steed and sabre.

When the Sultan's enemy Lord Tukunli received proof of Djerzelez Aliya's death he boasted:

Hey all of you in the city,
Did you hear how the Turkish Sultan I cheated,
How I got Aliya's dead head,
And his glorious steed of battle.   (282)

Moslem Collection, p. 16

Djerzelez Aliya is portrayed as a man who executes the Sultan's orders but in his own way. Just as Prince Marko fought with outlaws who threatened the Sultan's security, the epic Djerzelez Aliya defeated Lord Tukunli, a Hungarian who wanted to take over Constantinople:

Swiftly flees across the green fields,
After him pursues Djerzelez Aliya,
A bit hurries, but overtakes faster,
Aliya caught him alive,
Pulled him down from his black horse,
And tied his hands in reverse.   (373)

Moslem Collection, p. 18

The Sultan was overwhelmed by the victory of his faithful subject who cannot, however, forget the mistreatment he had suffered:

Hearken, Djerzelez Aliya!
Ask, brother, whatever you want,
Any land and whatever towns?   (409)

Moslem Collection, p. 19

While Prince Marko used to mock the Sultan and frighten him, Djerzelez Aliya carries his rebelliousness a step further when he answers to the
Sultan:

> I do not want a land or towns,
> But do not refuse me today,
> That in your Constantinople I do whatever I want,
> And let Cupriliya run the country.   (414)
>
> Moslem Collection, p. 19

Djerzelez Aliya is neither corrupt nor greedy and only means to avenge
himself. Thus:

> He easily leaps on his feet,
> Pulled out his sharp blade, Aliya,
> He beheaded forty viziers of the Sultan.   (418)
>
> Moslem Collection, p. 19

Djerzelez Aliya executed those viziers he considered to be the Sultan's
ill-intentioned advisors. He would have continued with the executions had
the Sultan not begged him to cease, showering him with many treasures
which Djerzelez Aliya took back with him to his native Bosnia.

This song clearly explains the extent to which the Bosnian Moslems felt
separate from the rest of the Turkish empire. These people served the Sultan,
but often disliked or disobeyed orders from Constantinople. Some Moslem
poems explicitly state that when Djerzelez Aliya visited Constantinople he
did not even understand the Turkish language. The epic Djerzelez Aliya was
very much a part of his Bosnian homeland where he fought the Hungarians
and Austrians and helped the Turks.

The song "Djerzelez Aliya, the Emperor's Champion," in Matica
Hrvatska 3, pt. 1, No. 1, has a very similar narrative to "Djerzelez Aliya,"
in *Moslem Heroic Songs*, by Frndič, No. 1. The main difference between the
two is that in the Matica Hrvatska song Djerzelez Aliya's adversary is
changed to the South Slavic hero Sibinyanin Yanko. The Moslem bards employ almost the same metaphor to describe Djerzelez Aliya's moustache as
Christian bards did for Prince Marko:

> Ah, what moustaches in Aliya are,
> As if he had a black lamb in his teeth!   (596)
>
> Matica Hrvatska, 3, pt. 1, No. 1

The same is the case with the description of Djerzelez Aliya's victorious ride
through the streets of Constantinople:

> Went the news through the white Constantinople,
> It went up to the palace of Mehmed Paša, the Bosnian:
> "Lo, what a rider rides as never before,
> His moustaches hang down the horse,
> Aslant, as if horse were a steer."   (812)
> Matica Hrvatska, 3, pt. 1, No. 1

Another parallel between the two heroes is that both decline the offer
to be given Turkish sultanas. In addition, Djerzelez Aliya displays a fierceness in slaying Turks across Constantinople that is very reminiscent of
Prince Marko:

> Thank you, Sir Emperor!
> Your sultanas are not for me,
> ....
>
> But I ask for your imperial seal,
> To walk across your Constantinople,
> From this hour to the third prayer,
> And that I may slay whomever I please.   (939)
> Matica Hrvatska 3, pt. 1, No. 1

In another remarkable song, "Marko Kralyevič and Djerzelez Aliya,"
in *Serbocroatian Heroic Songs,* by Parry and Lord, No. 2 (in synopsis), the
atmosphere is decidedly sympathetic toward the Moslem champion.[139] Here
Prince Marko and Djerzelez Aliya engage in various contests to determine
which of the two is the better warrior. Prince Marko lags behind in all the
tests. He also attempts to cheat on Djerzelez Aliya with the help of his sister,
"lovely Efimiya." Due to his greater strength Djerzelez Aliya eventually won
the competition, and as he takes his leave, he says in a dignified and superior
manner:

> Marko, my brother-in-God, let us say farewell!
> Marko, my brother-in-God, by my life,
> If it were not that I have eaten your bread,
> And that we are brothers-in-God,
> And that I have too much affection
> For my dear sister-in-God

To leave her without her brother,
I should kill you today!
I shall never come to see you again,
My brother-in-God![140]

                                        Parry, 2, No. 2, p. 2–1

So it happened that these two men from mutually hostile camps had respect for each other. The friendly ending of the song was composed by Moslem bards as a farewell speech to the Christian Prince Marko, both the
friend and adversary of Djerzelez Aliya. Moslem bards realized that the two
men would be divided by their places in two separate and warring worlds.
Despite the same blood and the deep, abiding sense of heroism shared by
the two men, they were inexorably separated by a fate symbolized in their
respective religions. It is a sad swan song of two heroes who long to be together, but who had no choice but to flee from each other because they belonged to different and hostile worlds.

EPIC DEATH

*A small boat managed to carry his body, in spite of the reefs
of the Eastern sea and the ambushing Turkish galleys. A fine
story which reminds me, of King Arthur's last crossing.*[141]

According to Constantine the Philosopher, Prince Marko died as a Turkish
vassal muttering a famous prayer to God, asking for the defeat of all the
Turks even at the cost of his own life.[142] These words were considered a vital
contribution to the subsequent and somewhat extraordinary popularity of
Prince Marko. Historical bits and pieces relating to the demise of King
Marko Mrnyavčević are fairly reliable with reference to the time and place
of his death.[143] The name of the Wallachian village of Rovine, where Marko
was killed in 1394, found its way into epic poetry as the Urvina Mountain,
most probably through written sources. The name Urvina, or Urvine, might
well have originated from the word Rovine, otherwise *urvine* in Serbian
means a "very steep crag from which rocks fall off at times."[144] The geographical term was applied to a locality near present-day Skopye in northern
Macedonia, which is fairly close to the actual residence of King Marko in
Prilep. In the words of Khalanskii, "epic poetry represents a better arrange-
ment of poetic models ... by focussing on those poetic or historico-geo-

graphic associations which overshadowed the specific intents of South Slavic singers and transferred the death of Marko from Rovine Field to the Urvina Mountain."[145]

Khalanskii points to those songs in the Bulgarian oral tradition which managed to preserve references to the town of Iurvin or Urvich, which was the point of the wedge of Turkish penetration into Bulgaria. According to the chronicler Paysiy, Urvich was a fortress belonging to the Bulgarian Emperor Šišman (1365–1393) who succeeded in resisting the Turks for years with the support of the citizens from Ohrid and the Serbian King Vukašin (Marko's father).

Several versions of Prince Marko's death exist in the folk tradition, one set relating that his death occurred in different places and under different circumstances. A second set suggests that Prince Marko never died at all, and is believed to be still living somewhere and waiting for the hour to return to his people.

Vuk Stefanović Karadžić presents the most comprehensive survey of all the versions:

> Different tales tell about the death of Prince Marko. According to several of them Marko was killed with a golden arrow, somewhere in the village of Rovine, by a Karawallachian duke named Mirčeta. The battle took place between the Turks and Karawallachians, and the arrow hit Marko in the mouth. Others say that Marko became lost in a swamp after the battle which was near the Danube River; fully armed, and together with his horse Šarac, Marko was bogged down in the mud and sank. In the Negotin March the story is told that this took place in a bog near Negotin, beneath Caričine Springs. Today a swamp and the walls of a ruined church stand there, the church having been allegedly erected on Marko's grave. Others still say that in the said battle so many were slaughtered that both the riders and the horses waded in blood. Marko then raised his arms to heaven and said: "O God, what shall I do now?" God heard Marko and in His grace miraculously transferred both Marko and his horse Šarac into a cave, in which they both live now.[146]

Similar approaches to the epic death of Prince Marko were expressed in the epic poetry although folk tales and oral tradition show more imagination in their selection of various deaths for Prince Marko.

Khalanskii enumerates the motifs related to the demise of Prince Marko, among these being: Prince Marko's death at the hands of his brother who kills him in ignorance; a murder by a jealous man; and death as a result of a fight with a man who tried to dishonor Prince Marko's sister (or in some cases his wife). The latter motif is derived from the legend of the hero Doyčin, who rises from his sickbed to successfully defend the honor of his sister, and then dies. There is also the motif of Prince Marko dying as a result of his stepmother's or a *vila's* deceit. Finally, Prince Marko's death may have come about as a consequence of his grievous sins which weigh upon him until they push him into his grave. The latter idea is reminiscent of the treatment of Marko the Accursed in the Ukrainian *dumy*.[147] These motifs are visible proof of the degeneration of epic songs relating to Prince Marko and their increasing tendency to depict the hero in a less favorable light. This was likely due to the influence of the written literature which was religious, didactic, and rationalistic in character.

Three motifs of Prince Marko's death were the most widespread: his dying of old age, death in combat as a warrior, and his immortality. The historical reminiscence can be found only in the second group although it was changed to such an extent that Prince Marko's death as a vassal was transformed into a heroic death while fighting the Turks.

The primary song which reflects the motif of old age by the hand of an inexorable God denying immortality to a hero is "The Death of Prince Marko," Vuk 2, No. 73. In this classical poem of great simplicity and beauty, the approach of the hero's death is foreshadowed by numerous supernatural signs and omens. One of these is a premonition experienced by Prince Marko's heroic horse Šarac, and its fears of impending death:

> Behold, Šarac began to stumble,
> To stumble, yea, and to shed tears.   (6)
>
> Low, No. 31

Then comes a fairy creature, the *vila*, who interprets the meaning behind Šarac's behavior and informs Prince Marko that the time has come for him to die:

> Wouldst thou know, brother, wherefore thy horse stumbleth?
> Šarac is heavy for thee, his master,
> For soon shall ye be divided.   (21)
>
> Low, No. 31

Prince Marko refuses to accept the inevitable. Indeed, he rebels, turning upon both Šarac and the fairy by boasting of his long, heroic life. Following Prince Marko's protestations that no one has ever been able to defeat him, the fairy's third and final premonition is presented. She agrees that Prince

Marko cannot be vanquished by any human hero or physical force, there being no one greater in might than Prince Marko himself. The fairy does, however, mention God—at whose hands Prince Marko must surely die. Eventually she is able to make the hero accept the fact that this time he cannot win.

The entire mood of this poem is achieved through a preternatural atmosphere which escalates in tension through the addition of many details: the fairy takes Prince Marko to a well of clear water situated between two slender fir trees and there he sees his face mirrored in the crystal surface and hears the fairy's words: "And thou shalt know when thou must die" (Low, No. 31).

Prince Marko's parting from his faithful horse and his weapons is poignantly described in his wish to be destroyed rather than running the risk of being caught by Turkish enemies. The motif of a hero killing his horse and destroying his weapons is common to heroic poetry throughout the world. Here was an opportunity for the South Slavic bards, in their discomfort over Prince Marko's vassalage to the Sultan, to emphasize once again their hero's great pride and his deep hatred of the Turks, a hatred even greater than his fear of death.

Notwithstanding their profound piety, South Slavic epic bards and their audiences keenly resented the universal law of nature which dictated that even their favorite hero had no choice but to ultimately die. In this sense, God himself becomes a temporary adversary since it is only he who can thwart the workings of Fate. Finally, in the realization of the transience of his heroic life and of ultimate defeat, Prince Marko suffers in this last battle. He says in his farewell speech:

> Deceitful world—thou wert a fair flower to me!
> Fair wert thou, but few the years of my sojourn.
> Three hundred brief years have I tarried;
> The hour now cometh that I must go forth of this world.   (68)
>
> Low, No. 31

With these words Prince Marko accepts the inevitable and, as most great heroes, is torn by the tragic conflict of being neither man nor god. During his heroic life he proved his worth by many heroic deeds. Prince Marko was in many ways a demigod who lived for "three hundred brief years," but who nevertheless lamented their temporal quality. In the end, Prince Marko is punished by God, "the Old Slayer," and dies like all mortals.

It is common for heroes of folklore to seek to conquer the unknown and to equal the gods themselves. In the Babylonian epic of the seventh century B.C., Gilgamesh gains his universal appeal through courage displayed in an attempt to escape from death and join the gods. In his quest for immortality, however, Gilgamesh fails to overcome death because it is both inevitable and destructive. In the Old English epic of the eighth century, Beowulf proves his superiority to all men by slaying monsters and a dragon. Twice Beowulf is able to conquer evil as symbolized by the dragon—only to succumb in the end. The implication is that neither darkness nor the unknown can be conquered solely by human hands. Thus, in the epics, death is portrayed as that single element which is simply beyond the reach of Beowulf, Gilgamesh, Prince Marko, or any other great hero.

The South Slavs did not fully accept Prince Marko's death and there existed a folk belief that he went to sleep. This ray of hope that Prince Marko is still alive is evident in the song, "The Death of Prince Marko." It is implied that he would somehow return when needed by his people:

> When my mace shall come up out of the sea,
> Another Marko shall appear upon earth!   (92)
>
> Low, No.

In a simplified popular concept of the death of a hero, bards had Prince Marko lie down upon some grass beneath a fir tree where he fell asleep forever. Those who happened to pass by would be careful not to disturb his sleep, speaking in hushed tones and taking other routes. At this point the influence of the Eastern Orthodox Church becomes evident once again. The abovementioned song describes how Abbot Vaso, from the Chilander Monastery on Mount Athos, discovers Marko and is the first to pronounce him dead. The Abbot's gentleness and sensitivity are manifested in the manner in which he speaks to his companion, the novice Isaiah:

> "Softly, my son," quoth he, "lest thou wake him,
> For Marko roused from slumber is evil-disposed,
> And might well make an end of both of us!"   (135)
>
> Low, No. 31

Epic bards tried to render Prince Marko as awesome and frightening in death as he was in life. Remembering Prince Marko's ill temper and the fierceness and haste with which he committed many an imprudent act, popular bards endeavored once more to evoke the hero in all his might. In addition, he was fully under the wing of the Church, a very important consideration since after the South Slavs lost their freedom and their state to the Turks, it was only the Church which continued to cultivate and maintain national ideals. Thus Prince Marko, the symbol of a whole national tradition, is ultimately carried away by Abbot Vaso, *Vasiliye*, and buried anonymously in the Chilandar Monastery where no one would know of his grave:

> But he left no sign thereon,
> That none should know the grave of Marko,
> And that his enemies should not revenge them on the dead.   (163)
>
> Low, No. 31

To this seemingly logical justification might be added a myth which was possibly created and certainly amplified by monks of the Chilandar Monastery. Kravtsov maintained that "localization of the hero and the attachment of Marko's death to the Urvina Mountain, as well as his burial in the Chilandar Monastery, were a result of monastic revision of songs relating to the death of Marko."[148]

It was in the monastery's interest to promulgate itself as the shrine of a hero, thus attracting donations and worshippers. One of the propagators of this theory was Joseph Bédier, who believed that the Roland legend was accepted and further developed by monasteries in France.[149] The same could have been true with the Prince Marko legend and the Chilandar Monastery. By associating the Prince Marko legend with itself the Church promoted its own interests but at the same time vastly contributed to the spread of Prince Marko's epic fame.

The influence of the Church is also reflected in Prince Marko's legendary last wish, written on a branch of the fir tree beneath which he died. According to the inscription, Prince Marko left three purses of gold, the first to the one who discovered his body and buried him, the second to the "adorning of churches," and

> The third I give to the maimed and the blind,
> That the blind may go into all the world,
> To sing and to celebrate Marko.   (108)
>
> Low, No. 31

This last wish of Prince Marko's is a direct request to epic singers, many of whom were actually blind and who had selected as their profession the chanting of epic songs about the ancient fame of the South Slavs.

10. A blind epic singer with the single-stringed instrument (*gusle*) as illustrated by Mirko Rački. From Narodno Delo, *Zbornik yunačkih epskih narodnih pesama* [Collection of Heroic Epic Popular Songs] (Beograd, 1930).

Prince Marko's burial in an unknown grave would seem justified by the need to protect that place from desecration by his enemies. Another reason concerns the parental curse. South Slavic epic poetry always sharply underlined the disagreements between Marko and his father, King Vukašin. The legend has Vukašin utter the following curse in the song "Uroš and the Mrnyavčeviĉes," Vuk 2, No. 33:

> Son Marko, may God slay thee,
> Mayst thou have neither grave nor posterity,
> And may thy soul not leave thee,
> Until thou hast served the Turkish Sultan! (249)
>
> Low, No. 3

South Slavs maintain a profound and deeply rooted belief that a parent's curse is always fulfilled, whether it is justified or not. Vukašin's words are almost a prophecy which was confirmed later in the song about Prince Marko's death. Bards remembered this curse well and repeated it as the stereotypical formula used by another epic character, the beautiful sister of Captain Leka who pronounced a similar curse upon Prince Marko when she rejected his proposal of marriage:

> For Marko holds of the Sultan,
> He fights and smites for the Turks,
> Never will he have grave nor burial,
> Nor o'er his grave will burial service be read! (464)
>
> Low, No. 6

The epic death of Prince Marko is reminiscent of descriptions of the death of Roland in the poem *La Chanson de Roland*. Khalanskii and Banašević drew parallels between the respective deaths of the French and South Slavic heroes. The horses of the two men, Veillantif and Šarac, foresee the approaching death of their masters. Both Roland and Prince Marko destroy their weapons before they die so as to prevent their falling into the hands of their enemies, the Saracens and the Turks. The motif of the weeping horse who mourns his master's approaching death was very popular in ancient and medieval times.[150]

The analogy between the deaths of Roland and Prince Marko is further emphasized by the fact that both heroes lie down beneath a tree to wait for death to arrive. Before expiring, each recalls his knightly adventures and sheds tears over his memories of past fame. Khalanskii describes the act of dying with a direct quotation from oral poetry in the song "The Death of Prince Marko," in Vuk 2, No. 73: "Then laid him down never to rise no more" (Low, No. 31), and compares it with Roland:[151]

> Then drooped his head upon his breast,
> And with clasped hands he went to rest.

Khalanskii reasoned that, although similarities do exist in the respective treatments of the deaths of Roland and Marko, Prince Marko's death cannot be explained by treating it as an imitation of or outright derivation from the Old French *chansons*. Khalanskii sees the possibility of professional medieval singers and troubadours (not to mention Crusaders during the Third and Fourth Crusades), bringing West-European cultural influence to the Balkan Peninsula.

A Bulgarian song deals with the topic of Prince Marko's surrender to the fate and inevitability of Turkish supremacy, titled "Marko's Death and the Loss of the Empire," in *Sbornik za narodno umotvorenia*, No. 14, p. 90–92.[152] It shows how Prince Marko becomes weaker and increasingly fails in his fights with the Janissaries in Anatolia in Asia Minor. This song further relates Prince Marko's return to his native land, Bulgaria. He has a prophetic dream which is interpreted by his mother as a sinister foreboding of the imminent Turkish invasion, during which the entire country will succumb along with Prince Marko's capital of Prilep:

> And there comes Marko's mother,
> Her eyes with a kerchief she covers,
> Her tears are reaching the ground
> Mournfully she talks to Marko:
> "Hey, my dear son Marko,
> So, my son, you go to fight far wars,
> You fight Turk Janissaries,
> But you don't know what happens here:
> Turk Janissaries are here,
> They conquered the Bulgarian land."

His mother advises Prince Marko to surrender to the Turks as all the others have done:

> All heroes surrendered keys of their towns
> And gave up the Bulgarian land

You too, my dear son Marko, will be asked
To surrender, my Marko, your keys,
The keys of the town of Prilep.

A pall of doom has fallen over the defeated homeland, but Prince Marko does not give up easily. When asked by the Janissaries to submit his keys he replies:

> When Marko the Bulgar falls,
> And when his horse Šarac falls,
> Then, you will get my keys,
> Then you will take hold of Prilep.
>
> *Sbornik za narodno umotvorenia*, No. 14

Prince Marko tries to alter the destiny of his people and goes off to Kossovo field. For three full days and nights he fights the Turks alone. Inexorable fate is fully at work when St. Elijah appears to Prince Marko ordering him to cease fighting: "in Prilep the Turks will rule."

Prince Marko comes to recognize his fate, and he accepts it, leaving Kossovo behind. Returning to Prilep he kills his family and horse so they would not fall into his enemies' hands. Then Prince Marko disappears. According to Iordanov, this song, which depicts the tragic fate of the Bulgarian people, is one of the finest products of Bulgarian epic poetry.[153]

The historical background of Prince Marko's death can be discerned in one other song which is geographically tied to Mt. Goleš near Kossovo.[154] "The Death of Prince Marko," Vuk 6, No. 28, narrates the events of the second Battle of Kossovo which took place in 1448, fifty-nine years after the first battle. In the battle of 1448 the Turks routed the Hungarian knights led by Yanoš Hunyady, the result being that in each of the two battles the Christians were thoroughly defeated. The song has Prince Marko arrive at Mt. Goleš and actively join in the battle against the Turks. Prince Marko is mortally wounded and summons a black raven to deliver a letter to the Abbot, asking him to hurry over so that Prince Marko may receive absolution before dying.

This motif evidently bears the signs of Church influence with its concern for last rites and death with the full sanction of the Church. The song is decidedly anti-Turkish in spirit and shows the presence of later layers of epic sentiment which emerged in the seventeenth century and reflected what became the unbearable oppression of Turkish rule. The dying Prince Marko's final words to his people were: "Beware of the Turks!" (Vuk 6, No. 27).

"The Death of Prince Marko" merged the legendary Battle of Kossovo Field with the myth of Prince Marko as the two single greatest pillars in the epic history of the South Slavs. Poetic licence was liberally applied to correct the embarrassment of Prince Marko's historical absence from the great battle in which the finest sons of the Serbian nation were lost. Ultimately, however, Prince Marko took his place alongside them and, according to a few songs, died a heroic death. As a symbol of their aspiration for freedom, the poets had Prince Marko buried at Kossovo, the place where freedom had been lost.

The idea of Prince Marko's immortality was very dear to the South Slavic people and the concept of immortality was popular not only in epic poetry but also in the entire oral tradition. Folk imagination, which always remained fascinated by Prince Marko, was especially active in the Macedonian area of Prilep, the region where King Marko ruled. There, according to tradition, Prince Marko still lives. Ostoyić writes: "The people in Prilep say that Marko is still alive. Together with his horse Šarac, Marko dived into the great blue sea, taking with him all his weapons. There Marko lives in a cave at the bottom of the sea. When Marko works around his horse Šarac, voyagers on the sea can clearly hear his curry-comb. At midnight, in the dead of night, Marko goes to his town Prilep and brings oats for Šarac from a shed."[155]

A collection of folktales by Vuk Vrčević contains a story about a Hercegovinian who meets Prince Marko on a country road and gives him wine. Marko drinks the wine and pays for it, telling the man that he is only waiting for the first appropriate opportunity to come back again and mingle with the Serbs. The Hercegovinian describes Prince Marko as a man huge in size, "as four grown men are today. His beard is gray and reaches down to beneath his waist, while the mustaches are long, each thrown across a shoulder, and hanging down along his back."[156]

According to a tale in the Brothers Miladinov collection Prince Marko never died at all, and is still living in a beautiful house on a deserted island. There he is visited by a man from Prilep, whom Marko receives very hospitably and to whom he says that very soon there will come a time when he will return.[157]

Ćorović claims that the idea of a hero's immortality is common to many epics, and that, as far as the Balkans were concerned, the concept was ascribed not only to Prince Marko, but to other heroes as well. The same idea recurs in traditional Armenian poetry, in which the great hero Mher fails to die decisively, but is rather doomed to spend eternity in a cave.[158] In this instance, the similarities with the Prince Marko theme are readily apparent and the aura of immortality associated with the hero seems logical.

The only anomaly in the case of the Armenian hero Mher is that he is con-demned to eternal life by the curse of the people of Sasoun, whose hatred he incurred because of a heroic strength which exceeded all measure.

Another case which fits well into the scheme of a hero's immortality in a kind of limbo relates to the German legend of Emperor Frederick Barba-rossa. He is said to still be in a cave on the Kyffhäuser Mountain in central Germany, awaiting the proper time to return to life and restore the greatness of his people.

The notion of a hero's immortality is the logical extension of a hero's glorious life. Those versions of Prince Marko's "death" which have rele-gated his posthumous existence to a secluded cave awaiting the hour of his return to the people conform perhaps to the more general theme of elevating a hero to the rank of a god. Just as Prince Marko's representation in his epic life was that of a highly composite figure, so too the death of the hero as-sumed a very complicated, sometimes even contradictory, form. The epic poets had him suffer several forms of death ranging from falling in battle to death from old age. In the long run, all of these together tend to seek a ne-gation of death and strive to understand heroism and epic heroes as the apotheosis of life itself.

Conclusion

He built a modern Centaur, creating a symbol of his people and country.[1]

The saga of Prince Marko, the warrior and the son of a king, managed to thrive among the South Slavic people from the fourteenth century to the present. Shaped by the anonymous epic bards Prince Marko became a living legacy enriched by heroism which was drawn from a lively interplay of popular legend and historical reminiscences.

In their pursuit of self-expression the South Slavic people captured a profound sense of suffering and immortalized it in their own image: Prince Marko the warrior. The epic singers built Marko into a towering, fearsome avenger of his rebellious people. Sometimes they presented Prince Marko as sinful and imperfect (as they were); on other occasions they transformed him into a paragon of human bravery and justice.

While the people maintained a wishful prophecy about Prince Marko's immortality, that he is asleep and will awake when his people need him, this myth has remained strong for more than six hundred years. One finds a surprisingly wide spectrum of Marko's admirers, not only in popular audiences who loved to listen to tales of his knightly encounters, but also in the great men and women of modern times.

In the nineteenth century Goethe envisioned Prince Marko as a South Slavic Hercules. The Brothers Grimm and other Romanticists were fascinated with folk literature in general and Prince Marko in particular. In the twentieth century one witnesses a renaissance of the Prince Marko legend among both prominent individuals and the popular masses.

The great Yugoslav sculptor Ivan Meštrović was an ardent admirer of the legendary hero Marko. From his childhood Meštrović was intoxicated by the powerful oral tradition and by the heroism of Prince Marko. In 1910, in an inspired creation, this son of the craggy Dinaric Mountains modelled an equestrian statue of Prince Marko, his first monumental memorial and more than fifteen feet high. The whole art exhibit in Zagreb that year centered around the symbol of Prince Marko and it was titled "In Spite of Unheroic Time."[2]

By venerating the years of the past and perceiving the present as bereft of heroes, Ivan Meštrović inspired a large group of young South Slavic artists. They worked together on sculptures of heroes for the so-called Kossovo Cycle to be presented to the world public at the International Fair in Rome in 1911. Entering into the Serbian pavillion,

> one finds himself in a totally different milieu and in a different time which lived with a different soul ... along a vista of rows of tonelessly weeping Caryatids all the way through to a Sphinx whose wings were frozen into rigidity by nightly vigil and waiting ... these are images of widows, in shoals of sorrow, griefing in hopelessness. Their lament is frozen in mute expressions of a primitive simple immediacy and motionless gestures of force ... and as a stunned visitor continues ... there in the middle of a hall was the gigantic figure of Prince Marko, the Hero, the Yugoslav Siegfried, almost welded to his ferocious neighing horse. Along the consoles were thrown asunder corpses of Turks, dominated by a frieze in which were sculpted images of the Serbian and Turkish fighters in combat.[3]

Meštrović's monumental statue of Prince Marko occupied a central location in the exhibition in Rome. Thanks to Meštrović's genius, he was able to translate his vision, consistent with the spirit of time, into a sculptural composition integrating Prince Marko with the people and the Earth. The hero and horse consolidate elemental oneness: it is a part of our Earth. Viewers understood that Meštrović's Marko is naked and weaponless, as were the people he symbolized. According to the literary critic and poet Matoš:

> From the epic poems Meštrović does not take anything else but that part which is heroic: the naked body and the Šarac horse ... Thus Marko was deprived of all such historical attributes as weapons and garments. From a historical figure Meštrović had made a hero who is outside and beyond history ... Furthermore, Meštrović had conceived Marko's horse Šarac as a mythical horse: frontside the horse was Greek, backside a long tail, a very long tail, indeed, with heavy broad rump the horse reminded on Florentine pre-Michelangelo's equestrian statues. Marko and Šarac are one, as is a statue of Centaur ... The horse is as heavy as is Earth and it amplifies the Centaurian power of the hero. ... Full of suppressed anger Marko

11. First study for the popular hero Kralyevic Marko, Ivan Meštrović, plaster, 1909 (National Museum, Belgrade). Reprinted from *The Sculpture of Ivan Meštrović* (Syracuse, N.Y.: Syracuse University Press, 1948).

climbed on horse's back, pressing on the horse's cruppers with his Cyclo-
pean primeval legs, simultaneously contracting his terrible Titanic fist into
a spiked mace. ... The light emphasizes Marko's irresistible vindictive
cramped arm, so that there is nothing more grandiose or monumental
than the transition from Marko's head along giant shoulder muscles, pro-
truding like distant mountains, to the quiet, almost petrified appearance
of the horse. This statue destroys and crumbles everything around itself.
And all of Marko's mien is nothing but anger. This is indeed a call of our
naked soul crying for revenge for all Kossovos, and for all betrayals and all
shameful defeats.[4]

The influence of Prince Marko's legend is felt in Western Europe today.
The late Belgian writer Marguerite Yourcenar, who was at home in many
lands and ages and was the first woman to become a member of the Aca-
démie Française, learned of the epic personality of Prince Marko many years
ago. In *Oriental Tales* (1985), Yourcenar told how often in her long life she
had thought of Prince Marko, in this case focussing on his death:

"The end of Marko Kralyević" is a story I had been wanting to write for
many years and finally completed in 1978. The inspiration for this tale was
a fragment of a Serbian ballad on the death of the hero at the hands of a
mysterious, unprepossessing, allegorical stranger. But where did I read or
hear this story about which I have so often thought? I no longer know, and
I cannot find it among the several books on the subject I have at hand,
which give many different versions of Marko Kralyević's death, but not
this one.[5]

Just as medieval bards constantly changed and developed the Prince
Marko legend, contemporary sculptors and writers addressed him in their
own ways. Meštrović interpreted Prince Marko according to his artistic in-
tuition. He creatively shaped heroism and gave a new dimension to the existing Marko legend—a Promethean terrifying power built in a modern
Centaur.

In the same vein but from her own viewpoint, Yourcenar unfolded the
Prince Marko legend and added her contribution as the many anonymous
epic singers did in the past. Yourcenar delineated Prince Marko incisively:
"He would have been recognized by the immoderate length of his shadow."[6]

She reflects on Prince Marko and the Turks in a forceful vision: "In this
savage Serb, we see a hero stripped bare. The Turks against whom Marko
launched his attack must have felt that a mountain oak was crashing down
on them."[7]

She describes Prince Marko's torture by the Turkish executioners, who are told: "You need more than a thousand nails and a hundred hammers to crucify Marko Kralyević."[8]

Finally she regards Prince Marko with such affection that she compares him with his Homeric counterpart: "Only the fish know of his trail in the water. Marko charmed the waves; he was as good a swimmer as Ulysses, his ancient neighbor from Ithaca."[9]

Prince Marko's heroic outlook varied, depending upon the time and conditions within which his legend flourished. His essence, however, is that of an epic hero who embodied the suffering of the South Slavic people who were left with few alternatives during the Turkish occupation. The South Slavs succeeded in finding a sustaining focal point in the epic personality of Prince Marko, in whom an acceptance of reality merged with dreams of ever-present greatness.

Notes

INU   Institut za narodnu umyetnost u Zagrebu (Institute for Folk Arts)

JAZU   Yugoslovenska akademiya znanosti i umyetnosti u Zagrebu (Yugoslav Academy of Sciences and Arts)

PMLA   Publications of the Modern Language Association of America

SAN   Srpska akademiya nauka u Beogradu (Serbian Academy of Sciences)

SUD   Srpsko učeno društvo u Beogradu (Serbian Learned Society)

INTRODUCTION

1. The town of Prilep is located in central Macedonia in Yugoslavia. The first fortifications of the Marko Tower date from the Hellenistic period. There are early Byzantine remains from the fifth and sixth centuries. Archaeological excavations beneath the Marko Tower revealed an early Slav settlement from the late tenth century. By the mid-twelfth century the churches of St. Demetrius and of the Holy Archangel had been built and decorated with frescoes. Prilep remained in Byzantine hands until 1334, when it was taken by the Serbian Emperor Dušan. It became King Vukašin's capital in 1366. After the battle at the Marica River in 1371, Prilep became the seat of King Marko, and after his death in 1394, the Turks seized and kept it until 1912. Marko's fortress is one of the best-preserved medieval castles in Macedonia. In *Treasures of Yugoslavia*, 1st ed. s.v. "Prilep."

2. Cecil Stewart, *Serbian Legacy* (New York: Harcourt, Brace, 1959), 63–64. See also Harold William Vazeille Temperley, who stated: "The Serbian peasant was a magnificent natural soldier . . . easily roused to moral enthusiasm by a reference to Marko Kralyević or Kossovo," in *History of Servia* (New York: Howard Fertig, 1969), 305.

3. *Treasures of Yugoslavia*, edited by Kosta Rakić (Beograd: Yugoslaviapublic, 1980), 558–59.

4. The oral composition of South Slavic epic poetry is discussed in a festschrift for Albert Bates Lord, *Oral Traditional Literature*, edited by John Miles Foley (Columbus, Ohio: Slavica Publishers, 1981).

5. "Although the content of the song is subject to constant change, the verse form, to some extent, preserves the song." Vido Latković, *Narodna knyiževnost* [Folk literature] (Beograd: Naučna knyiga, 1967), 18. Oral epic poetry was composed using the fixed metrical forms. The meters in the verses of heroic songs vary from seven to sixteen syllables. The most popular meter form among the South Slavs is the decasyllabic, consisting of five trochaic feet

with the accented and unaccented syllables falling at regular intervals. A short pause (caesura) divides every decasyllabic verse into four and six syllable sub-units. Each line of epic poetry is a syntactic unit ending in a pause which stresses the end of a thought. The decasyllabic meter fully reflects the solemn tone of the epic narrative in traditional South Slavic versification.

In addition to decasyllabic songs, which were also called "short-line" songs, were *Bugarštice*, or "long-line" songs, consisting of either fifteen- or sixteen-syllable meters in either seven or eight feet, with a caesura after the seventh or eighth syllable. The trochaic foot predominates, except that one dactyl precedes the caesura in the fifteen-syllable line. *Bugarštice* frequently contain refrains of six syllables added at the end of each line, at each alternate line, or every few verse lines. Refrains do not appear in the decasyllabic epic songs. While decasyllabic songs were sung to the accompaniment of an one-string instrument (*gusle*), it is not known whether the *bugarštice* were accompanied by any instrument, or if they were half-sung in a slow lamenting manner.

Rhythm is very important to epic songs because it creates a pattern of dramatic action and is a memory device. The inborn rhythm of decasyllabic verse usually places the dramatic upward movement of the line in the first part of the verse line and sometimes in the second part after the caesura.

Oral poetry is composed of formulas which consist of groups of words and group of phrases which are used recurrently in epic versification. The task of performing before an audience was facilitated for the illiterate bards through formulas in the oral composition. The formulas were built like modular blocks from simple repetitions of the fixed noun-adjective combinations to elaborate similes, the so-called Slavic antithesis. In the development of the oral-formulaic theory, new views appeared seeking to assert "syntactic definition of the formula." See J. M. Foley, *Oral Traditional Literature*, 67.

6. Svetozar Kolyević, *The Epic in the Making* (Oxford: Clarendon Press, 1980), viii.

1—SOUTH SLAVIC FOLK LITERATURE

1. Edward Gibbon, *The History of the Decline and Fall of the Roman Empire*, ed. H. H. Milman, 5 vols. (Philadelphia: Porter & Coates, 1845), 3:552.

2. Harold William Temperley, *History of Serbs* (New York: AMS Press, 1970), 9–17.

3. Ibid., 81–82.

4. Constantin Jireček, *Geschichte der Serben*, 2 vols. 1911–1918 (Reprint. Amsterdam: Adolf M. Hakkert, 1967), 1:128–32, 176–78.

5. The older Glagolitic alphabet was developed by Konstantin (later called St. Cyril) and his brother St. Methodius. These two Greek missionaries came from the vicinity of Salonica where the Macedonian Slavs were densely settled in the ninth century. It was from them that Cyril and Methodius learned the Slavic language. One of the oldest-preserved Glagolitic manuscripts, from the eleventh century, is the St. Mary's Gospel (*Codex Marianus*) or *Mariyinsko Yevandjelye*. The Cyrillic alphabet was introduced by St. Cyril's disciple, Kliment of Ohrid, who named the new alphabet after his teacher. It emerged in Preslav, Bulgaria, and was based on formal Greek uncial writing. One of the best-known Cyrillic manuscripts is Miroslav's Gospel, *Miroslavlyevo Yevandyelye*, which dates from the twelfth century and represents a masterful example of Slavic calligraphy, book illumination, and art.

The Glagolitic alphabet coexisted with the Cyrillic until the twelfth and thirteenth centuries and eventually the Cyrillic prevailed in Bulgaria, Serbia, Macedonia, and even in Russia.

By the tenth century the Cyrillic alphabet had been transferred to Bosnia where it was modified into a new sub-form called *Bosančica*, the Bosnian-Croatian Cyrillic. It was mostly used in the western part of the Balkan Peninsula, by the Bogomils and the Roman Catholics, and up to the nineteenth century by the Balkan Slavic Moslems.

The Glagolitic alphabet established deep roots in Dalmatia, the Adriatic Islands, Istria, and Coastal Croatia. During the fourteenth and fifteenth centuries, religious poetry in the Glagolitic script flourished in these areas and remained particularly strong among the Catholic village priests nearly until the nineteenth century. Still the Latin alphabet gradually succeeded in pushing out the Glagolitic and fully asserted itself in the sixteenth century among the Croats and Slovenes.

6. Arab is a generic term which often appears in South Slavic epic poetry, and it refers to a Moslem foreigner who is usually described as being of a black or dark coloring. The real Arabs came to be known in the Balkans only after the seventh century. The Bulgarians fought them near Constantinople from 716 to 718, and they are known to have frequently devastated the Dalmatian coast during the ninth century. From 1402 the Mongols, led by Tamerlane, attacked Turkey, the Serbs siding with the Turks. In this instance oral poetry called the assailants Arabs. Otherwise the term usually denotes an overseas, i.e., Mediterranean, Moslem, also often called Moor. *Cf.* Nikolai Kravtsov, *Serbskii epos* (Moskva: Academia, 1933), 112–13.

7. *Bogomils* were a religious sect which originated in Bulgaria around the tenth century and spread over the Balkan Peninsula, existing up to the fifteenth century. The *Bogomil* teaching represents a fusion of a dualistic neo-Manichean doctrine which was adopted from the Paulicians in Armenia and Asia Minor. *Bogomils* were against the matter and the flesh, believing that they were the product of the devil. The Serbian King Stefan Nemanya persecuted the *Bogomils,* and they found a refuge in Bosnia, known by the name of Patarenes. Bogomil heresy was accepted between the twelfth and fifteenth centuries by a majority of the Bosnian nobility and kings. *Cf.* Jireček, *Geschichte der Serben,* 1:223–25.

8. Jacob Grimm, the *Letter* to Serbian Prince Miloš Obrenović in Vuk Stefanović Karadžić, *Kleine Serbische Grammatik* (Leipzig: Reimer, 1824) (Reprint. Muenchen: Sagner; Beograd: Prosveta, 1974), [30–31].

9. Gibbon, *Decline and Fall,* 3:167–69.

10. Approximately twenty centuries ago, the whole area north of the Black Sea and east to the gap between the Urals and the Caspian Sea was referred to as Scythia. Around the second century A.D. massive inroads began between the Baltic and the Black Sea of Germanic, Slavic, Hun, Avar, and many other tribes which lasted for several centuries. Disregarding whether conquerors, refugees, or migrating settlers, they passed through Scythia and were often called Scythians. The ancient Slavs whose lands were in the present-day Ukraine were frequently called Scythians.

11. Gibbon, *Decline and Fall,* 3:167–68.

12. Voyislav Djurić, *Antologiya narodnih yunačkih pesama* [Anthology of folk heroic songs] (Beograd: Srpska knyiževna zadruga, 1969), 13–14.

13. *Polye yadikovo: antologiya crnogorskih narodnih tužbalica* [Field of sorrow: Anthology of Montenegrine folk laments] (Titograd: Grafički zavod, 1971), 31–32. See also Vuk Stefanović Karadžić, *Etnografski spisi* [Ethnographic notes] (Beograd: Prosveta, 1970), 102–3.

14. Milivoye V. Knežević, "O naystariyoy slovenskoy narodnoy pesmi" [On the oldest Slavic folk song] *Prilozi proučavanyu narodne poeziye* 6, No. 2 (Nov. 1939):268–69.

15. Ibid.

16. Domentiyan wrote *Život Svetog Save* [Biography of St. Sava] in 1243 or 1253. See Djuro Daničić, *Život Svetog Simeuna i Svetog Save napisao Domentiyan* [Biography of St. Si-

meun and St. Sava written by Domentiyan], 1865. Theodosius wrote *Život Svetoga Save* [Bi-ography of St. Sava] which is a popularized version of Domentiyan's, written after 1261, and noted in about sixty MSS in Serbia, Bulgaria, and Russia. See Djuro Daničić, *Život Svetoga Save od Teodosiya* [Biography of St. Sava by Theodosius], 1860. See also Dragolyub Pavlović, *Iz naše knyiževnosti feudalnog doba* [From our literature of feudal period] (Beograd: Pros-veta, 1968), 22–24, and Nikolai Kravtsov, *Serbskii epos* [Serbian epic] (Moskva: Academia, 1933), 66–67.

17. Theodosius, *Život*, in *Stara srpska knyiževnost*, vol. 2 [Old Serbian literature] (Novi Sad: Matica srpska, 1970), 136. See also Vido Latković, *Narodna knyiževnost* [Folk litera-ture] (Beograd: Naučna knyiga, 1967), 31.

18. The account about folk songs that Nicephorus Gregoras heard in the land of Serbs (called "Triballous") can be found in his *Letter*, No. 12, dated 1325–1326, and addressed to Andronicus Zaridas. The *Letter* is included in Vol. 8, 14, 375 of Gregoras' thirty-seven volume set of the *History*, which covers events that took place from 1204 to 1359. The primary source of the *Letter* is *Codex Urbinas*, gr. 151, 81r–87v, which is presently quoted from *Correspond-ance de Nicéphore Grégoras*, edited and translated by R. Guilland (Paris: Société d'Édition "Les Belles Lettres," 1927), i–xxii, [1], 36–37.

19. Benedikt Kuripešić, *Putopis kroz Bosnu, Srbiya, Bugarsku i Rumeliyu 1530* [Itin-erary . . .] (Sarayevo: Svyetlost, 1950):33.

20. Gibbon, *Decline and Fall*, 3:168.

21. Jireček, *Geschichte der Serben*, 1:75.

22. For information on the scholarship of the *Sermon* in Serbian, Bulgarian and Russian manuscripts and editions see ĬU. Begunov, *Kozma Presviter v slavianskikh literaturakh* [Cos-mas the Presbyter in Slavic literatures] (Sofiia: Izdatel'stvo Bolgarskoi Akademii Nauk, 1973).

23. Latković, *Narodna knyiževnost*, 31.

24. Svetozar Matić, "Otkad počinye naše epsko pevanye" [When does our epic singing date from] *Letopis matice srpske* 390, no. 1 (July 1962):6.

25. Kravtsov, *Serbskii epos*, 66–68, 88–89.

26. André Vaillant, "Les Chants épiques des Slaves du Sud," *Revue de cours et confér-ences* (Mar. 1932):306–46.

27. *Cf.* D. Karl Uitti, "Life of Saint Alexis" in *Story, Myth, and Celebration in Old French Narrative Poetry, 1050–1200* (Princeton: Princeton University Press, 1973), 3–64.

28. Dragolyub Pavlović, *Iz naše knyiževnosti feudalnog doba* [From our literature of feudal period] (Beograd: Prosveta, 1968), 126–32.

29. *Cf.* Radmila Marinković, *Srpska Aleksandrida* [Serbian Alexandriad] (Beograd: Filološki fakultet, 1969), 17–63.

30. Pavlović, *Iz naše knyiževnosti*, 126–32.

31. Djurić, *Antologiya narodnih*, in *Notes*, 692–93.

32. Ibid.

33. Latković, *Narodna knyiževnost*, 34.

34. "In the early fourteenth century minstrels were present in the houses of nobility and at royal courts. More respectable singers had been organized in companies, having had their own kings and ranks. They were paid according to their proficiency, they carried signs of their profession and maintained their dignity. They used to go from place to place; they served cities and towns, entertained at guildhalls and churches during religious festivities in cathedrals and monasteries, they congregated in great numbers at distinguished weddings or feasts of prom-inent noble families, they followed kings, participated in tournaments, theatrical performances and dances. They recorded and published important events. In other words they were a neces-sity for all." *Cf.* William Henry Scofield, *English Literature* (London: Macmillan, 1914), 19.

35. Dragutin Subotić, "Karakter, postanak i starina yugoslovenskih narodnih pesama"

[The character, origin and antiquity of Yugoslav folk songs], *Srpski knyiževni glasnik*, n.s., 51, no. 5 (July 1937):374.

36. Leopold von Ranke, *The History of Servia and the Servian Revolution* (London: Henry G. Bohn, 1853), 48.

37. Ibid., 266–69.

38. Ibid., 434–36.

39. Karel Horálek, "Quelques traits caractéristiques de la poésie populaire Bulgare," *Revue des études Slaves* 40 (1964):97–98.

40. Djurić, *Antologiya narodnih*, 11–12.

41. Vuk Stefanović Karadžić, *Narodne srpske pyesme* [Serbian folk songs] 2nd ed., 4 vols. Vols. 1–3 (Lipiska: Breitkopf i Härtl, 1823–24), vol. 4 (Beč: Štampariya Yermenskog manastira, 1833).

42. Vuk Stefanović Karadžić, *O srpskoy narodnoy poeziyi* [On Serbian folk poetry] (Beograd: Prosveta, 1968), 97.

43. Ibid., 151.

44. Nikola Banašević, *Ciklus Marka Kralyevića i odjeci francusko-italiyanske viteške knyiževnosti* [The cycle of Prince Marko and echoes of French-Italian chivalric literature]. (Skoplye: Skopsko naučno društvo, 1935), 167.

2—FACTUAL AND FICTIONAL IMAGES OF PRINCE MARKO

1. Dragutin Subotić, *Yugoslav Popular Ballads: Their Origin and Development* (Cambridge: University Press, 1932), 14.

2. Constantine the Philosopher—linguist, teacher and writer—lived in the fourteenth and fifteenth centuries. He came to Serbia after Bulgaria was conquered by the Turks. He lived at the court of the Serbian ruler Stefan Lazarević, whose biography Constantine wrote sometime between 1431 and 1435.

3. Mikhail Khalanskii, *Iuzhno-slavianskiia skazaniia o Kraleviche Marke* [South Slavic legends about Prince Marko] (Varshava: Tipografiia Varshavskago Uchebnago Okruga, 1894), 63.

4. Mauro Orbini gave the genealogy of King Marko's family in his Manuscript *Il Regno degli Slavi*, p. 273. According to chronicles of the Zographu monastery at Mt. Athos Vukašin's ancestors lived in Opanci village near Omiš (*Almissa*) in Dalmatia. Cf. Jireček, *Geschichte der Serben*, 1:423.

5. At that time Vukašin's name was pronounced *Vlkašin* and later changed to Vukašin and sometimes Volkašin.

6. In 1350 Vukašin (*Volcassinus*) became the Lord (*Župan*) of Prilep, and soon after was elevated to be the Ruler (*Despot*). Cf. Jireček, *Geschichte der Serben*, 1:423.

7. Since Emperor Dušan's son and heir Uroš was only nineteen years old when he inherited the Empire, Vukašin was either elected or selected to be the co-ruler. In November 1366 a Serbian state delegation arrived in Dubrovnik to negotiate on behalf of the Emperor Uroš (*dominus imperator Sclavonie*), as well as of King Vukašin (*dominus rex Sclavonie*). According to Orbini, it was Uroš who bestowed the royal title on Vukašin (*gli diede etiandio il titolo del Rè*). Jireček, *Geschichte der Serben*, 1:430.

8. King Vukašin's Charter in Poreč, 1370, giving commercial privileges to Dubrovnik, had two original copies: one at Serbian Court and the other in Dubrovnik. The latter is found in the "c.r. in Archivio Viennae, No. 62," Franz Miklošić, *Monumenta Serbica* (Wien: Brau-

mueller, 1858; reprint, Graz: Akademische Druck, 1964), 179–181. The author had in hand the document from Widener Library, Harvard University, published *Stare srpske povelye i pisma* [Ancient Serbian charters and letters], vol. 1, pt. 1: *Dubrovnik i susedi nyegovi* [Dubrovnik and its neighbors], collected by Lyubomir Stoyanović, 116, No. 122.

9. In April 1370, Pope Urban V sent letters to King Louis the Great of Hungary and to King Tvrtko of Bosnia about Marko's prospective marriage *"Filio magnifici viri regis Rassie scismatico."* Jireček, *Geschichte der Serben*, 1:430.

10. Ibid., 1:437.

11. Vukašin's and Uglyeša's bodies were never found. Ibid., 1:437–38.

12. Nikola Banašević, "O postanku i razvoyu Kosovskog i Markova ciklusa" [About the origin and development of the Kossovo and Marko cycles] *Srpski knyiževni glasnik* n.s. 47, no. 8 (April 1936):616.

13. Veliko Iordanov, *Krali-Marko: istoriko-literaturen priegled* [King Marko: A historical literary survey] (Sofiia: Carska Pridvorna Pechatnica, 1916), 4.

14. Tomo Maretić, *Naša narodna epika* [Our epic folk poetry] (Beograd: Nolit, 1966), 175.

15. Nikolai Kravtsov, *Serbskii epos*, 588.

16. Mauro Orbini, *Il Regno degli Slavi* (Pesaro, 1601), 290. See also Jireček, *Geschichte der Serben*, 2:105.

17. Jireček, *Geschichte der Serben*, 2:105.

18. In 1872 Andrei Nikolaevich Popov described A. I. Khludov's mansucript collection in the book, *Opisanie rukopisei i katalog knig tserkovnoi pechati biblioteki A. I. Khludova* [Description of MSS and the Catalogue of books of the Ecclesiastic Printing Office of the A. I. Khludov Library] (Moskva: V. Sinodal'noi tip., 1872).

19. In Khludov manuscript, No. 189. Also Lyubomir Stoyanović, *Stari srpski zapisi i natpisi* [Old Serbian records and inscriptions], 1:58–59, No. 189. In *Zbornik za istoriuy, yezik i knyiževnost srpskoga naroda*, Sec. I, vol. 1 (Beograd: Državna štampariya Kralyevine Srbiye, 1902). Also Jireček, *Geschichte der Serben*, 2:105–6.

20. Stoyanović, *Stari srpski*, 1:58–59, No. 189.

21. Stoyanović, *Stari srpski zapisi i natpisi*, 4:16, no. 6073 (151), 1379.

22. Ibid., 1:48, no. 151, 1379.

23. Jireček, *Geschichte der Serben*, 2:119–22.

24. Maretić, *Naša narodna epika*, 176.

25. The Battle of Rovine: "This conceited and majestical (Emperor Bayazet) decided to war against the Hungaro-Wallachians. So he raised all his forces, and brought them across the Danube River in 6903, and there fought against the great and self-governing Duke John Mircha, where enormous blood was spilt. It was then that there were killed King Marko and Constantine [Deyanović]. Among all those great commanders in this battle was also present Prince Stephen [Lazarević], about whom we write here. All of them did not go there by their own will, but by necessity fought on the side of the Ismaelites [Turks], that is why, it is stated, that the blessed Marko said to Constantine: "This is what I say and pray God to assist the Christians, even if I be the first among dead in this war." After returning home, the Emperor (Bayazet) made peace with them [Christians]." From Constantine the Philosopher, *Život despota Stefana Lazarevića* (Biography of the ruler Stephen Lazarević), translated by Lazar Mirković. In *Stara srpska knyiževnost* [Old Serbian literature], 3 (Novi Sad: Matica srpska, 1970), 203. See also: Jireček, *Geschichte der Serben*, 2:130–31.

26. Vuk Stefanović Karadžić, *Srpske narodne pyesme* [Serbian folk songs] 2nd ed. (Beograd: Prosveta, 1958), in *Notes*, 2:736–37.

27. Banašević, "O postanku i razvoyu Kosovskog i Markova ciklusa" [About the origin

and development of the Kossovo and Marko cycles], *Srpski knyiževni glasnik* n.s. 47, no. 8 (April 1936):614–16.

28. Yovan Tomić, "A. I. Jacimirski: Pesme o Marku Kralyeviću" [A. I. Jacimirski: Songs about Prince Marko], *Srpski knyiževni glasnik* 15, no. 2 (July 1905):155–56.

29. Aleksa Ivić, *Istoriya Srba u Voyvodini* [History of Serbs in Voyvodina] (Beograd: 1929), 210–44 *passim*.

30. The Balkan Slavs called Constantinople by the name of *Carigrad* (Imperial City). Through centuries the Greek-speaking population used simply "City," which in the Greek vernacular was *eis ten polin* ("Behold, the City"), which the Turks accepted after 1453 but pronounced as *Istanbul*, the official Turkish name after 1924.

31. Kostić, "Naynoviyi prilozi," *Srpski knyiževni glasnik* n.s. 48, no. 3 (June 1936):220.

32. Ibid., 272.

33. Jireček, *Geschichte der Serben*, 2:132–33.

34. Radosav Medenica, "Review of Dragutin Kostić: *Marko Barbadigo i naš epski Marko*" [Dragutin Kostić: Marko Barbadigo and our epic Marko] *Prilozi proučavanyu narodne poeziye 5*, No. 2 (Nov. 1938):305.

35. Aleksei Petrovich Storozhenko, *Marko Prokliatyi: poema na Malorossiiskom iazyke iz predanii i povierii Zaporozhskoi stariny* [Marko the Accursed: Poem in the Little Russian language from legends and folk beliefs of Zaporoshian Antiquity] (Odessa: Tipografiia L. Nitche, 1879).

36. Khalanskii, *Iuzhno-slavianskiia*, 738–40.

37. Ibid.

38. Ibid.

39. Jireček, *Geschichte der Serben*, 1:389–91.

40. Maretić, *Naša narodna epika*, 193–95.

41. Voyislav Djurić, *Antologiya narodnih yunačkih pesama* [An anthology of folk heroic songs] (Beograd: Srpska knyiževna zadruga, 1969), 31–33.

42. Jireček, *Geschichte der Serben*, 1:389–91. See also Djurić, *Antologiya*, 31–33.

43. In his book about Prince Lazar Hreblyanović, the historian Ilarion Ruvarac states that all historical sources dating from before the beginning of the second half of the eighteenth century referred to Miloš as Kobilić or Kobilović. It was not until 1754 that Vasiliye Petrović in his *History of Montenegro* used the name "Obilyević" for the first time. In 1765 Pavle Yulinac referred to Miloš as "Obilić," in a book on Serbian history. The two names, Obilyević and Obilić, suggested a person who is abundant with many good things. In Subotić, *Yugoslav Popular Ballads*. 88.

44. Maretić, *Naša narodna epika*, 200–201.

45. Benedikt Kuripešić, *Putopis Kroz Bosnu, Srbiyu, Bugarsku i Rumeliyu 1530.* (Sarayevo: Svyetlost, 1950), 30–37.

46. Jireček, *Geschichte der Serben*, 1:379–84. See also Maretić, *Naša narodna epika*, 205–06.

47. Jireček, *Geschichte der Serben*, 1:379.

48. Ibid., 1:382–84.

49. With respect to the custom of Slavic soldiers wearing wings Khalanskii stated: "The use of wings along with weapons was common in Slavic military life of the sixteenth and seventeenth centuries. South Slavic soldiers carried winged armor, as did the Polish Hussars. Moscovite *zhil'tsy* carried on their backs wings made of eagle's feathers fastened to their shoulders or waists. In one Russian tale soldiers are referred to as "winged." In Khalanskii, *Iuzhno-slavianskiia*, 165.

50. Kravtsov, *Serbskii epos*, 595.

51. Maretić, *Naša narodna epika*, 211–13.
52. Jireček, *Geschichte der Serben*, 2:180–81, 191–92.
53. Maretić, *Naša narodna epika*, 209–10.
54. Ibid., 150–55.
55. Kravtsov, *Serbskii epos*, 606.
56. Marguerite Yourcenar, *Oriental Tales* (New York: Farrar, Straus, Giroux, 1985), 52.
57. South Slavic genealogies originated at the end of the fourteenth century and expanded in the later medieval period of written literature. The most recent among them, *Tronoša Genealogy* (1791), is a combination of history and oral tradition with some literary value. See: Lyubomir Stoyanović, *Stari srpski rodoslovi i letopisi* [The Old Serbian genealogies and annals], 1927. The text of the *Tronoša Genealogy* was published in Yanko Šafarik, *Glasnik Društva srbske slovesnosti*, 5 (1853):17–112.
58. Djurić, *Antologiya narodnih*, in *Notes:765*.
59. Ibid., in *Forword:153*.
60. Svetozar Radoyčić, "O nekim zayedničkim motivima naše narodne pesme i nasheg starog slikarstva" [About some common motifs of our folk song and our old paintings] *Zbornik radova Srpske akademiye nauka*, 36, no. 2 (1953):159–78.
61. Djurić, *Antologiya narodnih*, in *Forword:58*.
62. *Cf.* Vladimir Iakovlevich Propp, *Morphology of the Folktale*, 2nd ed. (Austin: University of Texas Press, 1968), 9.
63. Ibid.
64. Djurić, *Antologiya narodnih*, in *Notes:765*.
65. Vido Latković, "Dragutin Kostić: pesma o vernom sluzi" [Dragutin Kostić: The song about the faithful servant], *Prilozi proučavanyu narodne poeziye* 3, no. 1 (March 1936):137–50.
66. According to Boris Tomashevskii, the definition of a "motif" is as follows: "An epic episode tends to break down into smaller parts which describe particular actions, events and things. Themes of such smaller parts which cannot be further divided are called *motifs. Cf.* Boris Tomashevskii, *Kratkii kurs poetiki* [Short Course on Poetics]: Russian study series, no. 70 (Chicago: Russian Language Specialties, 1969), 82.
67. *Cf.* Boris Tomashevskii, ibid. See also: *Teoriia literatury* (Moskva: Gosudarstvennoe Izdatel'stvo, 1928). (New York: Johnson Reprint Corp., 1967).
68. Johann Wolfgang von Goethe, "Serbische Lieder," *Kunst und Altertum* (Spring 1825).
69. Vuk Stefanović Karadžić, *Narodna srbska pyesnarica* [A book of Serbian folk songs] (Vienna: Pečatna Ioanna Shnirera, 1815), 95.
70. Tomo Maretić, "Kosovski yunaci i dogadjayi u narodnoy epici" [Kossovo heroes and events in the folk epic], *Rad Yugoslovenske akademiye znanosti i umyetnosti*, 97, no. 26 (1889):69–181, esp. 72.
71. Sreten Stoyković, *Kralyević Marko: literarno istraživanye uzroka nyegove slave i popularnosti u srpskom narodu* [Prince Marko: Literary research into the causes of his fame and popularity among the Serbian people] (Beograd: Državna štampariya Kralyevine Srbiye, 1907), 9.
72. Ćorović, "Kralyević Marko," *Srpski knyiževni glasnik* 22, no. 1 (Jan. 1909):44–48.
73. Khalanskii, *Iuzhno-slavianskiia*, 158–59.
74. Leopold von Ranke, *The History of Servia and the Servian Revolution* (London: Henry G. Bohn, 1853), 52.
75. Dragutin Kostić, "Starost narodnog epskog pesništva našeg" [The antiquity of our folk epic poetry], *Yužnoslovenski filolog* 12 (1933):45.

76. Maretić, "Kosovski yunaci," *Rad Yugoslovenske akademiye znanosti i umyetnosti* 97:72.

77. André Vaillant's article in *Revue des cours et conférence* (1932):636.

78. Nikola Banašević, *Ciklus Marka Kralyevića i odyeci francusko-italiyanske viteške knyiževnosti* [The cycle of Prince Marko and echoes of French-Italian chivalric literature] (Skoplye: Skopsko naučno društvo, 1935), 16–18.

79. Ibid., 18–37 *passim.*

80. Kravtsov, *Serbskii epos*, 40–41.

81. Ranke, *The History of Servia*, 52.

82. Leften Stavrianos, *The Balkans since 1453* (New York: Holt, Rinehart & Winston, 1958), 98.

83. Yovan Tomić, *Istoriya u narodnim epskim pesmama o Marku Kralyeviću* [History in epic folk songs about Prince Marko] (Beograd: Državna štampariya Kralyevine Srbiye, 1909), 152–54.

84. Ibid.

85. Maretić, *Naša narodna epika*, 246–48.

86. Karadžić, *Srpske narodne pyesme*, 2, No. 54.

87. Corović, "Kralyević Marko," 21, no. 12 (Dec. 1908):923.

88. Ivan Filipović, *Kralyević Marko u narodnim pesmama* [Prince Marko in folk songs] (Zagreb: St. Kugli, 1925), 9.

89. Mikhail Arnaudov, *Ocherki po Bulgarskiia Folklor* [Essays on Bulgarian folklore] (Sofiia: Drzhavna Pechatnitsa, 1934), 294.

90. Pavle Popović, "Iz naših narodnih pripovedaka" [From our folk tales] *Srpski knyiževni glasnik* 30, no. 9 (May 1913):673–76.

3—INTERPLAY OF LEGEND AND HISTORY IN EPIC SONGS ABOUT PRINCE MARKO

1. Edward Robert Bulwer-Lytton Owen Meredith, *Serbski pesme* [*sic*] : *or, National Songs of Servia* (London: Chapman & Hall, 1861), xxvii.

2. Mikhail Khalanskii, *Iuzhno-slavianskiia skazaniia o Kraleviche Marke* [South Slavic legends about Prince Marko]. (Varshava: Tipografiia Varshavskago Uchebnago Okruga, 1894), 44.

3. Ibid.

4. Ivan Filipović, *Kralyević Marko u narodnim pyesmama* [Prince Marko in folk songs] (Zagreb: S. Kugli, 1925), 21.

5. Svetozar Matić, *Notes and Explanations* in Vuk Karadžić *Srpske narodne pyesme* [Serbian folk songs] (Beograd: Prosveta, 1958), 2, 662–63.

6. Ibid.

7. David Halyburton Low, *The Ballads of Marko Kralyević* (Cambridge: Cambridge University Press, 1922. Reprint. New York: Greenwood Press, 1968). Whenever songs from the Vuk Karadžić collection are quoted in English they are given in Low's translation if available. Unless otherwise stated, the remainder are my own translation.

8. Whenever a poem is cited here, it will be identified by the name of the collection and the number in the collection. If the latter is not available, then the page is given.

9. Khalanskii, *Iuzhno-slavianskiia*, 6–13. Cf. D. Čiževskiy, *History of Russian Literature from the Eleventh Century to the End of Baroque* (The Hague: Mouton, 1960), 236.

10. The name of Beuves de Haumtone appears in various forms. In English it is Sir Beves of Hamtoun, in Italian Buovo d'Antona (or Antino).

11. Khalanskii, *Iuzhno-slavianskiia*, 19.

12. Vuk Stefanović Karadžić, *Srpske narodne pyesme*, 2, No. 33.

13. Cecil Bowra, *Heroic Poetry* (London: Macmillan, 1952), 399.

14. Svetozar Matić, *Notes and Explanations*, in V. S. Karadžić, *Srpske narodne pyesme*, 2, 647–48. See also Dragolyub Pavlović, *Iz naše knyiževnosti feudalnog doba* [From our literature of feudal period] (Beograd: Prosveta, 1968), 223–25.

15. Ibid. See also Stoyan Novaković, *Archiv fuer Slavische Philologie*, XI, 1888.

16. Veliko Iordanov, *Krali-Marko v bulgarskata narodna epika* [King Marko in Bulgarian folk epic] (Sofiia: Sbornik na Bulgarskoto Knizhovno Druzhestvo, 1901). *Cf.* Ivan Burin, *Bulgarsko narodno tvorchestvo* [Bulgarian Folklore], 12 vols. (Sofiia: Bulgarski pisatel, 1961), 1:116–22.

17. Veliko Iordanov, *Krali-Marko: istoriko-literaturen priegled* [King-Marko: A historical literary survey] (Sofiia: Tsarsko Pridvorna Pechatnitsa, 1916), 19–21.

18. Ibid., 23.

19. The South Slavic tribes found the Balkan Peninsula rich in remnants of the ancient Greek oral tradition, one which related to the *gigantes*, or South Slavic *gigovi*. Byzantine sources supplemented information concerning giants, or *djidovi* (as they came to be known among the South Slavs), who were poetically presented as the first inhabitants of the Earth. The motif spread over from the Balkans to Romania and the Ukraine during the sixteenth and seventeenth centuries. Khalanskii, *Iuzhno-slavianskiia*, 251–60.

20. Lazar Nikolić, *Srpske narodne pesme u Sremu* [Serbian folk songs in Srem], Marko Kralyević in eight folk songs, No. 5. In Khalanskii, *Iuzhno-slavianskiia*, 239–40.

21. Khalanskii, *Iuzhno-slavianskiia*, 243–44.

22. Sreten Stoyković, *Kralyević Marko* (Beograd: Državna štampariya Kralyevine Srbiye, 1907), 61.

23. "Ancient books" (*knyige starostavne*) referred to the old documents relating to law and public matters. Epic poets believed that such books were sacred and known only to the few chosen ones, since they served to protect the justice of God and Man. The Archpriest Nedelyko, who according to traditional belief gave the dying Emperor Dušan his last sacraments, was thought to have been the keeper of the "ancient books." *Cf.* Miodrag Lalević, "Veze izmedju usmene i pismene knyiževnosti: pisanye krvlyu i zlatom" [Connections between oral and written literature: Writing in blood and gold] *Prilozi proučavanyu narodne poeziye* 1, no. 1 (March 1934):76–77.

D. H. Low reported that Professor Pavle Popović informed him that "the ancient books" are supposed "to mean the old Serbian biographies (Sava, Domentiyan, Danilo and others). As these books deal chiefly with the Nemanya dynasty and do not admit any rival claim to the throne, Marko, as a loyal subject, gives no heed to the demand of his father and uncles, but declares in favor of Uroš, the last of the Nemanyićes." In Low, *The Ballads*, 13–14.

24. According to Kostić, the legend of the custom of throwing the crown into the air to determine the ruler, was most probably imported from Hungary where kings were thus elected. This legend also finds its way into Bogišić's songs Nos. 17 and 31. Kostić, "Naynoviyi prilozi" *Srpski knyiževni glasnik* n.s. 47, no. 4 (February 1936):264–65.

25. Nikola Banašević, *Ciklus Marka Kralyevića i odyeci francusko-italiyanske viteške knyiževnosti* [The cycle of Prince Marko and echoes of French-Italian chivalric literature] (Skoplye: Skopsko naučno društvo, 1935), 25–33.

26. Constantin Jireček, *Geschichte der Serben*, 1:440.

27. Karadžić, *Srpske narodne pyesme*, 2, No. 56, 334.

28. George Rapall Noyes, *Heroic Ballads of Servia* (Boston: Sherman, French, 1913), 115.

29. Kostić describes a numismatic discovery, a coin which carries the inscription *blagovyerne kralyi [ce] Evro [sime]* ("of the faithful que [en] Evro [sima]"), the Queen's name worn to the point of being undistinguishable. In Dragutin Kostić, "Naynoviyi prilozi proučavanyu narodne poeziye" [The latest contributions to research in folk poetry] *Srpski knyiževni glasnik* n.s. 48, no. 3 (June 1936):223.

30. Tomo Maretić, *Naša narodna epika* [Our epic folk poetry] (Beograd: Nolit, 1966), 177.

31. The *Slava* feast is a Serbian custom and the major annual religious and social celebration in honor of the family's patron saint.

32. Low, No. 11.

33. Jireček, *Geschichte der Serben*, 1:430.

34. Maretić, *Naša narodna epika*, 230.

35. The motif relates to a story in Russian polemic literary sources against the Roman Catholics. The story deals with a pope who is deceived by a woman he wanted and who entraps him into shaving off his beard. Realizing that he had been deceived and worried over his public image, the pope orders all bishops to shave, and justifies the order by pointing out that angels never have beards. In Khalanskii, *Iuzhno-slavianskiia*, 466–67.

36. Mauro Orbini, *Il Regno degli Slavi* (Pesaro, 1601), 290. See also Jireček, *Geschichte der Serben*, 2:105–06.

37. Ibid., 1:430.

38. D. H. Low, *The Ballads of Marko Kralyević*, xxix.

39. Marguerite Yourcenar, *Postcript* to *Oriental Tales* (New York: Farrar, Straus, Giroux, 1985), 145.

40. Ibid., 27.

41. Ibid., 29.

42. Ibid., 30.

43. Ibid., 31.

44. Ibid., 31–32.

45. Ibid., 33.

46. Ibid.

47. Khalanskii, *Iuzhno-slavianskiia*, 469–70.

48. Ibid., 251.

49. Ibid., 250.

50. Karadžić, *Srpske narodne pyesme*, 3, No. 25.

51. Felix Liebrecht, *Zur Volkskunde* (Heilbronn, 1879), S. 161, 167. 186. In Radosav Medenica, "Muž na svadbi svoye žene" [The husband at the wedding of his wife] *Prilozi proučavanyu narodne poeziye* 1, no. 1 (March 1934):59.

52. Karadžić, *Srpske narodne pyesme*, 3:123.

53. Jireček, *Geschichte der Serben*, 2:105–6.

54. Rikardo Ferdin, *Hrvatske narodne pyesme i pripovedke*, p. 89, in Khalanskii, *Iuzhno-slavianskiia*, 620.

55. Khalanskii, *Iuzhno-slavianskiia*, 620–23.

56. About the abduction of Prince Marko's wife see ibid., 614–23; about Prince Marko at his wife's wedding see ibid., 636–42.

57. N. F. Sumtsov, "Muzh na svad'be svoei zheny" [Husband at the wedding of his wife]

Etnograficheskoe obozrenie (Moscow):19, No. 4 (1893):21, in Khalanskii, *Iuzhno-slavian-skiia*, 641.

58. Banašević, *Ciklus Marka Kralyevića*, 114–16.

59. Karadžić, *Srpske narodne pyesme*, 2, No. 78.

60. Stoyan Novaković, *Monumenta Serbica* (1858):441, in *Glas* 22 (1890). See also Jireček, *Geschichte der Serben*, 2:197.

61. Ibid.

62. Karadžić, *Srpske narodne pyesme*, 2, No. 97.

63. Liebrecht, *Zur Volkskunde*, 193.

64. Maretić, *Naša narodna epika*, 252.

65. Voyislav Djurić, *Antologiya narodnih yunačkih pesama* [An anthology of folk heroic songs] (Beograd: Srpska knyiževna zadruga, 1969), in *Notes*:691–92.

66. The Poreč Charter from 1370 was published by Lyubomir Stoyanović, *Stare srpske povelye i pisma* [Ancient Serbian charters and letters], 1, pt. 1 *Dubrovnik i susedi nyegovi* [Dubrovnik and its neighbors]:116, No. 122. It is also published by Franz Miklošić in the *Monumenta Serbica* (1858):179–81. See also Jireček, *Geschichte der Serben*, 1:430. Also Maretić, *Naša narodna epika* [Our epic folk poetry]:177.

67. Stoyanović, *Stari srpski zapisi i natpisi* [Old Serbian records and inscriptions], 1:53–54, Nos. 165 and 166. In *Zbornik za istoriyu, yezik i knyiževnost srpskoga naroda*, Sec. I, vol. 1 (Beograd: Državna štampariya Kralyevine Srbiye, 1902). Also Vl. R. Petković, *Starine*:26 in Kostić, "Naynoviyi prilozi," *Srpski knyiževni glasnik* n.s. 47, no. 5 (March 1936):371.

68. When King Marko's brothers Andriya and Dimitar were settling the estate of King Marko *"Dymitras filius quondam regis Vochassini"* in a Dubrovnik court in 1399, he had to prove *". . . quod ipse Marchus non dimisit heredes legitimos,"* in Jireček, *Geschichte der Serben*, 2:106.

69. Khalanskii, *Iuzhno-slavianskiia*, 562–65.

70. Banašević, *Ciklus Marka Kralyevića*, 136–38.

71. Milovan Gavazzi, "Dva motiva iz narodne poeziye Gradišćanskih Hrvata" [Two motifs from the popular poetry of the Burgenland Croats] in *Zbornik radova* [Collection of works] (Zagreb: Filološki Fakultet, 1951), 1:189–90.

72. Petar Hektorović, *Ribanye i ribarsko prigovaranye* [Fishing and fishermen's conversations] (Venice, 1568) (photographic edition. Zagreb, 1953). See also Maretić, *Naša narodna epika*, 28–29.

73. Svetozar Kolyević, *Notes* in *Marko the Prince: Serbo-Croat heroic songs* (New York: St. Martin's Press, 1984), 31.

74. Ibid.

75. Stoyković, *Kralyević Marko*, 36–37.

76. Olinko Delorko, *Narodne epske pyesme* [Epic folk songs] (Zagreb: Matica Hrvatska, 1964), 1, Song No. 3; also in *Notes* 1:211.

77. Stephen and Dimitar Yakšić were sons of the Serbian Lord Djuradj Yakšić who emigrated later to Hungary. Stephen's daughter Anna was married to the Lithuanian Prince Glinskii. Their daughter Yelena was married to the Russian Grand Duke Basil III Ivanovich (1505–1533). Their son was Ivan IV Vassilyevich, the first Czar of Russia (1533–1584), Ivan the Terrible. In other words, Stephen Yakšić, whose life in the epic poetry was saved by Prince Marko, was the great grandfather of the first Emperor of Russia. In Jireček, *Geschichte der Serben*, 2:243.

78. Karadžić, *Srpske narodne pyesme*, 2, No. 41.

79. Jireček, *Geschichte der Serben*, 2:105–6.

80. Lyubomir Stoyanović, *Stari srpski zapisi i natpisi*, No. 189. Also Kostić, "Naynoviyi prilozi" *Srpski knyiževni glasnik* n.s. 48, no. 3 (June 1936):221–22.

81. Khludov manuscript, No. 189. (Moskva: V. Sinodal'noi tip. 1872). See also: Stoyanović, Ibid.

82. Ibid.

83. Ibid. See also: Yireček, *Geschichte der Serben*, 2:105.

84. Four okas = two gallons = ca. nine liters.

85. Cecil Bowra, *Heroic Poetry*, 198.

86. Ibid., 199.

87. The epic Philip the Hungarian was a historical person. He was Filippo Scolari called Pippo Spano (1369–1426), an Italian condottiere (a leader of mercenaries) who became Duke of Temešvar. See Maretić, *Naša narodna epika*, pp. 164–66.

88. Bowra, *Heroic Poetry*, 198.

89. Ibid., 115.

90. Kostić, "Naynoviyi prilozi" *Srpski knyiževni glasnik*, n.s. 47, no. 4 (Feb. 1936):280.

91. The anonymous chronicle from the twelfth century outlines the legendary story of Charlemagne, and it is assumed to have been composed as a part of the manuscript *Codex Calixtinus*. Printed editions include Ferdinand Castets, *Turpini Historia Karoli Magni et Rotholandi* (Montpellier, 1880); Ward Thoron, *Turpin's Chronicle* (Boston: the Merrymount Press, 1934); *Vita Karoli Magni*, ed. Gerhard Rauschen, in "Die Legende Karls des Grossen" (Leipzig, 1890), pp. 66–74. See also *The Pseudo-Turpin*, edited from Bibliothèque Nationale, by H. M. Smyser (Cambridge: Medieval Academy of America, 1937).

92. Banašević, *Ciklus Marka Kralyevića*, 48–53.

93. Krsto Lyumović, "Naynoviye prouchavanye ciklusa Kralyevića Marka" [The latest research of the Prince Marko cycle] *Glasnik yugoslovenskog profesorskog društva* 17 (1936/37):129.

94. According to Vuk Stefanović Karadžić there is some historical basis for this song. A prohibition to serve wine in cities was issued in 1671 in Turkey by Sultan Mohammad IV (1648–1687). This order was intended to stem demoralization of Turkish administration and increase public order in the seventeenth century. It is mentioned in the song that Prince Marko wears "green apparel," the color which had been forbidden for Christians. In Vuk Karadžić, *Notes and Explanations, Srpske narodne pyesme*, 2:745–46.

95. Kostić, "Naynoviyi prilozi" *Srpski knyiževni glasnik* n.s. 47, no. 5 (March 1936):359.

96. The songs in the Erlangen Manuscript are not titled. They are identified only by the sequence number of each song.

97. Gerhard Gesemann, *Erlangenski rukopis starih srpsko-hrvatskih narodnih pesama* [Erlangen Manuscript of old Serbo-Croatian folk songs] (Sremski Karlovci: Srpska manastirska štampariya, 1925), 159–60.

98. Auguste Dozon, *Poésies populaires serbes* (Paris: E. Dentu, 1859), 16.

99. Cecil Bowra, *Heroic Poetry*, 115.

100. Ibid., 114.

101. Low, *The Ballads of Marko Kralyević*, No. 24.

102. Banašević, *Ciklus Marka Kralyevića*, 54–55.

103. Khalanskii, *Iuzhno-slavianskiia*, 277.

104. Ibid., 210, 362.

105. Ibid., Maretić also accepted Khalanskii's opinion. See *Rad Yugoslovenske akademiye znanosti i umyetnosti*, 132:12–20.

106. Banašević, *Ciklus Marka Kralyevića*, 59.

107. Low and others frequently use the term "Moor" for "Arab" in the translations of the South Slavic epic songs. In this study both terms are used interchangeably.

108. Khalanskii, *Iuzhno-slavianskiia*, 275.

109. Banašević, *Ciklus Marka Kralyevića*, 62–63.

110. Bowra, *Heroic Poetry*, 132.

111. Karadžić, *Srpske narodne pyesme*, 2, No. 64.

112. Banašević, *Ciklus Marka Kralyevića*, 67.

113. Kostić, "Naynoviyi prilozi," *Srpski knyiževni glasnik* n.s. 48, no. 3 (June 1936):220.

114. Banašević, *Ciklus Marka Kralyevića*, 70–71.

115. Basilius Digenis Akritas was a Byzantine national hero who probably lived in the tenth century. The original Digenis epic is lost, but four poems are extant. The poem has been compared with the *Chanson de Roland* and the *Romance of the Cid*. *Cf.* the *Encyclopedia Britannica*, vol. 8, 11th ed. (Cambridge: University Press, 1910), 262.

116. Khalanskii, *Iuzhno-slavianskiia*, 447–52.

117. Kostić, "Naynoviyi prilozi," *Srpski knyiževni glasnik* n.s. 48, no. 3 (June 1936):220.

118. Kolyević, *The Epic in the Making*, 192.

119. Karadžić, *Srpske narodne pyesme*, 2, No. 66.

120. Yovan Tomić, *Istoriya u narodnim epskim pesmama o Marku Kralyeviću* [History in epic folk songs about Prince Marko] (Beograd: Državna štampariya Kralyevine Srbiye, 1909), 18.

121. Ibid., *cf.*, 146–77.

122. Ibid., 116–17.

123. Ibid., 98–99.

124. Banašević, *Ciklus Marka Kralyevića*, 94.

125. Ibid.

126. Ibid., 95.

127. Ibid.

128. Ibid., 94–100.

129. Ibid., 88–91.

130. Ibid., 102–3.

131. "People believe that dragons make clouds and hailstorms to destroy the crops. Consequently, when a dragon is buried in that place, there will be no wine or wheat, since the dead dragon may attract the hailstorm. It is evident that the feature which is discussed here was first narrated in the legends of St. George." In Maretić, *Naša narodna epika*, 249.

132. Tomić, *Istoriya u narodnim epskim pesmama*, 171–73.

133. Karadžić, *Srpske narodne pyesme*, 6, No. 59.

134. Dušan Maryanović, "Problem Djerzelez Aliye" [The issue of Djerzelez Aliya] *Prilozi proučavanyu narodne poeziye* 3, no. 1 (March 1936):92–101.

135. Vido Latković, "Dve studiye g. Olesnickog o ličnosti Djerzelez Aliye" [Two studies by Olesnicki about Aliya Djerzelez's personality] *Prilozi proučavanyu narodne poeziye* 2, no. 1 (March 1935):126.

136. Ibid., 124–25.

137. Ibid., 125–26.

138. Ivo Andrić, "Put Aliye Djerzeleza" [A journey of Aliya Djerzelez] *Pripovetke* [Short stories] (Novi Sad: Matica srpska, 1971), 28–29.

139. The song "Marko Kralyević and Djerzelez Aliya" was written down by Nikola Voynović, on July 24, 1934, in Novi Pazar in Serbia. *Cf.* Milman Parry and Albert Lord, *Serbocroatian Heroic Songs* (Cambridge: Harvard University Press, 1954) 1:198–201, 394–95.

140. Ibid., 1:201.

141. Marguerite Yourcenar, *Oriental Tales* (New York: Farrar, Straus, Giroux, 1985), 25.

142. Constantine the Philosopher, *Život despota Stefana Lazarevića* [Biography of ruler

Stephen Lazarevič]. In *Stara srpska knyiževnost* [Old Serbian literature], vol. 3 (Novi Sad: Matica srpska, 1970), 203.

143. Tomo Maretič, *Naša narodna epika* [Our epic folk poetry] (Beograd: Nolit, 1966), 180.

144. Mikhail Khalanskii, *Iuzhno-slavianskiia pesni o smerti Marka Kralevica* [South Slavic songs about the death of Prince Marko] (Sanktpeterburg: Tipografiia Imperatorskoi Akademii Nauk, 1904), 28.

145. Ibid., 29–32.

146. Vuk Stefanovič Karadžič, *O srpskoy narodnoy poeziyi* [On Serbian folk poetry] (Beograd: Prosveta, 1964), 48.

147. For a more detailed information see: Khalanskii, *Iuzhno-slavianskiia pesni*, 3–8; Khalanskii, *Iuzhno-slavianskiia skazaniia*, 558–59, 564; Storozhenko, *Marko Prokliatyi*, [Marko the Accursed] (Odessa: Tipografiia L. Nitche, 1879), 28, 47–49.

148. Nikolai Kravtsov, *Serbskii epos* [Serbian epic] (Moskva: Academia, 1933), 79.

149. *Cf.* Joseph Bédier, *Les légendes épiques* (Paris: 1912), 3:290, 374–85.

150. Vladimir Corovič, "Kraylevič Marko u srpskim narodnim pripoviyetkama" [Prince Marko in Serbian folk tales] *Srpski knyiževni glasnik* 22, no. 2 (Jan. 1909):120.

151. Khalanskii, *Iuzhno-slavianskiia pesni*, 32–36.

152. *Sbornik za narodno umotvorenia* [Anthology of folk lore] 14, 90–92. In Veliko Iordanov, *Krali Marko: Istoriko-literaturen priegled* [King-Marko: A historical literary survey] (Sofiia: Tsarsko Pridvorna Pechatnitsa, 1916), 43–44.

153. Ibid.

154. Khalanskii, *Iuzhno-slavianskiia pesni*, 14–15.

155. Tihomir Ostoyič, *Kralyevič Marko u narodnim pesmama* [Prince Marko in folk songs] (Novi Sad: 1904), 3:50.

156. Vuk Vrčevič, *Srpske narodne pripoviyetke, ponayviše kratke i šalyive* [Serbian folk tales, mostly short and humorous] (Biograd: 1868), 106.

157. Brothers Miladinov, *Bulgarski narodni piesni* [Bulgarian folk songs] (Sofiia: *Durzhavna Pechatnitsa*, 1942), 528–29.

158. Corovič, *"Kralyevič Marko u srpskim,"* 22, no. 2 (January 1909):120.

CONCLUSION

1. Ana Adamec, *Ivan Meštrovič, 1883–1962* (Beograd: Galeriya srpske akademiye nauka i umetnosti, n.d.), 50.

2. Ibid., 15.

3. Ibid., 17–18.

4. Ibid., 50–51.

5. Marguerite Yourcenar, *Postcript* in *Oriental Tales* (New York: Farrar, Straus, Giroux, 1985), 146–47.

6. Ibid., 26.

7. Ibid.

8. Ibid., 31.

9. Ibid., 26.

Select Bibliography

COLLECTIONS CONSULTED

Bogišić, Valtazar. *Narodne pyesme iz stariyih, nayviše primorskih zapisa* [Folk songs from ancient, mostly coastal manuscripts]. Vol. 1. Biograd: Državna štampariya, 1878.

Djurić, Voyislav. *Antologiya narodnih yunačkih pesama* [An anthology of folk heroic songs]. Beograd: Srpska knyiževna zadruga, 1969.

Dozon, Auguste. *Poésies populaires serbes*. Paris: E. Dentu, 1859.

Filipović, Ivan, ed. *Kralyević Marko u narodnim pyesmama* [Prince Marko in folk songs]. Zagreb: S. Kugli, 1925.

Gezeman, Gerhard. *Erlangenski rukopis starih srpskohrvatskih narodnih pesama* [Erlangen MS of old Serbo-Croatian folk songs]. Sremski Karlovci: Srpska manastirska štampariya, 1925.

Hektorović, Petar. *Ribanye i ribarsko prigovaranye* [Fishing and fisherman's talk]. Venice, 1568. *Pet stolyeća hrvatske knyiževnosti*, Vol. 7. Zagreb: Matica Hrvatska, 1968.

Karadžić, Vuk Stefanović. *Mala prostonarodna slaveno-serbska pyesnarica* [A little book of Slavo-Serbian folk songs]. Vienna: Pečatna Ioanna Šnirera, 1814.

———. *Narodna srbska pyesnarica* [A book of Serbian folk songs]. Vienna: Pečatna Ioanna Šnirera, 1815.

———. *Narodne srpske pyesme* [Popular Serbian songs]. Vols. 2–3, Leipzig: 1823; vol. 1, Leipzig: 1824; vol. 4, Vienna: 1833.

———. *Srpske narodne pyesme* [Serbian folk songs]. 4 vols. Vienna: Štampariya Yermenskog Manastira, 1841, 1845, 1846, 1862.

———. *Srpske narodne pyesme* [Serbian folk songs]. 9 vols. 'State Edition.' Beograd: Štampariya Kralyevine Srbiye, 1891–1901.

Laktinski, Blagoya. *Pesni za Krale Marko* [Songs about King Marko]. Skopye: Misla, 1968.

Low, David Halyburton. *The Ballads of Marko Kralyević*. Cambridge: Cambridge University Press, 1922. Reprint. New York: Greenwood Press, 1968.

Marko the Prince: Serbo-Croat Heroic Songs. Transl. from Serbo-Croatian by Anne Pennington and Peter Levi. New York: St. Martin's Press, 1984.

Matica Hrvatska. *Hrvatske narodne pyesme* [Croatian folk songs]. 10 vols. Zagreb: The Matica, 1896–1942.
Miladinov, Dimitur. *Bulgarski narodni piesni* [Bulgarian folk songs]. Sofiia: Durzhavna pechatnitsa, 1942.
Milutinović, Sima (pseudonym Čubra Čoykovič). *Pyevaniya cernogorska i hercegovačka* [Songs of the Montenegrins and Hercegovinians]. Budim: Kral. Sveučilište Ungarsko Pečatnia, 1835.
Noyes, George Rapall. *Heroic Ballads of Servia*. Boston: Sherman, French, 1913.
Parry, Milman, comp. *Serbocroatian Heroic Songs*. Edited and translated from Serbo-Croatian by Albert Bates Lord. 2 vols. Cambridge: Harvard University Press, 1953–54.
Petranović, Bogolyub. *Srpske narodne pyesme iz Bosne i Hercegovine* [Serbian folk songs from Bosnia and Hercegovina]. Beograd: n.p., 1867.
Slovenska Matica. *Slovenske narodne pesmi* [Slovenian folk songs]. Vol. 1. Lyublyana: Tiskanica Rudolfa Miliča, 1895–98.

BOOKS AND DISSERTATIONS

Angelov, Bozhan. *Trem' na bulgarskata narodna istoricheska epika: ot Momchila i Krali Marka do Karadzhata i Khadzhi Dimitra* [Introduction to Bulgarian historical folk epic: From Momchil and Krali Marko to Karadzhata and Khadzi Dimitra]. Sofiia: Chipev, 1939.
Arnaudov, Mikhail. *Baladni motivi v narodnata poeziia* [Ballad motifs in folk poetry]. Sofiia: Bulgarskata Akademiia na Naukite, 1964.
Banašević, Nikola. *Ciklus Marka Kralyeviča i odyeci francusko-italiyanske viteške knyiževnosti* [The cycle of Prince Marko and echoes of French-Italian chivalric literature]. Skopye: Skopsko naučno društvo, 1935.
Bowra, Cecil Maurice. *Heroic Poetry*. London: Macmillan, 1952.
Brault, Gerard J. *La Chanson de Roland*. University Park, Pa.: Pennsylvania State University Press, 1984.
Braun, Maximilian. *Das Serbokroatische Heldenlied*. Goettingen: Vandenhoeck & Ruprecht, 1961.
Broudy, Saul Frederick. "The Effect of Performer-Audience Interaction on Performance Strategies." Ph.D. diss., University of Pennsylvania, 1982.
Burkhart, Dagmar. *Untersuchungen zur Stratigraphie und Chronologie des Suedslavischen Volksepik*. Muenchen: Verlag Otto Sagner, 1968.
Chadwick, Munro H., and Chadwick, Kershaw N. *The Growth of Literature*. Vol. 2, *The Heroic Age*. Cambridge: The University Press, 1912.
Clawsey, Mary Crawford. "The Comitatus and the Lord-Vassal Relationship in the Medieval Epic." Ph.D. diss., University of Maryland, 1982.
Coote, Mary Putney. "The Singer's Use of Theme in Composing Oral Narrative Song in the Serbo-Croatian Tradition." Ph.D. diss., Harvard University, 1969.

Djordjević, Tihomir R. *Beleške o našoy narodnoy poeziyi* [Notes on our folk poetry]. Beograd: Državna štampariya, 1939.

Dundes, Alan, ed. *The Study of Folklore*. Englewood Cliffs, N.J.: Prentice-Hall, 1965.

Foley, John Miles, ed. *Oral Traditional Literature: A Festschrift For Albert Bates Lord*. Columbus, Ohio: Slavica Publishers, 1981.

Gal'kovskii, N. M. *Serbskii epos* [Serbian epic]. Moskva: Izdanie M.I.S. Sabashnikovykh, 1916.

Gibbon, Edward. *The History of Decline and Fall of the Roman Empire*. 5 vols. Philadelphia: Porter & Coates, 1845.

Golenishchev-Kutuzov, I. N. *Epos serbskogo naroda* [Epics of Serbian people]. Moskva: Akademiia Nauk SSSR, 1963.

Groeber, Karl, trans. *Der Koenigssohn Marko (Kralyević Marko) im Serbischen Volksgesang*. Wien: A. Hoelder, 1883.

Iordanov, Veliko. *Krali-Marko: istoriko-literaturen priegled* [King Marko: A historical literary survey]. Sofiia: Tsarska Pridvorna Pechatnitsa, 1916.

Jireček, Contantin. *Geschichte der Serben*. 2 vols. Gotha: F. A. Perthes, 1911–18.

Khalanskii, Mikhail. *Iuzhno-slavianskiia pesni o smerti Marka Kralevicha* [South Slavic songs about the death of Prince Marko]. Sanktpeterburg: Tipografiia Imperatorskoi Akademii Nauk, 1904.

————. *Iuzhno-slavianskiia skazaniia o Kraleviche Marke* [South Slavic legends about Prince Marko]. Varshava: Tipografiia Varshavskago Uchebnago Okruga, 1894.

Kilibarda, Novak. *Poeziya i istoriya u narodnoy knyiževnosti* [Poetry and history in folk literature]. Beograd: Slovo Lyubve, 1972.

Knežević, Milivoye V., ed. *Naša narodna poeziya* [Our folk poetry]. Subotica: Gradska štampariya, 1928.

Kolyević, Svetozar. *The Epic in Making*. Oxford: Clarendon Press, 1980.

Kravtsov, Nikolai. *Serbskii epos* [Serbian epic]. Moskva: Academia, 1933.

Latković, Vido. *Narodna knyiževnost* [Folk literature]. Beograd: Naučna knyiga, 1967.

Léger, Louis. *Le cycle épique de Marko Kralievitch*. Paris: E. Leroux, 1906.

Lockwood, Yvonne Rachel. "The Burgenland Croats: Oral Tradition and Historical Process." Ph.D. diss., University of Michigan, 1979.

Lord, Albert Bates. *The Singer of Tales*. Cambridge: Harvard University Press, 1960.

Lytton, Edward Robert Bulwer-Lytton [Owen Meredith]. *Serbski Pesme: or, National Songs of Servia*. London: Chapman & Hall, 1861.

Maretić, Tomo. *Naša narodna epika* [Our folk epic]. Beograd: Nolit, 1966.

Matić, Svetozar. *Naš narodni ep i naš stih: ogledi i studiye* [Our folk epic and our verse: Essays and studies]. Novi Sad: Matica srpska, 1964.

Miklošić, Franz. *Monumenta Serbica*. Wien: Wilhelm Braumueller, 1858. Reprint. Graz: Akademische Druck, 1964.

Misirkov, Krste P. *Iuzhno-slovianskiia epicheskiia skazaniia o zhenitbie Korolia Volkashina v' sviazi s' voprosom' o prichinakh' populiarnosti Korolia Marka sredi Iuzhnikh' Slovian'*. Odessa: Ekonomicheskaia Tipografiia, 1909.

Nedić, Vladan. *Narodna knyiževnost* [Folk literature]. Beograd: Nolit, 1972.

Orbini, Mauro. *Il Regno degli Slavi* (Pesaro, 1601) MS, Houghton Library, Harvard University, Cambridge, Mass.

————. *Kralyevstvo Slovena* [The kingdom of Slavs]. Transl. from Italian by Zdravko Šundrica. Beograd: Srpska knyiževna zadruga, 1968.

Ostojić, Tihomir. *Kralyević Marko u narodnim pesmama* [Prince Marko in folk songs]. Vol. 3. Novi Sad: n.p., 1901.

Petrović, Woislav M. *Hero Tales and Legends of the Serbians.* London: Harrap & Co., 1914.

Propp, Vladimir IAkovlevich. *Morphology of the Folktale.* 2d ed. Austin: University of Texas Press, 1968.

Ranke, Leopold von. *The History of Servia and the Servian Revolution.* London: Henry G. Bohn, 1853.

Stavrianos, Leften S. *The Balkans Since 1453.* New York: Holt, Rinehart & Winston, 1958.

Steinmetz, Devora. "From Father to Son: Kinship and Succession in Ancient and Medieval Literature." Ph.D. diss., Columbia University, 1984.

Storozhenko, Aleksei Petrovich. *Marko Prokliatyi: poema na Malorossiiskom iazyke iz predanii i povierii Zaporozhskoi stariny* [Marko the Accursed: Poem in the Little Russian (Ukrainian) language from legends and folk beliefs of Zaporozhian Antiquity]. Odessa: Tipografiia L. Nitche, 1879.

Stoyković, Sreten Y. *Kralyević Marko: literarno istraživanye uzroka nyegove slave i popularnosti u srpskom narodu* [Prince Marko: Literary research into the causes of his fame and popularity among the Serbian people]. Beograd: Državna štampariya Kralyevine Srbiye, 1907.

Subotić, Dragutin. *Yugoslav Popular Ballads: Their Origin and Development.* Cambridge: University Press, 1932.

Temperley, Harold William Vazeille. *History of Serbia.* New York: Howard Fertig, 1969.

Thompson, Stith. *Motif-Index of Folk Literature.* 6 vols. Bloomington: Indiana University Press, 1955–58.

Tomić, Yovan N. *Istoriya u narodnim epskim pesmama o Marku Kralyeviću* [History in epic folk songs about Prince Marko]. Beograd: Državna štampariya Kralyevine Srbiye, 1909.

Trayković, Nikola. *Legende o Kralyeviću Marku* [Legends about Prince Marko]. Beograd: Narodna knyiga, 1967.

Vogl, Johann Nepomuk. *Marko Kralyevits: Serbische Heldensage.* Wien: J. P. Sossinger's Witwe, 1851.

Zhirmunskii, Viktor. *Vergleichende Epenforschung.* Berlin: Akademie Verlag, 1961.

Žuković, Lyubomir. *Narodni ep o Marku Kralyeviću* [Folk epic about Prince Marko]. Beograd: Zavod za udžbenike i nastavna sredstva, 1985.

ARTICLES

Banašević, Nikola. "O postanku i razvoyu Kosovskog i Markova ciklusa" [About the origin and development of the Kossovo and Marko Cycles]. *Srpski knyiževni glasnik*, n.s. 47, no. 7 (Apr. 1936):523–34; no. 8 (Apr. 1936):611–22.

———. "O važnosti proučavanya motiva narodne poeziye" [On the importance of researching folk poetry motifs]. *Prilozi proučavanyu narodne poeziye* 2, no. 2 (Nov. 1935):169–73.

Ćorović, Vladimir. "Kralyević Marko u srpskim narodnim pripoviyetkama" [Prince Marko in Serbian folktales]. *Srpski knyiževni glasnik* 21, no. 9 (1908):678–85; no. 10 (1908):768–75; no. 11 (1908):844–50; no. 12 (1908):921–28; 22, no. 1 (Jan. 1909):43–50; no. 2 (Jan. 1909):119–24.

Djordjević, Tihomir. "Beleške iz naše narodne poeziye" [Notes from our folk poetry]. *Prilozi proučavanyu narodne poeziye* 2, no. 2 (Nov. 1935):206–16; 4, no. 2 (Nov. 1937):211–16; 5, no. 2 (Nov. 1938):193–98.

Ilijć, Dragutin. "O uzroku opadanya narodne poeziye" [On the cause of the decline of folk poetry]. *Letopis matice srpske* 136, no. 4 (1883):1–22.

Knežević, Milivoye V. "O naystariyoy slovenskoy narodnoy pesmi" [On the oldest Slavic folk song]. *Prilozi proučavanyu narodne poeziye* 6, no. 2 (Nov. 1939):268–69.

Komnenić, Petar. "Iz slovenačke narodne poeziye. Pripovetke, (epske) pesme: Kralyević Marko i nyegova ličnost u tim pesmama" [From Slovenian folk poetry. Tales, (epic) songs: Prince Marko and his personality in these songs]. *Glasnik yugoslovenskog profesorskog društva* 19 (1938):598–604.

Kostić, Dragutin. "Ko ye Marku pevao kroz Miroč" [Who did sing to Marko across the Miroč mountain]. *Prilozi proučavanyu narodne poeziye* 4, no. 2 (Nov. 1937):255–61.

———. "Naynoviyi prilozi proučavanyu narodne poeziye" [The latest contributions to research in folk poetry]. *Srpski knyiževni glasnik*, n.s., 47, no. 4 (Feb. 1936):264–280; no. 5 (March 1936):356–75; n.s. 48, no. 3 (June 1936):211–23.

———. "Nekoliko beležaka o narodnoy tradiciyi" [A few notes on folk tradition]. *Prilozi proučavanyu narodne poeziye* 2, no. 2 (Nov. 1935):156–68.

———. "Noviyi prilozi proučavanyu narodne poeziye" [Recent contributions to the research in folk poetry]. *Srpski knyiževni glasnik*, n.s. 47, no. 3 (Feb. 1936):196–209.

———. "Razlikovanye narodnih epskih pesama" [Classification of folk epic poems]. *Prilozi proučavanyu narodne poeziye* 2, no. 1 (March 1935):30–34.

———. "Review of '*Pesme o Kralyeviću Marku*'" [Review of *Songs about Prince Marko*]. *Srpski knyiževni glasnik*, n.s. 36, no. 3 (June 1932):231–34.

———. "Starost narodnog epskog pesništva našeg" [The antiquity of our folk epic poetry]. *Yužnoslovenski filolog* 12 (1933):47.

Krstić, Branislav. "Kony kao proročka životinya" [Horse as a prophetic animal]. *Prilozi proučavanyu narodne poeziye* 6, no. 2 (1939):245–51.

———. "Okultni motivi u našim narodnim pesmama" [Occult motifs in our folk songs]. *Prilozi proučavanyu narodne poeziye* 1, no. 1 (March 1934):62–70.

————. "Starost okultnih motiva u našim narodnim pesmama" [Antiquity of oc-
cult motifs in our folk songs]. *Prilozi proučavanyu narodne poeziye* 3, no. 1
(March 1936):116–17.
————. "Ženidba čoveka vilom" [Man's wedding to a *Vila*]. *Prilozi proučavanyu
narodne poeziye* 4, no. 1 (March 1937):99–118.
Lalević, Miodrag. "Dragutin Kostić: Starost narodnog epskog pesništva našeg"
[Dragutin Kostić: Antiquity of our folk epic poetry]. *Prilozi proučavanyu na-
rodne poeziye* 1, no. 2 (Nov. 1934):269–71.
————. "Veze izmedju usmene i pismene knyiževnosti: pisanye krvlyu i zlatom"
[Connections between oral and written literature: Writing with blood and
gold]. *Prilozi proučavanyu narodne poeziye* 1, no. 1 (March 1934):74–86.
Latković, Vido. "Dragutin Kostić: Pesma o vernom sluzi" [Dragutin Kostić: The
song about the faithful servant]. *Prilozi proučavanyu narodne poeziye* 3, no. 1
(March 1936):137–50.
————. "Dve studiye g. Olesnickog o ličnosti Djerzelez Aliye" [Two studies by Mr.
Olesnicki about Djerzelez Aliya's personality]. *Prilozi proučavanyu narodne
poeziye* 2, no. 1 (March 1935):123–26.
————. "O pevačima srpsko-hrvatskih narodnih epskih pesama do kraya xviii
veka" [Singers of Serbo-Croatian epic folk songs until the end of the 18th cen-
tury]. *Prilozi za knyiževnost, yezik, istoriyu i folklor* 20 (1954):184–202.
————. "Yedna ruska studiya o našim narodnim pesmama" [A Russian study on
our folk songs]. *Prilozi proučavanyu narodne poeziye* 1, no. 2 (Nov.
1934):263–69.
Lord, Albert Bates. "Notes on Digenis Akritas and Serbo-Croatian Epic." *Harvard
Slavic Studies* 2 (1954):375–83.
————. "Some Common Themes in Balkan Slavic Epic." *Actes du premier congrès
international des études balkaniques et sud-est européennes*. Sofiia, 1971, vii,
Separatum:653–62.
Lyumović, Krsto. "Naynoviye proučavanye ciklusa Kralyevića Marka" [The latest
research on the Prince Marko cycle]. *Glasnik yugoslovenskog profesorskog
društva* 17 (1936/37):124–33.
Maryanović, Dušan. "Problem Djerzelez Aliye" [The issue of Djerzelez Aliya]. *Pri-
lozi proučavanyu narodne poeziye* 3, no. 1 (March 1936):90–101.
Matić, Svetozar. "Beleška o epskoy improvizaciyi" [A note on epic improvisation].
Prilozi proučavanyu narodne poeziye 6, no. 1 (March 1939):70–75.
————. "Lični i kolektivni izraz u narodnom epu" [Individual and collective
expression in the folk epic]. *Prilozi proučavanyu narodne poeziye* 5, no. 2
(Nov. 1938):224–29.
————. "Markova legenda" [The Marko legend]. *Letopis matice srpske* 394, no. 1
(July 1964):540–56.
————. "Otkad počinye naše epsko pevanye" [When does our epic singing date
from]. *Letopis matice srpske* 390, no. 1 (July 1962):1–14.
————. "Snaga legende" [The force of the legend]. *Letopis matice srpske* 383, no. 5
(May 1959):411–19.

————. "Značenye geografskih detalya u narodnom epu" [The meaning of geographic details in folk epic]. *Prilozi proučavanyu narodne poeziye* 1, no. 1 (March 1934):12–15.

Matl, Yozef. "O pitanyu komparativnog proučavanya narodne poeziye balkanskih Slovena odnosno balkanskih naroda" [On the issue of comparative research in epic poetry of the Balkan Slavs, i.e. the Balkan Nations]. *Prilozi proučavanyu narodne poeziye* 3, no. 1 (March 1936):17–26.

Medenica, Radosav. "Dragutin Kostić: prenosi narodnih pesama s yednog yunaka na drugoga" [Transfer of folk songs from one hero to another]. *Prilozi proučavanyu narodne poeziye* 2, no. 2 (Nov. 1935):271–72.

————. "Muž na svadbi svoye žene" [The husband at the wedding of his wife]. *Prilozi proučavanyu narodne poeziye* 1, no. 1 (March 1934):33–61.

————. "Review of 'Dr. Nikola Banašević: *Ciklus Marka Kralyevića i odyeci francusko-italiyanske knyiževnosti* '" [Dr. Nikola Banašević: *The Prince Marko Cycle and the Echoes of French-Italian Literature*]. *Prilozi proučavanyu narodne poeziye* 3, no. 2 (Nov. 1936):300–304.

————. "Review of 'Dragutin Kostić: *Marko Barbadigo i naš epski Marko*' " [Dragutin Kostić: *Marko Barbadigo and Our Epic Marko*]. *Prilozi proučavanyu narodne poeziye* 5, no. 2 (Nov. 1938):305.

Pavlović, Dragolyub. "O podeli naše narodne knyiževnosti na periode" [On the division of our folk literature into periods]. *Prilozi za knyiževnost, yezik, istoriyu i folklor* 20 (1954):5–13.

Polenaković, Haralampiye. "Steyićeva variyanta narodne pesme o Kralyevićiu Marku i vili brodarici" [Steyić's variant of the folk song about Prince Marko and *Vila* of the river]. *Prilozi proučavanyu narodne poeziye* 4, no. 2 (Nov. 1937):270–71.

Popović, Pavle. "Iz naših narodnih pripovedaka" [From our folk tales]. *Srpski knyiževni glasnik* 30, no. 9 (May 1913):668–76.

Prodanović, Nikola. "Kralyević Marko i Lyutica Bogdan: a poem" [Prince Marko and Lyutica Bogdan]. *Letopis matice srpske* 286, no. 2 (1912):21–30.

Redjep, Yelka. "Razvoy motiva o ženidbi Vukašinovoy" [Development of the motif of Vukašin's wedding]. *Zbornik matice srpske za knyiževnost i yezik* 14–15, pt. 2 (1966/67):364–70.

Šaulić, Novica. "Tayna Marka Kralyevića" [The secret of Prince Marko]. *Prilozi proučavanyu narodne poeziye* 4, no. 2 (Nov. 1937):261–64.

Schmaus, Alois. "Helge Duerrigl: Die Marko-gestalt in der mazedonisch-bulgarischen Volksepik." *Prilozi za knyiževnost, yezik, istoriyu i folklor* 21 (1955):357–59.

Stanisavlyević, Vukašin. "Naša narodna knyiževnost" [Our folk literature]. *Knyiževnost i yezik* 16, no. 1 (1969):69–72.

Stanoyević, Stanoye. "Nekoliko beležaka o narodnoy tradiciyi" [A few notes on folk tradition]. *Prilozi proučavanyu narodne poeziye* 2, no. 1 (March 1935):1–7.

————. "O nekim motivima u našim narodnim pesmama" [About some motifs in our folk songs]. *Prilozi proučavanyu narodne poeziye* 1, no. 1 (March 1934):5–12.

Stefanović, Svetislav. "O naynoviyim proučavanyima narodne srpske poeziye" [Concerning the latest research in Serbian folk poetry]. *Letopis matice srpske* 345, no. 2 (Mar./Apr. 1936):199–210.

Subotić, Dragutin P. "Karakter, postanak i starina yugoslovenskih narodnih pesama" [The character, origin and antiquity of Yugoslav folk songs]. *Srpski knyiževni glasnik*, n.s. 51, no. 4 (June 1937):262–72; no. 5 (July 1937):371–78; no. 6 (July 1937):431–44.

Timčenko, Nikolay. "Dve pesme o Kralyeviću Marku u Erlangenskom rukopisu" [Two songs about Prince Marko in the Erlangen MS]. *Knyiževnost i yezik* 14, no. 3 (1966):311–15.

Toholy, Sava. "Naša narodna epika" [Our folk epic]. *Glasnik yugoslovenskog profesorskog društva* 15 (1934):36–55.

———. "Zaklyučivanye o starosti epskih pesama po nyihovoy sadržini" [Conclusion about the antiquity of epic songs according to their contents]. *Prilozi proučavanyu narodne poeziye* 2, no. 2 (Nov. 1935):227–37.

Tomić, Yovan N. "Review of 'A. I. Yacimirski: *Pesme o Marku Kralyeviću*' " [A. I. Yacimirski: *Songs about Prince Marko*]. *Srpski knyiževni glasnik* 15, no. 2 (July 1905):155–56.

Vaillant, André. "Les Chants épiques des Slaves du Sud." *Revue de cours et conférences* (Mar. 1932):306–46.

———. "Marko Kralyević et la *Vila*." *Revue des études Slaves* 8 (1928):81–85.

Velyković, Momir. "Legenda Kralyevića Marka" [The Prince Marko legend]. *Prilozi proučavanyu narodne poeziye* 4, no. 1 (March 1937):122–25.

Index

Index of Songs

PRINCE MARKO

was composed in 10-point Sabon, with two points of leading, on a Linotron 202
by Partners Composition;
printed by sheet-fed offset on 50-pound, acid-free Glatfelter Natural Hi-Bulk,
bound over binder's boards in Holliston Roxite C,
with dust jackets printed in 2 colors,
by Braun-Brumfield, Inc.;
and published by

SYRACUSE UNIVERSITY PRESS
SYRACUSE, NEW YORK 13244-5160